FIGHTING THE IDEOLOGICAL WAR

FIGHTING THE IDEOLOGICAL WAR

WINNING STRATEGIES FROM COMMUNISM TO ISLAMISM

ESSAYS BY

Patrick Sookhdeo
Stephen Ulph
John H. Moore
John Lenczowski
Robert R. Reilly
Thomas Joscelyn
Sebastian L. Gorka

EDITED BY

Katharine Cornell Gorka
Patrick Sookhdeo

The Westminster Institute
Isaac Publishing

Fighting the Ideological War:
Winning Strategies from Communism to Islamism

Published in the United States by Isaac Publishing
6729 Curran Street, McLean, Virginia 22101

For more information about obtaining additional copies of this
Westminster Institute publication, please visit the Institute's website at
www.westminster-institute.org or call 1-703-288-2885.

Library of Congress Control Number: 2012934903

ISBN: 978-0-9853109-0-5

Book design by Lee Lewis Walsh, Words Plus Design

Printed in the United States of America

CONTENTS

INTRODUCTION:
IN THE BATTLEFIELD OF IDEAS

Patrick Sookhdeo
and Katharine Cornell Gorka

From the earliest days of the United States' founding, Americans have been committed to the notion that they would not allow the state to meddle in religious affairs nor judge one another on the basis of belief. Arguably, this commitment is the basis for America's global stature as a defender of individual freedom, as well as its centuries of relative domestic peace and stability. But this laudable impulse to keep religion free from interference by the state has resulted in the now dangerous outcome that our government and military leaders have proscribed examination of the religious dimension, or even the broad set of beliefs, of today's enemy. Critical analysis of the ideas animating Islamic terrorists is further forestalled by the fact that today's leaders are fearful of provoking the ire of the Muslim world with the impression that the West has declared war on Islam. The result is an unwillingness to engage in the battle of ideas and a widespread confusion, even doublespeak, in the way policymakers talk about Islam.

When a violent and political strain of Islam burst onto the scene in 1979, there was no lack of clarity in the U.S. response. In the course of that year, the Shah was overthrown in Iran and Ayatollah Khomeini returned from exile in France to set up an Islamic Republic. On November 4th, 66 Americans were taken hostage by Islamist students and militants. On November 20th, Islamists seized the Grand Mosque in Mecca and held it for two weeks. Khomeini blamed the latter event on "criminal American imperialism," and as a result, the U.S. embassy in Islamabad, Pakistan, was burned to the ground and the U.S. embassy in Libya was also attacked. Given these events in 1979, it was easy for both Carter and then Reagan categorically to condemn Muslims with theocratic aspirations as antagonistic to Western values and interests. But subsequent events in Afghanistan clouded the picture. While the events of November 1979 loomed large in the American conscience, they were viewed as acts of terrorism and vengeance, not as acts of jihad that might have made administration officials think twice about supporting Islamists elsewhere. The Soviet occupation of Afghanistan, which began on December 24, 1979, was by far the greater concern. The Soviet Union was the greatest threat to the United States and indeed was seen as an existential threat. Therefore it was believed that Soviet occupation of Afghanistan must be resisted at all costs. Taking the position that the enemy of my enemy is my friend, the Carter Administration began providing support to the holy warriors, the *mujāhidīn*.

It can be argued that the United States must have badly misunderstood jihad if it was foolish enough to support the Islamist fighters who were the *mujāhidīn*, and indeed it was probably true that U.S. policymakers and defense and intelligence experts had limited knowledge of Islam. But to be fair, the concept of jihad at that time was also understood differently by the fighters themselves. As one analyst put it, under the *mujāhidīn* "...the ultimate legitimacy to rule draws upon military strength, but the contest itself is called jihad simply because Islam is the sole language of political legitimacy."[1] The fact that the *mujāhidīn* were Muslim was secondary to the fact that they were Afghans fighting Soviet occupation. It was only in the course of that war that Islam became the guiding principle, and jihad primarily a religious fight, rather than a strictly political one.

Inspired by the struggle in Afghanistan, the political aspirations of Islam grew dramatically in numbers and in the sophistication of their rhetoric through the 1980s. While ideologues such as Sayyid Qutb and Sayyid Abul A'la Al-Mawdudi had already built a framework for an Islamist resurgence, it was Abdullah Azzam, a Palestinian who had obtained his PhD in Islamic jurisprudence from al-Azhar University, who helped these ideas go viral. Azzam declared that the struggle in Afghanistan was a model for future struggles, the goal of which would be the re-establishment of the Caliphate, which would one day encompass the globe. Azzam transformed the notion of jihad into a personal obligation (*fard'ayn*) for all Muslims and thereby inspired thousands of Arab Muslims to come to Afghanistan to fight against the

Soviet occupation. Osama bin Laden, Azzam's disciple, took Azzam's notion of jihad as a personal obligation one step further—not only was it required as a defensive action, but now it would be required offensively as well. In his infamous fatwas of 1996 and 1998, he called on Muslims everywhere to take their jihad to the enemy, to attack Americans wherever they could be found.

At the same time that the rhetoric of Islamism was changing dramatically, providing a rationale for offensive violent jihad based on authoritative texts, Islamist parties saw significant wins both on the battlefield ("defeating" the Soviet Union in Afghanistan in 1988), and at the ballot box (in Turkey, Jordan, Kuwait and Algeria). Yet ironically, the rise of Islamism was greeted not with a commensurate rise in condemnation and confrontation from the West, but rather, the very opposite. The more strident the Islamists became, the more accommodating became the West. One of the first major U.S. government statements on fundamentalist Islam was delivered on June 2, 1992, by Assistant Secretary of State Edward Djerejian, under President George H. W. Bush. The Soviet Union had collapsed just a few months earlier, and the speech marked a major shift in U.S. foreign policy from one of containment in a world divided by conflict to one of collective engagement, in which former enemies could now work together to bring about global peace and stability. The pre-eminent concerns were now the Arab-Israeli conflict and the security and stability of the Persian Gulf. But Djerejian spoke with an overall tone of optimism that in the new spirit of cooperation even these issues could be resolved. Importantly, he directly addressed the issue of Islam:

> A cover of a recent issue of *The Economist* magazine headlined its main story, "Living with Islam" and portrayed a man in traditional dress, standing in front of a mosque and holding a gun. Inside the magazine, we are told that "Islam Resumes its March!" and that "one anti-western 'ism' is growing stronger." If there is one thought I can leave with you tonight, it is that the U.S. Government does not view Islam as the next "ism" confronting the West or threatening world peace. That is an overly simplistic response to a complex reality… The Cold War is not being replaced with a new competition between Islam and the West.[2]

In the new spirit of cooperation, seeking to avoid any sense of conflict, Djerejian presented the view of Islam as one of the three great Abrahamic faiths and said the Crusades had been over for a long time. Given this perspective on Islam, it is not surprising that he then signaled a U.S. acceptance of a growing role for Islam: "In countries throughout the Middle East and North Africa, we thus see groups of movements seeking to reform their societies in keeping with Islamic ideals. There is considerable diversity in how these ideals are expressed. We detect no monolithic or coordinated international effort behind these movements. What we do see are believers living in different countries placing renewed emphasis on Islamic principles and governments accommodating Islamist political activity to varying degrees and in different ways."

The question that the Bush Administration was facing at the time, and which Djerejian was answering, was whether to support democracy, which would entail supporting the Islamists, or whether to fight the Islamists, which would entail supporting authoritarian regimes. Bush chose the former, based at least in part on the optimism derived from the collapse of the Soviet Union. But this stance was also based on the way the Bush Administration viewed the United States: Djerejian said they did not want to impose an American model on others, as if the U.S. model of equality under the law and freedom was just one among many—all equally good. "Each country must work out," he said, "in accordance with its own traditions, history, and particular circumstances, how and at what pace to broaden political participation." Therefore a system of government grounded in Islamic principles would not be a problem. The Bush Administration did not view Islam, even in a radical form, as a theologically rooted ideology that might pit itself in a death match against the United States. If Islam did lean toward radicalization, this was viewed as a social condition that could be solved through aid, education, and economic reform.

This position was essentially maintained under President Bill Clinton, in spite of the fact that the World Trade Center was bombed just one month after he was inaugurated, and Islamist terrorists had been tracked by the FBI for months in anticipation of the attack. In the first clear statement of the Clinton policy, the Acting Coordinator for Counterterrorism, Laurence Pope, stated in April 1993, "The misuse of Islamic political rhetoric ... should not cause us to confuse in our own minds terrorism and Islam... What we're talking about is terrorism and not political ideologies, and certainly not Islam."[3]

The strategy set first by George H.W. Bush and maintained by Clinton, that of segregating terrorism from Islam and maintaining a pristine image of Islam, has remained consistent for the nearly two decades that have followed. After the attacks of September 11th, 2001, George W. Bush veered briefly away by citing the transcendent, spiritual nature of the attack: "This is a new kind of evil," Bush declared on September 16, 2001. "This crusade, this war on terrorism…" he called the response. But the verbal firestorm that erupted from political and religious leaders alike quickly pushed him back in line. Bush's use of the word "crusade," said Soheib Bensheikh, Grand Mufti of the mosque in Marseille, France, "was most unfortunate… It recalled the barbarous and unjust military operations against the Muslim world" by Christian knights, who launched repeated attempts to capture Jerusalem over the course of several hundred years. The very next day, Bush was obliged to appear at an Islamic center in Washington and recant, saying, "the face of terror is not the true faith of Islam. That's not what Islam is all about."[4]

Even *The 9/11 Commission Report*, which is often cited for its frank reference to the role of Islam in the attacks, exercises great discretion in how it interprets that role. The authors write, "Despite his claims to universal leadership, Bin Laden offers an extreme view of Islamic history designed to appeal mainly to Arabs and Sunnis."[5] The authors would seem to be suggesting that Bin Laden has a limited reach since he is appealing only to Arabs and Sunnis. But there are about 300 million Arabs in the world, while there may be as many as 1 billion Sunni. So in fact al Qaeda might have extensive appeal. The report also states, "Most Muslims prefer a peaceful and inclusive vision of their faith, not the violent sectarianism of Bin Laden." Is that based on researched and documented fact, or on wishful thinking? So while *The 9/11 Commission Report* at least acknowledges the Islamic roots of the ideology driving al Qaeda, its overall message remained consistent with the prevailing viewpoint of U.S. officials—that bin Laden represented a distortion of Islam, not true Islam, and in fact that terrorism had nothing to do with Islam.

Eventually, the effort to divorce terrorism from Islam led to the excision of *all* mention of Islam from the United States' national security lexicon. While *The 9/11 Commission Report*, released in July 2004, used the word Islam 322 times, Muslim 145 times, jihad 126 times, and jihadist 32 times, The *National Intelligence Strategy of the United States*, issued in August 2009, used the term Islam 0 times, Muslim 0 times, jihad 0 times. Similarly, the FBI's *Counterterrorism Analytical Lexicon* makes no reference to Islam, Muslims, or jihad. In the most recent documents put out by the Obama Administration, it is acknowledged that Islam has a part to play in terrorism, but (echoing the language used by earlier administrations) only to the extent that the terrorists have misappropriated and distorted Islam. The *National Strategy for Counterterrorism*, released in June of 2011, states that the preeminent security threat to the United States is "al-Qa'ida and its affiliates and adherents," not

Islamism, radical Islam, or global jihad. The doctrine espoused by al Qaeda is a *distortion* of Islam, their belief a *"fabricated* legitimization of violence (emphasis added)."[6] In other words, al Qaeda's doctrine is not truly Islamic, and that then justifies the exclusion of Islam from all national security discourse.

While any number of factors may have contributed to the policy of previous administrations in trying to portray terrorism as unIslamic, under the Obama Administration three distinct factors can be discerned. First, the Administration has made clear, albeit quietly, that it is trying to undermine al Qaeda's legitimacy by calling it unauthentic, a grave condemnation in Islam. If this were the only motivation for defining al Qaeda as unIslamic, or as a distortion of Islam, it would be a commendable act of psychological warfare, one with strong potential for delegitimizing the enemy and disillusioning possible recruits. But two other factors are also at work here, which undercut whatever strategic advantage might be gained by the first factor. First, key policymakers inside the Administration are operating under the assumption that there are "good" Islamists and there are "bad" Islamists, and that we should empower the former in order to defeat the latter. This view is elucidated by Quintan Wiktorowicz, who joined Obama's National Security Council in July 2011 as the senior director for global engagement. Wiktorowicz makes the distinction between what he calls the purists (non-violent Salafists) and the jihadis (violent Salafists) and says we should invest in the former:

> In terms of U.S. strategy, the primary concern should be how strategy can influence these interpretations of context to empower the purists. Although the purists are strongly anti-Western (and anti-American), they are also the least likely to support the use of violence. To the extent that the United States can amplify the purist contextual reading at the expense of the jihadis, the movement of Salafis toward the radical extremists will likely slow.[7]

But this is a problematic argument. As Wiktorowicz himself explains, it is not the attitude toward violent jihad that separates the reformists or purists from al Qaeda, but rather the tactical decision over the timing of jihad:

> For reformist Salafis, there is great concern that the Muslim community is not ready to engage in jihad, either against incumbent Arab regimes or the United States. It is not that jihad is rejected as a tactic of religious transformation, rather, reformists believe that several prior

phases are necessary before a jihad is permissible... The central component of the reformist counter-discourse on jihad is that unless
Muslims follow the straight path of Islam and the Salafi manhaj[8], they
will be unable to engage in a successful jihad, since God rewards only
the true believers. A lack of effective Salafi propagation and concomi-
tant divisions within the Muslim community creates weakness that
will prevent a successful jihad against Western countries led by the
United States. Any premature movement toward the use of violence is
therefore doomed to fail.[9]

In other words, the Administration has a strategy of working with non-
violent Islamists in the hope that this will keep them from becoming violent,
even while one of the administration's leading experts acknowledges the so-
called purists have not foresworn violence, but only call for a different timing in the use of violence. The fundamental problem is that these deep internal contradictions in the administration's reasoning with regard to Islam and
the policies based upon them are having far-reaching consequences both
abroad and at home. The U.S. has supported the creation of constitutions
based on shari'a law in Afghanistan and Iraq, with very negative consequences for minorities and for the democratic process itself. The U.S. has also
demonstrated a willingness to provide support for Islamists such as the
Muslim Brotherhood throughout the Middle East as more secular regimes
have been overthrown. Obama, like both Bushes and Clinton, has gambled
on the hope that the so-called reformers throughout the Middle East would
move away from violence and toward democracy. But now that "the reformers" are coming into power, the gamble seems ill-founded. Each successive
outbreak of violence, each attack on Christians, minorities, and moderate
Muslims suggests that Islamism may not be the way to peace after all.

The second factor of concern that is shaping the official U.S. approach
toward Islam is the participation of Islamists in the crafting of both policy
and narrative. The decision to engage Salafists has brought Islamists into the
United States' national security apparatus, both in key staff positions and
through such vehicles as the Homeland Security Advisory Council.[10] Top
Justice Department officials have repeatedly met with Islamist activists who
have lobbied for cutbacks in anti-terror funding, changes in the content of
anti-terrorism training, and the blacklisting of trainers whose interpretation
of Islam they take issue with.[11] The White House has virtually shut down all
domestic counter-terrorism training on Islam as a result; it has shut the door

to moderate Muslims, and it has shifted local law enforcement away from intelligence-led policing toward community policing. In August 2011 the White House published *Empowering Local Partners to Prevent Violent Extremism in the United States*, in which it stated:

> Protecting American communities from al-Qa'ida's hateful ideology is not the work of government alone. Communities—especially Muslim American communities whose children, families and neighbors are being targeted for recruitment by al-Qa'ida—are often best positioned to take the lead because they know their communities best.[12]

Part of the outreach effort has meant not conducting any military or law enforcement training that Muslims might find in any way offensive. The National Security Staff (NSS), a part of the Executive Office of the President, initiated a sweeping review process of all counter-terrorism training conducted by the U.S. Attorney's offices, the FBI, and by all branches within the Department of Defense. The DoD memo announcing the review acknowledged the importance of understanding and attacking AQ's ideology, but then undercuts its strategic value by misrepresenting the relevance of that world view:

> …a successful strategy against al-Qa'ida must focus on undermining and inhibiting the group's ideology… A central tool in countering that ideology is knowledge—knowledge of the complex religious, cultural, and social context in which al-Qa'ida long has sought to conflate its narrow ideological worldview—which draws the support of a tiny fraction of the global Muslim population—with an authoritative religious perspective for all Muslims.[13]

Again, Wiktorowicz's analysis pulls the rug out from beneath the claim that al Qaeda is isolated and has minimal support:

> As the United States engages in the new global threat of the twenty-first century, it is important to contextualize bin Laden and his followers as a movement operating within a broader transnational community of Islamic activists. While it is tempting to dismiss bin Laden and other radicals as outside the boundaries of Islam, such assertions underestimate the spiritual, ideological and human relationships that connect those who espouse a violent jihad against the United States

with more moderate elements within particular segments of the Muslim community.[14]

Thus the internal contradictions of U.S. policy toward terrorism and its relationship to Islam abound. Yet this approach, as illogical as it is, has run through successive administrations for more than two decades: much of the world's terrorism today is carried out in the name of Islam, yet we cannot discuss Islam or analyze Islam or look closely at the way Islam inspires acts of violence or even authoritarianism and oppression. The end result is that United States has barely engaged in a war of ideas. And yet it must, because the war against Islamist terrorism cannot be won solely on the battlefield. The ideological foundation that al Qaeda is built on allows it to recover from tactical defeats and constantly renew its personnel, resources and moral authority. Moreover, unlike communism, Islamism is not likely to burn itself out through faulty economic policies. Indeed, given the natural resources held by those Islamic countries that support or tolerate terrorist and extremist groups, they can easily outspend the United States if they so choose. And unlike Anarchism, radical Islam does not eschew political organization, therefore condemning itself to inevitable dissolution for lack of institutionalization. Rather, the Islamists have the force of the OIC (Organisation of Islamic Cooperation) and its 57 member states behind them, pushing for ever greater recognition of Islam and its demands, and, in its own words, promoting and coordinating Muslim solidarity in economic, social, and political affairs.

In short, Radical Islam, or Islamism, which has declared itself at war both with the West and with moderate or secular Muslims, is well organized, well funded, and grounded in the authority of religious texts. The United States therefore has a particularly difficult battle to fight. It is engaged with an enemy that cares first and foremost about the ideological battle—rebuilding a distinct Muslim identity and strengthening the *umma*. Without understanding and directly confronting the ideology driving such groups as al Qaeda, the United States will never be able to defeat the Islamist threat. And yet the Administration has declared that particular battlefield off limits. Therefore, non-governmental institutions have a vital role to play. At this moment, it is largely outside of official institutions that the ideological aspect of the war against Islamism can be acknowledged and properly studied. This collection of essays is intended to provide much needed historical background and comparative analysis to the current generation of those tasked with defending America.

In this initiative, we have taken particular inspiration from the life of an economist named Warren Nutter, whose story is told here by John Moore. In the 1930s and 1940s, the Soviet economic model of central planning was being hailed as more efficient and more humane than the Western capitalist model. Many, particularly those in Western academia, embraced that argument. One economist, Warren Nutter, was tasked with evaluating Soviet industrial output for the National Bureau of Economic Research. Importantly, Nutter was not part of the Soviet Studies establishment, which was dominated by those who believed the Soviet system was capable of maintaining high rates of growth. After extensive study, Nutter came to the conclusion that the Soviet economy's rate of growth was in fact slowing and indeed that the U.S. model might be a better one after all. For this he was excoriated. He was attacked for not being a Sovietologist, for not knowing Russian, for being biased in favor of capitalism. But Nutter was correct, and in the long run his views were vindicated. As John Moore writes, "The NBER study represents the earliest public indication of the inherent weaknesses of Soviet socialism." Moreover, it had far-reaching consequences:

> In breaking the stranglehold of conventional wisdom about Soviet economic performance, the NBER study opened the door to a widespread critique of socialism and socialist central planning that, in turn, played an important role in the demise of the Soviet Union.

The parallels to the situation today should be obvious. Apologists for Islamism currently have the dais. They have the microphone both in government and in universities, many of which, it should be added, are receiving funding from the very fundamentalists they are meant to be objectively studying. Conventional thinking in the United States at this moment is that Islamists are viable partners, and that politics shaped by Islam will lead to democracy and peace. Those who would challenge those views are sidelined and criticized. But we take heart from the story of Warren Nutter and others like him. They were not afraid to examine what was in front of them and to tell a different story, one that in the end proved to be true.

This is one of several important lessons to be learned from the ideological battles of the past. John Lenczowski, who served as Director of European and Soviet Affairs at the National Security Council from 1983 to 1987, makes the point that Reagan's success in ultimately defeating the Soviet

Union, which had threatened America's annihilation for over half a century, grew out of his shift from a focus on the enemy's tactics to its founding ideology—the set of beliefs from which all of its actions and tactics derived. Reagan believed that the threat to the United States would be eliminated only when the ideological nature of the Soviet system could be changed. Lenczowski tracks how that task was accomplished.

Robert Reilly, who worked both as a Special Assistant to President Reagan and as Director of Voice of America, looks at the central importance of messaging in the "war of ideas." The United States Information Agency and Voice of America received a lions' share of manpower and resources in order to promote "the American idea" and to challenge the counter-narrative of the Soviets. This stands in sharp contrast to today, where USIA has been dismantled and the current notion of messaging entails broadcasting Britney Spears, J.Lo, and Eminem into the Arab world. Both Reilly and Lenczowski put a premium on the importance of language in describing both the enemy and ourselves. As Robert Reilly writes, "Words and the restoration of their relationship to reality were critical to the Communist collapse."

The absence of accuracy and truth in how we talk about Islam today and about the threats that emanate from parts of the Muslim world are further illustrated in Thomas Joscelyn's essay on state-sponsored terrorism. For much of the Cold War, the CIA refused to accept the idea that the Soviet Union was sponsoring left-wing terrorism, in spite of ample evidence. As a result, the United States did little to deter these smaller-scale acts of provocation, and Soviet sponsored terrorism continued unabated. Today it is the role of Islam that is downplayed as a motivator for acts of terrorism. But unlike the past, when terrorism was just one tool and indeed a minor tool in the war against the West, today terrorism is the principal tool used by violent jihadists. Without an explicit message of delegitimation and deterrence, the United States will not be able to stop jihadist states from allowing or sponsoring attacks against the West and Western targets, and no amount of airport screening or barricading of U.S. installations will be able to keep Americans safe.

The starting point for all these strategies is the correct use of terminology and an accurate assessment of the enemy's threat doctrine. Patrick Sookhdeo sets us on that road by directly challenging the assertion of U.S. officials over the past two decades that Islamism is not a new ideology out to challenge the West. He traces the rise of the ideology behind radical Islamism, in both its violent and non-violent forms, and he states, unequivocally, that until the West directly confronts the ideology driving these movements, it will never be able to defeat the threat of Islamist terrorism.

Stephen Ulph's essay looks at the parallels between Islamism, Nazism and communism not for the lessons in how the United States responded to these ideologically driven threats but for the clues to vulnerabilities in the ideology, the chink in the armor. Comparing Islamism with other totalitarianisms weakens the important claim of the Islamists to an authenticity that is uniquely Islamic and divinely sanctioned. This is turn weakens their overall cause and justification. But again, if the West is unwilling to allow open discussion and examination of the Islamist claim, and insists instead that it is merely "man-made disasters," or "violent extremism" that we are battling, then the ideology of the Islamists, which is the version of Islam that generates the most heat, will remain the sun around which all other lesser constellations will be forced to orbit.

Finally Sebastian Gorka writes that the ideology of global jihad is very much influenced by Western totalitarian ideologies of fascism and communism, and that today, despite bin Laden's death, the ideology is alive and well, in fact growing in popularity if one looks to the events of the last twelve months in the Middle East and North Africa. This ideology is not just driving the violent jihadists but also their far more numerous and potentially more dangerous non-violent compatriots, typified by the Muslim Brotherhood. Gorka argues that the United States and its allies, advocates for freedom and the rule of law, must understand that the non-violent and violent jihadists are united in their strategic objective of realizing a global caliphate under shari'a law. Moreover, this is a form of warfare that the West can lose without another shot ever being fired or another plane being hijacked.

Sun Tsu stated two-and-a-half-thousand years ago that the aim of warfare is not to destroy the enemy but to bend his will, and that the primary target in any war is not the enemy's organization but his strategy. Today America must attack global jihad at the level of its strategy, which means engaging in the battlefield of the mind and destroying the ideology of the enemy, just as America once destroyed the evil ideology of the Soviet Union. It is our hope and our intention that this collection of essays will challenge the prevailing denial of the enemy's ideology, and that by looking to the successes of the past in defeating those who would rob us of our freedom, we can find a way to a secure and peaceful future.

PART I

Identifying the Enemy
after the Death of bin Laden

THE WEST, ISLAM, AND THE COUNTER-IDEOLOGICAL WAR

Patrick Sookhdeo

Wars of subversion and counter-subversion are fought, in the last resort, in the minds of the people.[1]

The struggle with revolutionary Islam will only be won when the West begins to methodically analyze the ideological religion that empowers it and forms its basis.[2]

INTRODUCTION

Islamic religiosity, under current conditions, almost invariably entails an ideological vision.[3]

The killing of Osama bin Laden was undoubtedly a great success in the ongoing battle against Islamist terrorism. However, it will not of itself remove the underlying causes that continue to inspire jihadi terrorism. *The 9/11 Commission Report* concluded that the ultimate requirement for eliminating the danger posed by al Qaeda is "prevailing in the longer term over the ideology that gives rise to Islamist terrorism."[4] This statement rightly pinpoints the fact that it is the ideology promoted by Osama bin Laden and his associates that binds together the disparate, multi-ethnic movement that is al Qaeda, a movement described by one expert as "the ideological organization par excellence."[5]

Al Qaeda, however, is but one of many ideological terrorist organizations embedded in a wider base of Islamist movements with specific doctrines and goals. They view Islam as a political ideology and are linked to mainline, traditional Islam by their reliance on the Islamic source scriptures (Qur'an and Hadith), the model of Muhammad, and the history of the early Islamic state (the Caliphate), which is seen as paradigmatic by most Muslims. It is this link to traditional Islam that gives them legitimacy and serves to attract sympathy, resources and recruits to their cause. As Stephen Ulph explains:

> Al-Qaeda has derived much of its power to penetrate into Muslim societies from the fact that it cannot be glibly written off as something alien, or external to the broad spectrum of Islamic beliefs. Violent jihadists have not constructed for themselves a doctrine ex nihilo. Doctrinal opponents of al-Qaeda, in highlighting its 'errors,' have to concede that its jihadism, doctrinally speaking, lies deeply embedded within a succession of concentric circles of religious doctrine.[6]

The ideological battle is therefore in many ways more important than the kinetic battle. It is easier to kill radical Islamist jihadists than to eliminate their Islamist ideology. It is ideology that gathers resources and recruits new fighters to replace those who have been killed. Kill the ideology, and the terrorism-inspiring movement withers and dies.

Some experts see in the current struggle against radical Islam a parallel to the Cold War, which was a long-term ideological struggle against communism. There were some who saw its ending as the end to all ideological wars:

> The surrender of the Soviet Union was an ideological surrender rather than one forced by military defeat, but it was a surrender nonetheless, and marked the eclipse of the most potent challenger to the liberal world order following the defeats earlier in the century of Germany and Japan... Francis Fukuyama captured the moment with his declaration that Hegel had been right all along, if premature, and that history had now definitely ended, by which he meant amongst other things that the long ideological civil war in the West was over, and that liberalism had won. There was now no alternative to liberal capitalism and democracy, and no serious challenger left.[7]

However, the reality is that Islamism has replaced communism as the most significant ideological opponent of the Western liberal world order.

Radical Islamist movements have declared war on the West as well on other Muslims. They are well organized, well funded, and grounded in the authority of religious texts. Their goal is the rebuilding of a distinct Muslim identity, the strengthening of the *umma* (the global Islamic nation), and the defeat of the West both materially and spiritually. Without directly confronting the ideology driving these movements, the West will never be able to defeat the threat of Islamist terrorism.

Some Western governments have realized that security measures are not enough and that Islamist ideology must be faced.[8] Thus in Britain, following the July 2005 London bombings, Tony Blair clearly recognized that the enemy was an ideology that needed to be confronted in a battle of ideas:

> What we are confronting here is an evil ideology. It is not a clash of civilisations—all civilised people, Muslim or other, feel revulsion at it. But it is a global struggle and it is a battle of ideas, hearts and minds, both within Islam and outside it.[9]

Ten years after 9/11 Tony Blair was still adamant that the real danger was the radical Islamist ideology, of which al Qaeda was but a small margin at its edge. The real problem, he said, was not a small isolated group of terrorists, but the broader ideology that sustained them. Moreover, he also said it was deeply naive to believe that it was the West's response which had radicalized Muslims. "It is not because of something we are doing to them. They believe in what they believe in because they believe their religion compels them to believe in it." Blair warned the threat would therefore end only when "we defeat the ideology":

> I think it will take a generation, but the way to defeat this ideology ultimately is by a better idea, and we have it, which is a way of life based on openness, democracy, freedom and the rule of law.[10]

Yet while many now acknowledge that the ideological battle is vital, widespread confusion persists as to which approach should be taken in response. Western policymaking is hampered by uncertainty about the definition of the hostile ideology, confusion as to its linkages both to mainline Islamist movements and to traditional Islam, and ambiguity as to how it should be countered in the realm of ideas. While it is important to clarify that this is not a "war on Islam," of which Islamists are quick to accuse the West, it *is* imperative to acknowledge that the war against Islamist terrorism is a war of ideas, ideologies and worldviews.

THE IDEOLOGY OF ISLAMISM

Jihadism is neither flimsy nor merely a modernist by-product of 20ᵗʰ century stresses, but rather makes a point of rooting itself deep within the body of Islamic tradition and is very adept at negotiating the seams. By understanding the potency of its attraction and taking it seriously as an intellectual movement, the hope is that a more thorough groundwork can be laid to the construction of a consistent counter-message to Islamist radicalism, one that will benefit from greater penetration and higher precision.[11]

International terrorism carried out by Muslims in the name of Islam is a small visible part of a much larger ideological movement known as "Islamism" (also called "political" or "fundamentalist" Islam). "Islamism" is an umbrella term for a wide variety of radical religious-political, ideological and transnational movements. These movements and their discourses are committed to Islam as a political ideology, a totalitarian system and way of life, and an alternative to Western secular ideologies.[12] They operate across all areas of human society and all over the world and have defined grievances and goals.[13]

Delwar Hussein, a researcher on South Asian communities in Britain, defines Islamism as a set of political ideologies intent on reshaping the state and placing it under shari'a:

[Islamism] refers to the set of political ideologies derived from conservative formulations of *sharia* law. It holds that Islam is not only a religion, but also a political system that governs the legal, economic and social imperatives of the state, the community and the individual. Islamist movements generally seek to reshape the state by implementing this formulation of *sharia* law.[14]

The *Almuslih* website for a reformed Islam defines Islamism as a radical ideological movement intent on fundamentally changing the structures of state and society:

At its core, Islamism is an ideological movement with a program that seeks to fundamentally alter the religious, intellectual and political complexion of Muslims worldwide towards a more pristine and "Islamically authentic" form—an original, divinely sanctioned, winning template that will restore the lapsed political, military and economic fortunes of the Muslim world. Islamism's primary obligation is to ensure that Islam defines the political, legal and public space of Muslims, but the corollary of Islam's religious universalism means that the political implications of this universalism must perforce embrace the global arena too.[15]

It is important to realize that religious doctrine is the life-blood of Islamist movements. They offer a complete intellectual architecture and educational program based on religious doctrine, which are constructed to reconfigure the self-image and identity of Muslims from passive observers to zealous religious ideologues.[16] As the former Bishop of Rochester, Michael Nazir-Ali, explains:

> Although we need carefully to distinguish between Muslims, Islam and Islamism, we must also recognise that there is considerable overlap here. A devout and pietistic Muslim can be influenced by extremist ideology, and Islamism certainly uses much in the fundamentals of Islam to argue its case.[17]

Islamism first appeared in the first half of the 20th century. It grew out of the Islamic reform movements of the 19th century, which were reacting to the perceived weakness of Islam under Western domination. These movements argued that Muslims must return to the original Islamic sources and to the Golden Age of early Islam in order to revitalize modern-day Islam. Islamism therefore adopted the expansionist drive of early Islam and sees itself as the vanguard of a revived, revolutionary, true Islam.[18] It is its link to the sources of Islam and Islam's early history that maintains Islamism's vitality and enables it to propagate itself and gain recruits and resources wherever Muslims are found.

> Islamism is defined here ... as synonymous with "Islamic activism," the active assertion and promotion of beliefs, prescriptions, laws, or policies that are held to be Islamic in character. There are numerous currents of Islamism in this sense: what they hold in common is that they found their activism on traditions and teachings of Islam as contained in scripture and authoritative commentaries.[19]

Islamists see themselves as reformers of a degenerated, modern Islam that has deviated from its original purity. They hold that this degeneration is the cause of the decline in Islam's political and economic power evident in the past three centuries. To reverse that decline and revive Islam's power and glory, Muslims must return to the pure doctrines and practices established by Muhammad and the *salaf* (the pious ancestors).[20] These include the purifying of society from what Islamists view as un-Islamic practices and teachings, and the establishment of an ideal Islamic state modeled on that of Muhammad and his Companions: a unified worldwide "Islamic state" (*khilafa*), in which shari'a is the basis and sole source of all legislation.[21] Islamist reform includes the restoration of Islam's universal mission to dominate and Islamic hegemony in both the domestic and global arenas.

Islamism utilizes a strand of radicalism and violence inherent in much of traditional Muslim theology and history. Like the other strands in Islam, it is based on selected passages in the Muslim source texts, on Muhammad's example, and on early Muslim history. As the distinguished scholar of Islam, Bernard Lewis, notes:

> From the earliest times, the reported events of Islamic history, supported by the precepts of Islamic tradition and law, reflect two distinct and indeed contradictory principles. The one we have called authoritarian and quietist; the other might be called radical and activist... the radical activist tradition is also old and deep-rooted, and is acquiring new significance in our day, with the emergence of the idea of an Islamic Revolution, and of leaders and movements devoted to its accomplishment... The exponents of both traditions naturally looked to the life and teachings of the Prophet for guidance and inspiration; both concentrated their attention on the political actions which the prophet found necessary to undertake in order to accomplish his religious mission."[22]

The well-known Egyptian scholar, Nasr Hamid Abu Zayd, also makes note of the religious roots of Islamist terrorism:

> If we follow the rules of interpretation developed from the classical "science of Koranic interpretation," it is not possible to condemn terrorism in religious terms. It remains completely true to the classical rules in its evolution of sanctity for its own justification. This is where the secret of its theological strength lies.[23]

The truth, unpalatable though it may be, is that Islamists and Islamist terrorists are authentically Islamic, emphasizing specific texts and offering literalist interpretations of the sources. They cannot be undermined with the simple claim that what they are doing is unIslamic.

Moreover, Islamists strive to ensure that Islam will define the political, legal and public space everywhere.[24] To achieve this goal, Islamist movements seek the Islamization of the entire social and political system of their societies, their states, the whole Muslim world and ultimately the entire globe.[25] Islamization involves bringing everything under Allah's sovereignty, rule and law (as perceived by Islamists) and its integration within a total Islamic system in which implementation of shari'a is the crucial element. Islamists emphasize *Tawhīd*, the traditional doctrine of the unity of Allah. In their interpretation, however, this becomes a unitary and uniform vision of Allah, universe and society: one god, one people, one law. Just as Allah's physical laws are imposed on the universe, so Allah's religious law (shari'a) must be imposed on society.

The state is seen as the most efficient instrument for implementing this vision of an Allah-pleasing society under shari'a and as the guarantor of its survival. Islamists therefore concentrate their efforts on capturing the state, its centers of power and its instruments of violence, either legally within the democratic framework, or violently by revolution or coup d'état.[26]

Islamists have revived the classical doctrine of jihad as a main plank of their ideology. Gradualists, who include the Muslim Brotherhood, aim at implementing jihad in all spheres of human activity, including violent military jihad when the situation calls for it. Radicals, such as al Qaeda and affiliated movements, emphasize the necessity of immediate violent jihad as the only method that Muslims today should consider using.

For many Islamists the modern nation states, even Muslim ones, are contrary to Allah's will, were imposed by Western imperialists and should not elicit any real loyalty from Muslims. At best they are merely a stage in the process of establishing the divinely commanded universal Islamic state governed by shari'a and encompassing all Muslims worldwide. The final stage will see the *umma* and the Islamic state once again converge as they did in the glorious early history of Islam under Muhammad and the rightly guided Caliphs.[27]

To achieve their goals, Islamists strive to polarize relations between Muslims and others, pushing the concept of a permanent religious, cultural and civilizational conflict between the two and that of Muslims as perennial victims. Their discourse has deeply affected all levels of Muslim societies, leading to widespread feelings of victimhood and a flourishing of conspiracy theories. The West is blamed for all problems faced by Muslims today: their fragmentation, their backwardness, their humiliation and their inability to unite and regain their former glory. This view is similar to the Huntington paradigm of a "clash of civilizations," but was advocated long before Huntington by Islamist leaders and thinkers such as Sayyid Qutb and Abu'l A'la Mawdudi. In this view the global Muslim *umma* has been under a perpetual attack since its birth by an aggressive Christendom bent on the total destruction of Islam. Muslims must respond by resisting Western cultural influences and by reviving authentic Islam. They must shed their defeatist posture and return to the triumphant confidence of Muhammad in Medina, rejecting Western worldviews and judging the world only by authentic Islamic norms. Muslims must regain their self-confidence, affirm Muslim exceptionalism, and regenerate by persistent efforts to rebuild the strength of the *umma*.[28]

Islamism has thus succeeded in turning its main ideological concepts into accepted Islamic tenets among many Muslims. At the same time its operatives have largely taken control of many important Muslim institutions and organizations, and have assumed powerful positions in state and society, even in the military of some states, such as Pakistan.

ISLAMISM AND EXPANSION IN THE WEST

In the West, Islamists are able to operate and pursue their objectives legally because of a democratic system that does not practice censorship and policing of ideas. Western states that include large and growing Muslim diaspora communities are seen by Islamists as a source of financial support, political shelter, and new recruits as well as an active arena of expansion. This program includes the radicalization of Muslims living in non-Muslim majority states, a highly dangerous development for the security and stability of these states.[29]

While some mainline Islamists promote Muslim participation in Western politics to increase Islamist influence and power, others employ the tactic of disengagement from civic participation and promote cultural self-isolation in order to protect the purity of the community. These radicalized communities reject participation and demand ever-greater concessions to Islamic exceptionalism. Accession to these demands gradually undermines the social coherence of the democratic state, and eventually even its legal and security mechanisms. This erosion of social coherence makes the non-Muslim citizens vulnerable as Islamists prepare for the stage in which liberal democracy and secularism will be directly confronted.[30]

GRADUALIST AND RADICAL ISLAMISTS

Islamist groups may share a number of long-term aims and political incli-nations, but they differ in their short-term and mid-term priorities.[31]

What sets non-violent Islamists apart from the violent groups is their doc-trine of gradualism, which includes a tactical willingness to work within the legal system of their countries in order to further their strategic goals. Their tactical goals include the Islamization of Muslim societies at the grass-roots level, the building of a committed vanguard of elites and the mobilization of the masses. Gradualist movements advocate a comprehensive multi-faceted system of jihad, which includes struggle on all fronts—economic, cultural, political—in order to mobilize Muslims and gather Islamic strength for the final struggle, which might include the use of force.

Radicals (such as al Qaeda) diverge from the gradualist mainstream (such as the Muslim Brotherhood) in justifying the immediate use of force to achieve their aims. They reinterpret traditional and classical Islamic concepts to justify indiscriminate violence against all perceived enemies, both Muslim and non-Muslim, arguing that this is divinely ordained jihad.

Thus Ayman al-Zawahiri, al Qaeda's main ideologue and now its leader (following the death of Osama bin Laden), argues that jihad is an individual obligation on all capable Muslims everywhere. Indeed it is the main duty for all Muslims, standing above all other religious duties. It is defensive, because infidels have occupied Muslim lands. At the same time, offensive jihad is still an obligation when the circumstances are right, as jihad is obligatory until "all religion is God's alone and there is no more conflict in the land." Mistakes made in jihad are no reason for stopping jihad, which must contin-ue because it is ordained to go on forever. Jihad follows the example of Muhammad and his Companions, and is based on the Qur'an, Sunna and shari'a and on the consensus of all Muslim scholars. There is simply no excuse for abandoning jihad, as it is an obligation "on which no two scholars have disagreed throughout the last 14 centuries." According to this view, Islam is a religion of power, prestige, awe, strength and honor, and it will be lost if the sword is lost; it cannot triumph without jihad. Weakness is a crime, and Muslims too weak to change the situation by force are still obligated to prepare and help create the conditions for jihad.[32]

In contrast, gradualists accept the classical limitation that only the legitimate ruler is authorized to declare jihad. They stress the defensive nature of jihad. However, in the case of attack by non-Muslims on Muslim land, they argue that jihad becomes an individual duty on every Muslim, annulling the need for the leader's declaration of jihad. The differences between the two views are obvious, but they are partly semantic and open to a wide spectrum of interpretations. Gradualists have supported violent insurgency in Iraq, Afghanistan and Palestine, including suicide bombings.

The border between mainline, gradualist Islamists and the violent radicals is thus not clear-cut and defined, but flexible and permeable in both directions. While there is agreement on ultimate goals, there is constant argument over how best to achieve those goals. The radical organizations might differ with the mainline movements on matters of tactics and medium-term strategies, but do not differ on matters of core religious doctrine and ultimate goals. They can thus be viewed as manifestations of a single collective ideology, whose common aim is the establishment of the global Islamic State, the Caliphate.[33] Because the distinction between the two camps is often merely one of tactics, the movement from one camp to the other does not require a tremendous leap.

'Abdullah 'Azzām, bin Laden's mentor, is one example of this shift from gradualism to radicalism. Originally a member of the Muslim Brotherhood, he became radicalized by the Soviet invasion of Afghanistan. He then glorified jihad as one of the main pillars of Islam and as the solution to all problems faced by Muslims. He came to believe that jihad is the divine method of establishing Islam in the world and therefore must be both defensive and offensive.[34] In 'Azzām's words:

> We are terrorists. Every Muslim must be a terrorist. Terrorism is an obligation as demonstrated in the Koran and the Sunna. Allah Most High said: "Muster against them [infidels] all the men and cavalry at your command, so that you may strike terror into the heart of your enemy and Allah's enemy" [Q. 8:60] Thus terrorism is a [religious] obligation. And the Messenger of Allah is the first terrorist and the first menace.[35]

Islamist ideology tends to produce a paranoid world view. Islamists indulge in conspiracy theories and scapegoating, identifying enemies who are viewed as seeking at all times and all places to destroy Islam. The outcome of this mentality is that Islamists see themselves as being involved in a permanent conflict between the *umma* and everyone else. For them there is a constant requirement to "fight in Allah's way" (jihad) and to show perseverance in the struggle to liberate and unify the *umma* and to bring humanity under Allah's rule. As we have seen, gradualists concentrate on the various requisite stages in this struggle while radicals focus on immediate violence and terror.

UTILIZATION OF IDEOLOGY FOR MOBILIZATION AND COMMUNICATION

Counterterrorism cannot be conducted effectively without full knowledge of the process of jihad radicalization on the worldwide Web. Whether this process started with the seizure of the Grand Mosque in Mecca or Iran's Shiite revolution, or before, is immaterial. Today, co-option on the 'Net is where it's at. Those not computer literate in Arabic and English cannot begin to understand a multi-dimensional global groundswell of jihadi revenge.[36]

Islamist ideology, both gradualist and radical, is communicated and spread by influential Islamist networks. Each of these networks originated in a specific part of the Muslim world, but they have now spread globally and are influential throughout the Muslim world and the West. These networks aim to influence all aspects of society—politics, law, finance, media and education—using the most modern means of communication.

Globalization, especially globalized communication, has helped Islamists to revive the concept of the one global *umma*. It has promoted the unifying and universal aspects of a text-based Islam while diminishing the impact of local cultural varieties.[37] Globalization, mobility, mass media and the internet have helped create a "virtual" *umma* in cyberspace that can be accessed regardless of international borders. This has given rise to an influential, ideologically driven, Islamist *umma*-elite that creates and distributes vast amounts of information about the *umma*.[38]

The "virtual mosque" now supplements the traditional mosque as a locus of jihadi subversion.[39] The internet is used to publish and distribute texts and promote radical Islamist views as normative for all Muslims, resulting in their widespread acceptance by many Muslims across the world. This cyberspace community provides a global forum for collective action across borders. Local crises are exaggerated and presented as evidence for the global victim-hood of all Muslims. Calls for communal protest actions are organized inter-nationally via the internet and social networks. The violent responses to the Danish cartoons affair in 2005-2006, for example, were stage-managed by Islamist instigators who managed to mobilize the Muslim masses. This out-burst of manipulated Muslim anger further soured relationships between Muslim and Western states and further impeded the integration of Muslims into Western society.[40]

The manipulation of alleged threats, humiliations and insults and the glorification of jihad and resistance result in radicalization and greater Muslim paranoia and resentment against non-Muslims. Radical responses are intentionally provoked, including violent demonstrations and demands for censorship and apologies. A climate is created in which new terrorist attacks seem justified and moderate Muslim voices are marginalized and suppressed. As a result Muslim regimes are forced, often against their will, to fall in line or face the danger of being swept away by the inflamed masses.[41]

Salafi-jihadis especially are surfing the new cyber wave and have become masters at deploying the rhetoric of the global *umma* via the internet to rad-icalize Muslims and gain support and recruits. They have set themselves up as the true defenders of the *umma*, fighting the evil powers threatening Muslims everywhere: Western Crusaders and Zionists as well as infidel and corrupt Muslim regimes that must be toppled and replaced.[42] This propagan-da has caused many Muslims to identify with Islamist ideas and some to become actively involved in jihadi causes.

Since 2005, al Qaeda has reorganized its overall approach to jihad, focus-ing on media operations over terrorist attacks. This rebranding and strategic reframing has also enabled al Qaeda's ageing senior leadership to reclaim a role as the main ideological inspirers of the globally dispersed jihadist move-ment, which is now dominated by younger leaders.[43]

The new generation of media-savvy radical Islamist communicators is exemplified by Anwar al-Awlaki (a Yemeni American), who, prior to his recent death, had a huge presence on the internet. Though he lived in Yemen, he was able to directly inspire many jihadis because of his skillful use of the internet. He mentored Major Nidal Hasan, the Fort Hood gunman. Commenting on the attack by Nidal Hasan on the US army base at Fort Hood, al-Awlaki posted this statement: "No scholar with a grain of Islamic knowledge can defy the clear cut proofs that Muslims today have the right—rather the duty—to fight against American tyranny."[44] Al-Awlaki was also linked via the internet to the young Nigerian, Umar Faroul Abdulmutallab, who attempted to blow up Northwest Airlines Flight 253 to Detroit in December 2010.

GROWING IMPACT OF ISLAMISM

Over the last four decades radical Islamist ideology has made its voice increasingly audible among the currents of contemporary Islamic thought and continues to maintain the initiative, to the point of displaying greater public vitality than any other trend in the Muslim world.[45]

Gradualist Islamist movements are involved in a process of building worldwide alliances and networks at every level: international, regional, and national. They are active in every sphere: religious, political, economic, cultural, and social. As they Islamize Muslim states and regimes, they are also active in non-Muslim states, strengthening isolationist trends among Muslim-minority communities, taking over Muslim institutions and increasing their influence in politics, media, culture and economics. They are adept at changing their discourse and their organizational formats in order to deepen their penetration of state power centers. In the West, they strive to take a leading role within Muslim communities and to present themselves as their only real, authentic representatives and the main interlocutors between governments and Muslims.

As Olivier Roy argues, the traditional concepts of the *umma*, the sovereignty of Islam in the state, and the supremacy of shari'a as revived by Islamists have become a major driving force in contemporary Islam, both in Muslim states and among Muslim minorities elsewhere. The ubiquitous message of contemporary Islamists has resulted in a perceptible shift from national to transnational Islamic identity.[46] Many Muslims now accept the Islamist view that the contemporary *umma* is defective and weak, needing a strong defense against perceived cultural and political attacks.

As Sami Zubaida notes, this ideological mode of thought has become the dominant one among Muslims:

Umma nationalism seems to be, currently, a dominant mode of thought for many Muslims, in the west as well as the Muslim world. It conceives the political world as one of confrontation between

Muslims on the one side and hostile Christians, Jews and Hindus on the other. It is a variant of the "clash of civilizations." It is a totalizing vision which eliminates actual politics. The complexities of Iraq or Afghanistan or Palestine/Israel, of the ethnic politics of Europe, of the struggles of Chechnya, all these are collapsed to a single dimension of religious/communal confrontation. This discourse of umma nationalism seems to be widely held, not only by committed ideological or religious Muslims, but also casually by many nominal Muslims.[47]

This Islamist worldview has even been adopted to a large extent by the Organization of Islamic Cooperation (OIC, formerly the Organization of the Islamic Conference), the powerful global alliance of Muslim states.[48] They put forth the argument that solidarity and common goals must be harnessed to serve the interests of the whole *umma* rather than those of individual Muslim states. By pooling all the available resources of its constituent parts, it might begin a new civilizational cycle in which the *umma* is at the forefront of human power.[49] We have already seen that the Islamist emphasis on the global *umma* tends to lead to a jihad mentality. The Mecca Declaration adopted by the 3rd Islamic Summit of the OIC in January 1981 had indeed adopted Islamist jihadi language, threatening perceived enemies of Islam:

> We are equally determined to engage in *Jihad* with all the means at our disposal, to liberate our occupied territories, to support one another in defending our independence and territorial integrity, in vindicating our rights and in eliminating the injustices wreaked on our nation, depending on our own strength and firm solidarity.[50]

A more recent OIC document repeats Islamist claims that the *umma* is engaged in a civilizational confrontation with the West, which started in the 19th century with the spread of Western imperialism into all Muslim states. Western imperialism corrupted the Muslim world, according to their argument, humiliated it and destroyed its willpower. This however is a temporary stage. The *umma* has experienced many cycles of crisis and recovery in its long history, and it now needs to be revived by applying the true principles of Islam and thereby recovering its essential character and power.[51]

Yet while the OIC makes no secret in many of its official documents of its aim to strengthen Islamism and Islamist ideology across the globe, in other instances it uses politically correct language which will be acceptable to the West in order to obscure its intentions. For example, the OIC has criticized Canadian Prime Minister Stephen Harper for stating that "Islamicism" and "Islamic terrorism" were still the greatest threats facing Canada. The OIC General Secretariat argued that his words were misleading and could create controversy. OIC Secretary General Ekmeleddin Ihsanoglu denounced Harper's remarks as impeding efforts to address intolerance, "bigotry and hatred between religions and diverse cultures."[52]

Confusion in the West

In spite of the ample evidence of a gradualist, non-violent Islamist movement, one which is active across the globe, at both the state and supra-state levels, in the West there is a general failure to understand Islamism and its ideological and intellectual infrastructure. Most analysts focus on the activities of the militant, violent fringe and ignore the massive Islamist social engineering project undertaken by Islamist ideologues and movements. Furthermore, acting in the name of tolerance, Western support for Islamism has undermined the status of moderate Muslims. This has enabled Islamists to prevent a true debate on the acceptable expressions of Islam, thus helping to erode democratic culture in the name of political correctness.[53]

Clearly extreme caution should be exercised in order not to give the impression that the West is at war with Islam. On the other hand, suggesting that the war is limited to al Qaeda is misleading, counterproductive and dangerous. Yet this is what the current administration has done. According to President Obama's National Security Strategy, 2010: "We are at war with a specific network, al-Qa'ida, and its terrorist affiliates."[54] This focuses on only one narrow part of the Islamist whole. The focus should not be limited to al Qaeda, or even to the terrorist ideology promoted by al Qaeda. The focus needs to be broader so as to include the wider Islamist ideology that provides the justification for Islamist terrorism by calling for Islamic dominance and placing the doctrine of jihad at the center of Islam.

Underestimating Ideology

Part of the problem for Western policy-makers is that they have underestimated how long ideological battles last and how resilient ideologies can be, especially if they are embedded in culture and religion. A superficial understanding of how tightly bound Islamist ideologies are to Muslim populations has led some to make premature claims that the ideological battle has been won. In 2008 former CIA Director Michael Hayden asserted that there had been "significant setbacks for al-Qaida globally—and here I'm going to use the word "ideologically," as a lot of the Islamic world pushes back on their form of Islam.[55]

More recently many commentators have seen the Arab Spring as a severe setback to al Qaeda and Islamist jihadi terrorism in general.[56] As the well-known Middle East specialist Mai Yemeni explained:

> Fortunately, bin Laden's death comes at the very moment when much of the Islamic world is being convulsed by the treatment that bin Laden's brand of fanaticism requires: the Arab Spring, with its demands for democratic empowerment (and the absence of demands, at least so far, for the type of Islamic rule that Al Qaeda sought to impose).[57]

However, while the core of al Qaeda may seem to have been weakened by the death of bin Laden and other key leaders, radical Islamism remains a significant threat. The evidence for this is clearly shown by the continued plots and strikes in the West (including on US soil) as well as in Muslim countries, the establishment of new bases (in Yemen, East Africa and the Sahel), the consolidation of existing strongholds and the influx of fresh recruits. Above all al Qaeda and its affiliates have succeeded in their strategy of bleeding Western economies, especially that of the US, as they respond with massively expensive countermeasures to attacks that cost the terrorists very little to launch.[58] Successes such as the death of bin Laden will therefore not have a fundamental impact on the underlying issues that continue to make Islamist radicalism an ongoing threat.

THE PROBLEM OF "ROOT-CAUSE" THEORY

One of the key reasons for the failure of the West adequately to understand and address Islamist ideology is the continuing focus by many Western media and analysts on the erroneous "root-cause analysis" of Islamist terrorism. They assume the primacy of Western responsibility for causing Islamist radicalism, and they ignore the self-definition of radical Islamists. The root causes are explained in terms of socio-economic and political factors such as unemployment, poverty, discrimination, cultural displacement or US and Western foreign policy towards Muslim states. Western analysts argue that Islamist extremism is the product of Western policies, including counter-terrorism policies. A "we know better," patronizing attitude rejects what

Islamists write and say about themselves and their ideology as irrelevant, or as religious idiom hiding the real social, political and economic causes of terrorism.[59] Some argue it is all about politics, others that it is all about economics, others still that it is all about power relations and oppression. The most common conclusion is that Islamist violence is exaggerated and that Muslims are being unfairly targeted. This leads to confusion concerning the nature of the threat and weakens the prospects for counter-terrorism and the promotion of reform.[60]

DENIAL OF THE RELIGIOUS DIMENSION OF ISLAMIST VIOLENCE

Many Western policymakers also mistakenly deny the religious legitimacy of Islamism and Islamist terrorism. In an act of wishful thinking, they dismiss the irrefutable evidence of the link between Islamism, radicalization and terrorism.[61] For example, John O. Brennan, Barack Obama's Assistant for Homeland Security and Counterterrorism, describes jihad as a "legitimate term" that should not be applied to the actions of Islamist terrorists:

> Even as we condemn and oppose the illegitimate tactics used by terrorists, we need to acknowledge and address the legitimate needs and grievances of ordinary people those terrorists claim to represent.
>
> Using the legitimate term jihad, which means to purify oneself or to wage a holy struggle for a moral goal, risks giving these murderers the religious legitimacy they desperately seek but in no way deserve.[62]

President Obama's National Security Strategy of May 2010 again tried to undermine the Islamic credentials of Islamist terrorists:

> ...we reject the notion that al-Qa'ida represents any religious authority. They are not religious leaders, they are killers; and neither Islam nor any other religion condones the slaughter of innocents.[63]

The problem with this misrepresentation is that it implies that Islamists have no connection to classical Islamic traditions. But members of al Qaeda are strongly motivated, indeed utterly consumed, by their religion. To claim that they are not is an absurd distortion. Furthermore, their willingness to slaughter those whom others would see as innocents is specifically justified by their religiously inspired ideology and by religious scholars (*ulama*) of the Salafi-jihadi school.

CONFUSION AS TO THE NATURE OF THE THREAT

The ability of policy-makers in the West to understand the true nature of Islamist ideology is hampered by a stifling political correctness, a sense of post-colonial and post-modern guilt that leads to blaming only "oppressive" Western culture and wishful thinking about the likelihood of Islamists becoming more moderate. Policy decisions have been influenced by an over-riding desire to show that the West is not "at war with Islam," even if this means that security services must deny the influence of certain interpreta-tions of Islamic teachings upon Islamist terrorism. Western confusion has allowed Islamist activists freedom to pursue their strategy to make Islamism the established form of Islam both in Muslim-majority states and among the Western diasporas.[64]

Equally damaging has been the desire for a quick fix and the reluctance to engage in a long-term struggle against the ideological structure that nour-ishes and promotes Islamist terrorism. The difficult decisions and the hard struggle that this battle would entail have frequently been avoided. Others assume that non-violent Islamist movements are equivalent to Western ("Christian democratic") conservative parties eager to participate in the polit-ical struggle against dictators and willing to back secular, democratic regimes in their countries. Indeed, the head of US National Intelligence, James Clapper, recently explained to Congress that the Muslim Brotherhood is a largely secular and moderate group. It has "eschewed violence," decries al Qaeda as a "perversion of Islam," and just wants "social ends" and "a better-ment of the political order in Egypt."[65]

Other politicians, such as British Prime Minister David Cameron, do rec-ognize the ideology of Islamism as the real enemy, but have misconstrued the relationship between Islamism and Islam, arguing that Islamism is a perver-sion of true Islam:

> We need to be absolutely clear on where the origins of these terrorist attacks lie—and that is the existence of an ideology, "Islamist extrem-ism." And we should be equally clear what we mean by this term, dis-tinguishing it from Islam. Islam is a religion, observed peacefully and devoutly by over a billion people. Islamist extremism is a political ide-ology, supported by a minority. At the furthest end are those who back terrorism to promote their ultimate goal: an entire Islamist realm, governed by an interpretation of sharia. Move along the spec-trum, and you find people who may reject violence, but who accept

various parts of the extremist world-view including real hostility towards western democracy and liberal values. It's vital we make this distinction between the religion and the political ideology.[66]

The inability of Western politicians to see the links between radical Islamism, gradual Islamism and traditional Islam makes it difficult for them to recognize what kind of ideological counterattack is needed. They are understandably afraid of offending moderate Muslims or seeming to imply that Islam is a violent religion. However, they must be willing to support the progressive, reformist Muslims who recognize these links and want to reform Islam away from Islamist doctrines and traditional teachings that support them.

CONFUSION AS TO NON-VIOLENT ISLAMISM

In Western states threatened by violent Islamist terrorism, two views have emerged as to how the West should relate to non-violent Islamist groups. Some Western experts (the so-called optimists) recommend that governments accept non-violent Islamists as reliable partners who will help Muslim integration and limit radicalization in Muslim communities. It is argued that only Islamists are engaged at the grassroots and have the credibility effectively to influence large segments of the Muslim community. Their marginalization might trigger a dangerous radicalization, while their engagement will lead to their moderation.[67]

Other experts (the pessimists) call on governments to exclude Islamists from any engagement. They argue that Islamists are deceitfully intent on destroying the very freedoms that allow them to operate in the West. Their organizations should be marginalized and not receive any state recognition, support or funding. It is foolish for governments to grant monopolistic control of the Muslim community to self-appointed groups and leaders with an Islamist ideology opposed to the liberal ethos of the democratic state. Government support will simply enable them to gain control over the Muslim community and marginalize more liberal and secular elements within it.[68]

A recent study by the independent thinktank Demos has named these two views as "moral policing" and "moral oxygen":

The relationship between these groups and individuals that commit terrorist acts is unclear. Broadly speaking, there are two approaches to this issue. On the one hand, the "moral oxygen" argument suggests that radical groups—even when non-violent—provide an environment of intolerance that sustains the inspiration and tacit support for terrorist activity and serves as a recruiting ground... On the other hand, the "moral policing" argument suggests that non-violent radicals provide an important buttress *against* violent action and are best placed to stop people getting involved in terrorist activity. And although some may go on to support or undertake terrorist activity, the vast majority do not.[69]

Some Muslim intellectuals support the view that Islamists are better positioned to prevent terrorism than are moderate Muslims. Sheikh Michael Mumisa, a PhD candidate and Special Livingstone Scholar, University of Cambridge, explains:

The Taliban, Al-Qaida and their affiliate organisations justify their violence by drawing upon Deobandi and Salafi interpretations of Islamic texts. Thus, Deobandi and Salafi fatwas against violent extremism are more effective in delegitimizing extremist groups than fatwas and theological arguments from Sufi scholars such as Tahir al-Qadri and others however well-meaning they may be.[70]

Politicians, academics and media of the optimist "moral policing" view have formed alliances with non-violent Islamist groups and are lobbying government and public opinion in their favor. Some Christians are found in this group too, often influenced by liberation theology.[71] In spite of deep ideological differences, what seems to unite them is a deep aversion to right-wing politics. Many are pro-Palestinian, anti-Israel and anti-American, who view Islamism positively as an authentic Muslim resistance movement that best represents the voice of oppressed Muslims and their desire for liberation.[72]

There are proponents of this view even in the police forces. The London Metropolitan Police Force established the Muslim Contact Unit (MCU) in 2002, comprised of a dozen highly trained police officers whose task was to interact with the local Muslim communities in London. The MCU attempted to establish trust-based relationships with community leaders who could help prevent terrorist attacks and counter the radicalization of local Muslims. Under the leadership of Robert Lambert, the MCU decided to partner with a variety of Islamists, including some of the most radical voices in London's Salafi community.[73] Lambert argued that the "ideal yes-saying" Muslim leaders lack credibility in their communities and have no knowledge of radicalism. He therefore advocated "police negotiation leading to partnership with Muslim groups conventionally deemed to be subversive to democracy." According to Lambert, only these groups have the credibility to challenge the narrative of al Qaeda and its influence on young Muslims. Under the Channel Project, for example, Salafi imams worked with police officials to identify youths undergoing a radicalization process and attempt to divert them from violent extremism. Lambert argues that nonviolent Salafis have the capacity to prevent young men from becoming terrorists and hence are necessary counterterrorism assets.[74] He also argued that the Brixton Salafis were the most effective group fighting London-based violent extremists in the 1990s.[75] This has created suspicion of the Metropolitan Police amongst other British groups such as Sikhs, Hindus and moderate Muslims, who no longer feel comfortable to pass information to the police and have lost confidence in them because of their close relationship and support of Islamist groups. Within the police force itself, some senior officers have also viewed this development with great concern. However, British Home Secretary Theresa May criticized the Prevent program initiated by the previous Labour government as a part of its "Contest" strategy for counter-terrorism. The strategy had four aspects: Prevent (to stop people from becoming terrorists or supporting terrorism), Pursue (to stop terrorist attacks), Protect (to strengthen protection against terrorist attack), Prepare (to mitigate the impact of an attack where it cannot be stopped). May described Prevent as a "flawed programme" that allowed the possibility of public funding by central and local authorities to reach extremist groups. She said that it "failed to tackle the extremist ideology that not only undermines the cohesion of our society, but also inspires would be terrorists to seek to bring death and destruction to our towns and cities." Lord Carlile of Berriew, the independent reviewer of the Prevent review, described revised Prevent plans as "a template for challenging the extremist ideas and terrorist actions which seek to undermine the rule of law and fundamental British political values and institutions."[76]

HOW TO COUNTER THE ISLAMIST IDEOLOGY

Global Islamism with its multifaceted jihad must be countered. But how? First, Western governments must get over their discomfort with religion. The return of the religious dimension to domestic and international affairs must be recognized and accepted. Western leaders and policymakers must acknowledge that they are engaged in a long-term ideological struggle based on religious dogma, which has affinities to the ideological wars against Fascism, Nazism and communism. Given the centrality of ideology to this battle, Western leaders must then make a commitment to winning the war of ideas. To do so requires a three-pronged strategy:

1. Understand the ideology
2. Directly counter the Islamist threat
3. Promote reform within the Muslim world

1. Understanding the Ideology

First and foremost, the West must do a better job of understanding the ideology of Islamism. As we have seen, after a period of sidestepping this issue, Britain has now come back around to putting the ideology front and center. According to the new British policy, a revised version of the Prevent strategy, Britain would first, "respond to the ideological challenge of terrorism and the threat from those who promote it." "In doing so," the report goes on to say, "we must be clear: the ideology of extremism and terrorism is the problem..."[77]

But while the UK is going one direction, the United States is going the opposite way. The U.S. has had a decade-old strategy of dissociating talk about terrorism from any mention of Islam, believing that this would help mollify the Muslim world and prevent further radicalization. In keeping with this tactic, the Obama Administration calls its counter-terrorism program Countering Violent Extremism (CVE), not, for example, Countering Global Jihad, or Countering Islamist Violence, which would have been a more accurate descriptor. In recent months, the Obama Administration has taken this policy to new extremes. In the fall of 2011, the White House initiated a widespread review of all counterterrorism training in both the military and domestic law enforcement. Slides that mentioned Islam in the context of terrorism were deemed "incendiary," and trainers who had focused too much on the ideology of Islamism were barred from further training.[78] The focus of counter-terrorism efforts, as laid out on the December 2011 document, *Strategic Implementation Plan for Empowering Local Partners to Prevent Violent Extremism in the United States*, is not to understand and to fight the ideology driving would-be jihadis, but rather to empower "local stakeholders to build resilience against violent extremism."[79]

Yet Islamism and Islamist terrorism cannot be understood and tackled without identifying their religious core. Policy-makers in the West must avoid the self-deception and wishful thinking involved in pretending that these are not religiously inspired and not legitimized by religion. Thankfully, this has now been recognized in Britain and Canada, where, as noted above, senior politicians have acknowledged that ideology is the key element that needs to be addressed in the war against terrorism. The question is: will American policy-makers eventually move down this road as well? Political correctness must be avoided, because it obscures a clear definition and identification of the enemy. The close links between mainstream Islam, Islamism and jihadism must be acknowledged, as it is clear that the legitimacy Islamist ideology has among Muslims derives from classical Islamic theology.

It is also important to accept the linkage between Islamism and early and classical Islam, which is the main cause of its influence on ordinary Muslims.[80] It is therefore essential carefully to study and analyze Islamist ideology, history and practice, and the reasons for its wide appeal to ordinary Muslims. At the same time its vulnerabilities and weaknesses must be analyzed and strategies developed to utilize them. Methods must be employed to counter its appeal and a sophisticated strategy developed to challenge Islamist assertions about ideology, Islam and politics.[81]

2. Promoting Reform within the Muslim World

Unless Muslims make a stand and reclaim Islam from Islamists, then future generations of Muslims will adopt a political ideology as their religion.[82]

Ultimately the war against terrorist ideology will be won or lost by Muslims. Muslim governments, Muslim religious leaders and Muslim intellectuals are far more influential than any of their Western counterparts in reaching Muslim minds and hearts. Muslims must be encouraged to undertake a far-reaching reform of Islam that will cut off the violent roots that nourish Islamism. As the prominent Muslim-American reformer Zuhdi Jasser has stated:

Political Islam has a viral recurrence in the form of an infection which needs a Muslim counter-jihad in order to purge it. Thus, we cannot win this ideological war without the leadership of Muslim anti-Islamists. The radical and political ideologies of Islamism, Wahhabism, Salafism, Al Qaedism, Jihadism, and Caliphism, to name a few, cannot be defeated without anti-Islamist, anti-Wahhabi, anti-Salafist, anti-Al Qaedist, anti-Jihadist, and anti-Caliphist devout Muslims.[83]

A new hermeneutic of the violent Medinan verses in the Qur'an used by radicals and accepted as more authoritative than the peaceful ones is necessary. Most Muslims still accept the traditional doctrine of abrogation that justifies the radical interpretation of the Qur'an. Without a thoroughgoing reform of Islam, assertions that "Islam is a religion of peace" are not convincing.[84] Should such a reinterpretation be accepted by the majority of Muslims worldwide, the violent radicals and the ideologies sustaining them might be marginalized.

The Progressive Muslim Challenge to Islamism

It is worth noting that Islamism is being challenged from a number of different quarters within the Muslim world and employing a number of different arguments. Perhaps most significant of these is the challenge by progressive Muslims. They represent a wide variety of approaches to the challenges of modernity and are generally characterized by a peaceful approach to Western and other non-Muslim cultures. Most see themselves as good Muslims who oppose atheistic ideology but embrace the separation of religion from state and politics. They accept what they consider to be a core of basic Islamic values, distilled from the Islamic source texts, as spiritual and moral norms that override coercive political and social interpretations. However, they are willing to ignore traditional Islamic concepts and interpretations that contradict modern values of freedom and equality. They see a need radically to change traditional, orthodox Islam in such a way as to integrate liberal humanistic values at its very core.[85]

Progressive reformers aim to liberalize Islamic teaching on jihad, shari'a and the relationship of religion and state. They reject a literal interpretation of the Islamic sources, especially on the subjects of jihad, the Caliphate and non-Muslims. They weaken the authority of the Hadith, and interpret violent passages in the Qur'an and Hadith as normative only in their immediate historical contexts and therefore not applicable today. They view Muhammad as a fallible human who sinned in the violent episodes of his life, and they reject the classical view that his example is to be emulated in every detail by Muslims in every age. They spiritualize the Islamic teaching on jihad, seeing it as a moral battle against personal sin, and they explicitly deny the validity of military and violent aspects of jihad for today.

Progressive reformers include Sayyid al-Qimny, Abd al-Hamid al-Ansary, Hassan Mneimneh, Latif Lakhdar and Muhammed al-Sanduk, whose views can be seen on the Almuslih website.[86] Many others could be mentioned as well, including the Malaysian "Sisters in Islam," the British publicist Ziauddin Sardar, the late Nasr Hamid Abu Zayd (Egypt), Abdou Filali-Ansary (Morocco), Abdelmajid Charfi (Tunisia), Farid Esack (South Africa / USA), Ebrahim Moosa (USA), Asghar Ali Engineer (India), Abdullahi an-Naim (Sudan / USA), Amina Wadud (USA), Fatima Mernissi (Morocco), Leila Babès (France), Khaled Abou El Fadl USA), Nurcholish Madjid (Indonesia), Farish Noor (Malaysia), and Ömer Özsoy (Turkey).

These contemporary, progressive Muslim reformers are active, but they are under great pressure from traditionalists and Islamists and lack resources and security. Progressive reformers remain largely marginalized. Progressives, however, represent the best hope for a liberal, tolerant and terrorist-free Islam. They urgently need recognition and help from academia, media and governments. They also need their voice to be heard within the Muslim communities. It is to be hoped that their versions of Islam will develop and that they will be able to organize and create grass-roots movements that can represent larger segments of Muslim society.[87]

The Traditional Muslim Challenge to Islamism

A very different set of arguments comes from what could be called traditional Muslims. Whereas the progressive Muslims look to the future and an Islam that can adapt to the challenges of modernity, the traditionalists look more to the past and to an uncorrupted Islam. In that sense they sound like to Salafists, but they differ in that they see in the very foundations of Islam a way of inhabiting the world peacefully and living beside people of other faiths or even those who chose to leave Islam. They condemn modern-day extremists by drawing a parallel between violent, offensive jihadists and the Kharijites, an historical sect dating from the 4th Caliphate, who withdrew their support from the Caliph on the grounds that his actions did not conform to the Qur'an. They became violent and fanatical and dismissed as infidels or apostates all those who did not demonstrate strict adherence to the faith. Like the Kharijites, today's Islamists accuse "moderate" (non-violent or non-Salafist) Muslims of deviation and misguidance, of not being true Muslims. The response of the traditional Muslims is to criticize these *takfiris* (in this case, Islamists who accuse peaceful Muslims of not being good Muslims) and jihadis for dividing the *umma* and for killing good Muslims.

Several conferences have been organized condemning *takfir* as un-Islamic and contrary to shari'a law. One such was the International Islamic Conference convened in Amman, Jordan, July 4-6, 2005, which issued a united statement (also called a fatwa) that forbade calling any Muslim a *kafir*.[88] King Abdullah II of Jordan has been a staunch supporter of these efforts, declaring in December 2009:

> Jordan is determined to carry on with its legitimate and historic role to confront the campaign of distortion being waged against our honourable religion by rejecting extremism, violence, and *takfiri* thought. We will continue to convey the true principles of Islam, the religion of moderation and tolerance.[89]

However, most policies countering Islamist terrorist ideology are carried out by traditionalists who are not prepared to tackle the deeper theological legitimacy that terrorism derives from classical Islam. They are unwilling to argue that aggressive texts in the sources should be contextualized and that some sources and models are not applicable to the modern world. Faced with Muslims committing acts of terror in the name of Islam, many traditional Muslim leaders continue to deny that this has anything to do with Islam.

Professor Peter Riddell, of the Melbourne School of Theology, argues that the denial mentality characteristic of traditional Muslim leaders leads them to whitewash the Muslim sacred texts, suppressing any offending elements. This denial allows them to continue to project the blame on factors external to Islam, such as the foreign policies of Western states, Israel, and the invasions of Afghanistan and Iraq. He calls on traditional Muslim leaders to take the bold step of reinterpreting the verses in the Qur'an and Hadith used by radicals to justify their actions.[90]

The Former Jihadist Challenge to Islamism

Finally, a third source of pressure on the Islamists from within the Muslim world is the case of former Islamists and jihadis who have publicly recanted. Notably, Said Imam al-Sharif, also known as "Dr Fadl," once a main leader of Egyptian Jihad and one of al-Zawahiri's early mentors, published a book in 2007 entitled *Document of Right Guidance for Jihad in Egypt and the World*. In the book he denounced al Qaeda as a "criminal" movement that had failed Islam and he renounced his previous commitment to the violent jihadist ideology.[91] Several senior leaders of Al-Jama'a al-Islamiyya in

Egypt form another group of revisionists, who have recently published several books recanting their pursuit of violence against the state as misguided and renouncing its future use.

The effectiveness of critiques by such prominent former jihadis is reflected by the energy with which jihadis try to refute their arguments. Thus, following the publication of Imam Sharif's book, no less a figure than Ayman al-Zawahiri felt compelled to write a refutation.[92]

3. Directly Countering the Islamists

Yet even while reform of Islam, or at least a disavowal of the exclusivist, supremacist Islamist ideology, will have to come from within the Muslim world, that does not mean that the West has no role to play. Indeed it is critical that West engage in the war of ideas, not least because it is the current lack of engagement and adequate understanding that has led to the state of confusion and contradiction we find ourselves in. Islamists must be identified and isolated wherever they are and in whatever form they disguise themselves. They must be isolated from ordinary Muslims and prevented from penetrating their institutions and Western centers of power, as well as from broadcasting their propaganda. This is the first step in the counter-insurgency strategy that Julian Lewis describes as "identify, isolate, neutralize and negotiate" (double-I, double-N strategy).[93] Effective counter-propaganda is important in this venture. Lewis asserts that "systematic use against one's opponents of their own words, promises and predictions has always been a most effective propaganda tool."[94]

Western discourse must discredit arguments that Islam is under attack from the West while delegitimizing Islamism by presenting it as a totalitarian political ideology detrimental to Muslims. The weakness of Islamist ideas and the broadcasting of Islamist failures and brutalities must be widely communicated. Islamists should be isolated and subverted wherever possible. To discredit the Islamists it is vital that "all who need to resist them be made aware of what they believe, declare and intend to do."[95] However, this approach has many pitfalls and can backfire, especially as non-Muslim channels of communication are automatically suspect to many Muslims. The appeal of the Islamists is rooted in the Islamic source texts and this makes it very difficult to discredit them in the eyes of Muslims. The development of deradicalization approaches within the Muslim world by Muslim scholars has gone some way to meeting this need.

Negotiation, unlike the other three elements, can be used only periodically and only from a position of strength or at least stalemate. It cannot be attempted when the radicals appear to be winning. When conditions are appropriate, deals can be proposed ranging from granting a simple amnesty to requiring genuine concessions. In Islamic countries other aspects can come into play, for example, bringing in the family or appropriate Islamic leaders.

The West must intensify the anti-Islamist propaganda or information war and make it more sophisticated and efficient. As Julian Lewis asks, "Where is the Western response to the extensive output of the [Islamist] message via the Arab media and the Internet?" Islamists must also be neutralized by sophisticated measures that deny them any propaganda victories and popular sympathy.[96] Western public sympathy for terrorists' causes, such as the view that terror is the only weapon of the "oppressed" and the "wretched of the earth" who have no other choice, serves only to legitimize their immoral and criminal acts and to strengthen their cause. Therefore in addition to confronting the Islamist movements and individuals directly, we should also delegitimize all Western groups, individuals and movements that support and sustain Islamist discourse and power.

Stephen Ulph, a leading Western scholar on jihadist ideology, stresses the central importance of knowing jihadist thinking well enough to identify its weaknesses and vulnerabilities.[97] We must create centers of research on the political dimension of the Islamist movement; we must read radical Islamist polemics and self-analysis. Through that process, the weak spots in the Islamists' argument can be identified. In their own self-criticism, and in the doubts raised by other Muslims about Islamist doctrine and practice, their vulnerabilities are revealed. These then form the foundation in the construction of a counter-ideology program. Such a program can be further enhanced by identifying legal points of controversy and weakness, sources of prestige, and the emergence of trends and ideas that challenge and compete with the Islamist ideology. But without an extensive and ongoing understanding of the Islamists' narrative, their ideology cannot be countered and defeated.

CONCLUSION

The fact of a long-term ideological struggle must be accepted. This struggle includes not only Islamist attacks on Western targets but also the battle within the Islamic world about what type of Islam will be dominant. Breakthroughs such as the killing of bin Laden are important, but the prospects for defeating the Islamist terrorist ideology depend critically upon being able to define the ideology clearly and precisely—its aims, the movements and organizations involved, and the methods by which it draws support and creates legitimacy. It is vital to investigate ways to defeat the Islamist ideology, analyze the sources of Islamist resilience and target its vulnerabilities. This process includes studying the internal weaknesses of the various groups involved and their claims to Islamic authenticity. To reverse the radicalization of Muslims by Islamists will require a long-term strategy. A bolder and deeper reform in the Muslim world must be encouraged in order to break the hold of Islamism and the cycle of violence. This reform must be focused in particular upon a change in the way the sources and texts of Islam are interpreted. Progressive voices within the Muslim community should be encouraged while the radicals are delegitimized, both from inside and outside Islam. The Muslim community leadership that has a progressive and irenic interpretation of Islam must be supported, rather than marginalized, as is currently the case, while those who espouse Islamist ideologies must be isolated and disenfranchised.

The Arab Spring is rapidly turning into an Islamist Summer as Gulf States such as Saudi Arabia and Qatar back the emerging Islamist movements that they have already been nurturing for years with financial and ideological support. As Arab countries throw off the yoke of authoritarian and dictatorial governments, so political Islam has begun to shape their societies with a new totalitarianism. The West must take note. For both Saudi Arabia and Qatar have also been involved in Western countries, reshaping the ideologies of their co-religionists in these countries and gradually transforming what was previously a peaceful and almost privatized Islam into an Islam that is more concerned with shaping the political agenda than with developing the piety of the believers. The challenge for the West, given their commitment to the Gulf States, will be how, on the one hand, to continue to work with them on geopolitical, military, economic and energy issues while, on the other hand, reducing their influence in Western countries and countering their efforts to radicalize Muslim minorities in the West.

The West and Islam are currently at a crossroads—whether they clash or move forward together peacefully has yet to be determined. But without a meaningful discussion of the ideas at stake, the current conflict has little hope of resolution. The West's insistence on denying the deeper roots of current Islamist terrorism, no matter how well intentioned, does a disservice both to the West and to Islam. It hampers the West's ability to undermine its enemies and thereby ensure its own safety, and it gives primacy to those who carry the biggest stick—the violent and non-violent Islamists. Censoring all mention of Islam from debate is a service to no one, and whatever sense of self-satis-faction that may arise in those who feel they are doing Islam a favor will be short-lived indeed. The future for both the West and for Islam lies in honest discussion, no matter how painful or uncomfortable that discussion might be at times.

ISLAMISM AND TOTALITARIANISM: THE CHALLENGE OF COMPARISON

Stephen Ulph

This paper is an analysis of the parallels between the ideology of radical Islamism and the European totalitarian ideologies of the 20th century. It explores how a comparison between the deeper intellectual underpinnings of Islamism with those of historical western totalitarianisms may allow us a point of entry to deconstructing the ideology. A neutral research endeavour on the points of similarity would establish the nature and extent of the parallels, and to what extent these are due to direct contacts or simply to parallel trajectories of thought that express deeper instincts. It would at the very least establish that the Islamist intellectual infrastructure does not represent a pure, unmingled standalone Truth, as its exponents claim, but is rather to be seen as a typical product of a broader spectrum of human ideological speculation.

An association of political totalitarianism with Islam is neither unknown nor particularly new. As far back as 1920 Bertrand Russell was intrigued by the parallels between the nascent Bolshevism and Islam. "Among religions," he wrote,

Bolshevism is to be reckoned with Mohammedanism rather than with Christianity and Buddhism. Christianity and Buddhism are primarily personal religions, with mystical doctrines and a love of contemplation. Mohammedanism and Bolshevism are practical, social, unspiritual, concerned to win the empire of this world.

Russell went on to observe that

Bolshevism combines the characteristics of the French Revolution with those of the rise of Islam... Marx has taught that Communism is fatally predestined to come about; this produces a state of mind not unlike that of the early successors of Mahommet... *what Mohammedanism did for the Arabs, Bolshevism may do for the Russians.*[1]

In a similar vein, Carl Jung and Karl Barth were making comparisons between fascism and Islam in the late 1930s: "We do not know whether Hitler is going to found a new Islam," wrote Jung. "He is already on the way; he is like Muhammad. The emotion in Germany is Islamic, warlike and Islamic. They are all drunk with a wild man."[2] Barth's view was that "*it is impossible to understand National Socialism unless we see it in fact as a new Islam, its myth as a new Allah, and Hitler as this new Allah's Prophet.*"[3] In 1937 Edgar Alexander Emmerich published *The Hitler Mythos,* in which he compared National Socialism with "Mohammedanism" and found similarities between them, although he stated that his interest in the comparison was on external organizational forms, mass psychological effects and militant fanaticism.

Historically the parallel has been employed as a criticism of these totalitarian systems, not of Islamism. "Communism," wrote Jules Monnerot in the 1950s, was "the Islam of the 20th century" in that it was both "a *secular religion*" and a "*universal state.*"[4] In 1963 Manfred Halpern noted how the Islamist ideology of the Muslim Brotherhood and its reconstruction of society through the "spiritualization of politics" was not in itself a unique phenomenon. It was, instead, a

Middle Eastern version of fascism ... stamped ... by a kinship with certain religio-political movements which spread in Western Europe at the beginning of its modern age.[5]

At the time such a parallel was not recognized, since there was no compelling evidence of an expansionist program of Islamist totalitarians on which to base the comparison, while contemporary developments in the emergent Islamist politics were still far below the horizon and of interest to only a few

Orientalists. The Orientalist and former communist Maxime Rodinson at the time considered Monnerot's views as "paradoxical, almost heretical", but later came to believe that with respect to its "coercive orthodoxy" "Islam and communism display an astonishing similarity." Monnerot's work is now increasing in relevance, but with his argument inversed: Islamism is now the "communism of the 21st century." Similarly, as Walter Laqueur illustrates, Manfred Halpern's analysis of the fascist nature of the neo-Islamic totalitarian movements such as the Muslim Brotherhood was not considered at the time, since they appeared on the wane. They were, however, "to some extent prescient."[6]

The comparison of Islamism and totalitarianism is not without its critics. The association with Fascism has been particularly controversial, but much of the criticism has had to do with superficial understanding of the ideologies of both Fascism and Islamism, so that the issue became irrelevantly bound up with the historical manifestation of Nazism, of race exclusivism[7] and charismatic leadership. How, for instance, can a fully totalitarian conception of society be compared with Islamism's category of *dhimma* status for those who do not wish to participate fully in the ruling ideology?[8] And where, critics could ask, does self-sacrifice fit in?[9]

With Communism the association has fared little better, with objections raised that there is in Islamism no ideology of "the state," yet if Islamists eschew loyalty to an existing state, this does not prove that they are anti-statist. In fact the preoccupation of forming an Islamic state, voiced by al Qaeda and the Taliban, contradicts this objection. Indeed the formation of the Islamic state is a prerequisite for fulfilling the goals of a supra-state designed to embody the supremacy of the Islamic faith. Both communists and Islamists aim to create totalitarian supra-states and believe that the interests of the individual should be subordinated to the interests of this state. In both ideologies, this state is considered to be a temporary phase serving a further purpose. Far from an ideology of no state, therefore, Islamism actually maintains an ideology of *one sole permitted state.*

Attempts to associate Islamist movements with these 20th century totalitarianisms have tended to focus on the organizational aspects of the parallelism, or the mere fact of political alliances. For instance, references to Muslim Brotherhood founder Hassan al-Bannā's modelling of his movement's organizational structure on Mussolini's Blackshirts, or the close relations between Palestinian Mufti Hajj Muhammad Amin al-Husseini and Adolf Hitler, while interesting in themselves, do not prove a conclusive influence on the deeper ideological level. For the purposes of countering the ideology, these are less illuminating than investigating the *intellectual* processes that are paralleled between the systems. For it is this type of comparison, one that goes beyond the manifestation in political programs, that can highlight how the Islamists and European totalitarians follow parallel mental trajectories, and answer to parallel—human—pre-occupations.

By observing these common mental trajectories the discussion can examine the implications of this commonality for the claims made by the Islamists to a divinely sanctioned legitimacy for their ideology. This type of discussion is key to a successful counter-ideology since, unlike any other approach, it argues by using the terms of reference of the extremists themselves. Within these terms of reference it specifically targets the following claims:

- The uniqueness of the Islamists' model for an Islamic society;
- The divine origin of the doctrines underpinning the ideology;
- The uniqueness of the political applications of their ideology.

That is, it penetrates to the vitals of Islamist extremism and its militant expression in jihadism: the pretension to an unassailable Islamic "authenticity".

THE IMPORTANCE OF AUTHENTICITY

Why is this targeting of authenticity important? First of all, any targeting of the ideological infrastructure of jihadism has major implications for a counter-ideology response in that while military reverses can be explained away by the appeal to a struggle that is taking place on a long-term scale, ideological justification cannot brook defeat at any point. Secondly, and more importantly, one of the basic building blocks of that justification—a *Leitmotif* in the vast corpus of their literature and a core formula for jihadist resilience—is *authenticity*. This is the arbiter of their moral authority on all matters, the yardstick for determining what constitutes for them, and for their propaganda message, the difference between true or counterfeit Islam. The authenticity pre-occupation is therefore key to Islamism and the resilience of the jihadists.

To understand why this is so we should look at what constitutes the intellectual cradle of Islamism. In response to what they see as a progressive globalization of ideas that conflict with some fundamentals of Islamic belief, Islamist radicals claim to be providing the "true model" for a Muslim to live his life. Their claim is that their model of Islam is the authentic one, because it is based on the words and deeds of *al-salaf al-sālihūn* (the "virtuous pred-ecessors"), that is, the earliest Muslim community. The behaviour of these predecessors is considered to set the pattern to be emulated, precisely because they are "authentic" and pre-date the compromises made in Islamic medieval and modern history with the practical exigencies of mundane power. This is the position of the *Salafiyya*, those who follow the practices of the *Salaf*, and is the spectrum of thought from which the *Salafiyya-Jihādiyya* school derives (the school to which al Qaeda associates itself) and which it sees itself as perfecting.

The authenticity pre-occupation grants the *mujāhidīn* considerable resilience. It allows them to justify their ideological standpoint—the reacti-vation of militant jihad—on the grounds that:

- as Muslims they are commanded to imitate the Prophet and the early community, and given that the Prophet and the early Companions waged *jihad*, their argument is made for them;
- since they are therefore simply following the Prophetic precedent as outlined in the Hadith and *sīra* literature—their behavior and exam-ple is more authoritative. This means that in a contest over what con-stitutes true Islam, if fought over with the text, the jihadists are likely to win;
- since they are returning to a pristine template they are not obligated to follow (*taqlīd*) the directions of the legal schools which clearly have abandoned the template through corruption over the course of history. Anti-radical scholars are therefore collaborators with the *jāhiliyya* ("the Age of Ignorance")[10] and thus have no authority over them.

If authority depends on authenticity as understood by the Salafist prece-dent, it spells out immunity to alternative streams of Islamic thought, a fact that goes some way to explaining why de-programming initiatives have to date yielded mixed results. For without any challenge being mounted to this authenticity the jihadists can retain an unassailable resilience. The problem is, if the *mujāhidīn* do have the scriptural texts behind them—at least to their own satisfaction—what is it that could damage their claims to authenticity?

Behaving Like the Infidel

The one arena of debate which overrides the hermetically sealed, logocentric mental universe of the Islamists, in which they feel themselves supremely confident, may be summed up by the legal principle *al-shabīh bil-munkar makrūh*—"that which resembles something forbidden is loathsome." This is a general Islamic principle, but under the more orthodox and uncompromising stipulations of the doctrine of *al-walā' wal-barā'* ("Loyalty and Renunciation") the "true Muslim" does not assimilate into the enemy's society or imitate its ways on even the most trivial level, even to the point of speaking, dressing or eating and drinking like the infidel, since according to the Prophet's saying: *"anyone who associates with a polytheist and lives with him is like him"*[11]—let alone sharing their intellectual political conceptions. In the Islamist system, expelling as far as practically possible every element of western cultural influence is therefore a basic instinct.

This basic instinct is of considerable value for a counter-ideology initiative. If the political program of the Islamists is claimed to be unique as a divinely sanctioned endeavour, it should be fairly well Islamic from *Alif* to *Yā*. Therefore, if it can be conclusively established that the mindset and the tendencies of Islamists lack this uniqueness, and if it can be conclusively proved that the ideology of Islamism demonstrates identical patterns of thought to man-made infidel political systems unconnected with Islam, or even with religious faith at all, then the claim to their endeavors being "in God's path" is severely, if not terminally, compromised. The question that the Islamists must answer is why a divinely ordered system should end up resembling so closely some mid-20th century European, infidel totalitarian collective ideologies, such as those represented by the Italian or German Fascisms or Marxism-Leninism.[12]

By calibrating the parallels (and differences) by means of a comparative approach we may be able to draw a sharper focus on these claims to uniqueness and Islamic authenticity. The comparison can be applied by degrees:

- *on the parallels with sacralized political totalitarianisms,*
- *on the parallels with fascistized religious movements,* and
- *on the parallels with doctrinally absolutist non-Muslim religious movements.*

As is in the nature of comparisons the fit will not be seamless on all fronts. But since theirs is a movement that strenuously defines itself as *authentic, uniquely Islamic* and *divinely sanctioned,* Islamists are obligated to engage in the discussion and demonstrate why the comparison *at any level* is inappropriate.

Ultimately, the aim of this approach is to replace the understanding promoted by Islamists of a Clash of Cultures with one that may be more appropriately seen as a *Clash of Chronologies*, that is, an issue of civilizational development, sharing features held in common with the political and religious development of other, non-Muslim, societies.

THE PROPRIETY OF THE COMPARISON

At the outset we should remove the reticence to group totalitarian ideologies and religious belief in the same discussion. A religious belief is no more immune than any other system to being passed through a totalitarian filter by believers who have their own preconceptions on how it should be practiced and applied. To demonstrate this it would be useful to take a look at some core terms employed in the comparison.

Firstly, a baseline definition for totalitarianism:

> The term "totalitarianism" can be taken as meaning: an experiment in political domination undertaken by a revolutionary movement, with an integralist conception of politics... it seeks the subordination, integration and homogenisation of the governed on the basis of the integral politicization of existence, whether collective or individual.[13]

By directly mobilizing the "people" or working through an élite who speak for the "true" members of the community, the task of the new breed of revolutionaries is to achieve cultural hegemony for their new system of values. From this position, the aim is to control the channels of opinion and education for the ultimate purpose of bringing about the total rebirth of the nation (however this is conceived) from its present decadence. This rejuvenation or re-birth of the nation, conceived as an organic total, constitutes the "mythic core" to this political ideology in all its various permutations.

Secondly, due to some controversies registered on the subject of Islamism's relation to the fascist expression of totalitarianism, it is worth establishing some background.

"Fascism" originally referred to the corporatist society promoted by Benito Mussolini in Italy, to describe a system whereby the state would function as one organic whole. As a result of the priorities of Marxist academics, writings on fascism have tended to stress its elements of nihilism, reaction, deviant pathology, personal megalomania and the lack of a cohesive ideology, along with a muddled re-configuration of national history and myth. Beyond that broad definition there is a lack of unanimity between theorists of Fascism as to what constitutes the core, defining elements of the term.[14]

Given that there were considerable divergences between the authoritarianisms of Hitler, Mussolini and Franco it is not surprising that the attempts to make parallels between Fascism and Islamism have excited controversy and opposition. But since the early 1990s comparative studies in Fascism as an international phenomenon, one that takes Fascism as a *movement* rather than as a series of geographically defined political struggles, have coalesced theories of a generic Fascism, one that can be taken as a type of mentality[15] or a series of intellectual tendencies, with some consistent features identifiable in each of its political manifestations. For instance, the Italian author and academic Umberto Eco in his essay *Ur-Fascism* argued that one could eliminate from a fascist regime one or more features, and it would still be recognizable as fascist:

> Take away imperialism from fascism and you still have Franco and Salazar. Take away colonialism and you still have the Balkan fascism of the Ustashes. Add to the Italian fascism a radical anti-capitalism (which never much fascinated Mussolini) and you have Ezra Pound. Add a cult of Celtic mythology and the Grail mysticism (completely alien to official fascism) and you have one of the most respected fascist gurus, Julius Evola.[16]

For Roger Griffin[17], such an approach that pares down the analysis to intellectual mechanisms

> arguably has other merits too as a heuristic device. It highlights the existence of the mythopoeic matrix which determines how the ideology of a particular form of fascism has often been synthesized from a bewildering range of ideas, both left and right, conservative and anti-conservative, national and supranational, rational and anti-rational.[18]

Therefore, more than a matter of charismatic leaders, mass rallies and militarism, a common baseline denominator suitable for defining the ideology of fascism may be given as "*palingenetic populist ultra-nationalism,*"[19] that is:

a revolutionary form of nationalism, one that sets out to be a political, social and ethical revolution, welding the "people" into a dynamic national community. The core myth that inspires this project is that only a populist, trans-class movement of purifying, cathartic national rebirth (palingenesis) can stem the tide of decadence.[20]

Thirdly, the relationship between these political systems and religious belief: that there was a religious dimension to politics was overtly claimed by totalitarian thinkers themselves. "*Il fascismo è una concezione religiosa*," according to Benito Mussolini and Giovanni Gentile writing in 1932, without their intending any metaphor. For these, a human was defined by his relation to a "superior law, an objective Will that transcends the particular individual and elevates him to becoming a conscious member of a spiritual society."[21]

The last fifteen years has seen the study of totalitarianism theory adjusting its focus in this very direction, towards theories that penetrate deeper into Fascism's core motivation as a "political religion."[22] As the noted historian of Fascism Professor Emilio Gentile[23] explains:

> The concept of political religion does not refer solely to the institution of a system of beliefs, rites or symbols; it also relates to other fundamental aspects of the totalitarian experiment, that is, to the conquest of society, the homogenisation of the society formed by the governed, an anthropological revolution.[24]

The characteristic of the totalitarian political religion, he maintains, is the extremist and exclusive nature of its historical mission:

> Political religion does not accept coexistence with other political ideologies and movements; it denies the autonomy of the individual while affirming the primacy of the community; it sanctifies violence as a legitimate weapon in the struggle against those it considers internal and external enemies.

This violence is employed to force the process of transformation as an instrument of a collective regeneration:

> ... it imposes obligatory observance of collective regeneration; it imposes obligatory observance of its commandments and participation in the political cult.[25]

These elements—the rebirth of a new type of individual subordinated to a homogenized collective purpose, in a society that is conceived as spiritual, one that has been imposed by conquest and that denies legitimacy to all other forms of belief or social structure—form the basis of this renewed focus on the core generic features of totalitarianism.

Since the raw material for this type of study is largely European, there is naturally yet to develop a comparable body of literature focusing on its manifestation beyond this cultural arena. However, as renewed studies of totalitarianism (and Fascism in particular) converge like this with the study of political religion,[26] it would seem logical that a study of a similar convergence in the modern ideology of radical, politicized Islam should find a broader acceptance than it currently enjoys.

Generic Parallels Between Islamism and Totalitarianism

Given the problems with defining the exact contours of the totalitarian systems, it will therefore be more useful to take their more common generic elements in order to illustrate any parallels that exist with Islamist ideology. Taking as starting point the ideology of Islamism, and its overt militant expression in jihadism, a number of features stand out, features such as:

- the withdrawal and disengagement from contemporary culture and social relations;
- the promotion of a single, supreme ideology as a universal explanation and filter, through which all phenomena are interpreted and processed;
- the goal of transforming not only the political and social order but the very intellect of the individual in the new order;
- the promotion of communal over individual rights and the gradation of rights based on loyalty to a belief-system;
- the demotion of universal rights, the suppression of diversity and the vehement opposition to democracy, pluralism and liberal thought;
- the calls for an expansionist supra-state.

Many who look at these features, particularly in Europe, soon become aware of broad similarities with political experiments familiar from their recent history. The salient points of resemblance between Islamist and European, totalitarian ideologies—taken on the deeper level, and stripped of their geographical or cultural particularities—may be listed as follows:

- the crisis of the contemporary world;
- a global, universalist cause;

- "re-birth" and the "anthropological revolution";
- the sacralisation of community and state;
- no separation between private and public life;
- collective (not individual) rights;
- the top-down process of empowerment.

We may take these generic parallels and examine them in some more detail:

The Crisis of the Contemporary World

The common feature of totalitarian ideology is its response to an existential crisis, born of what are perceived to be the failed values of the liberal society, one that is atomized, pluralistic, and "purposeless". The fascist totalitarian's conception of the crisis and its cure has a familiar ring:

Fascists promise that with their help the national crisis will end and a new age will begin that restores the people to a sense of belonging, purpose, and greatness. The end result ... they believe, will be the emergence of a new man and new woman. This new man and new woman will be fully developed human beings, uncontaminated by selfish desires for individual rights and self-expression and devoted only to an existence as part of the renewed nation's destiny.[27]

The verdict of history is that of inexorable decline, due to the essential anomaly of western liberalism from the true nature of Man. For Sayyid Qutb "the phase of the white man is now ended,"[28] its power is an illusion and the world stands "on the edge of the abyss," at a point of transition from darkness to the light of truth. This tone was explicitly set by the founder of the Muslim Brotherhood Hasan al-Bannā' in his 1947 work *Toward the Light*:

We assert that the Western civilization, which was for a long time brilliant by virtue of its scientific perfection subjugating the whole world with the products of this science, is now in ruin... Strange ideologies and widespread revolutions are undermining its social foundations. Its people are at a loss as to the cure and have strayed far of the path... All of humanity is tormented, wretched, worried and confused, having been scorched by the fires of greed and materialism.

To remedy this crisis entails more than reform, it means a total abolition of the failed system and the cultural values that support it. It is these structures of the repudiated civilization, its institutions of repression, that are keeping Mankind in slavery. To create, therefore, one must first destroy, but in the logic of rebirth it is a "creative destruction" of false behavioural habits and cultural identities to something more universal, and eternally "true". Hasan al-Bannā' elaborates the salvific role of the warriors of the new order:

> They are in dire need of the sweetness of True Islam to wash from them the filth of misery and to lead them to happiness... all it requires is a strong Eastern power to exert itself under the shadow of Allah's banner, with the standard of the Qur'an fluttering at its head, and backed up by the strong soldiers of unyielding faith; then you will see the World living under the tranquillity of Islam... This is not in the least a product of the imagination: It is no other than the true verdict of history.[29]

A Global, Universalist Cause

The cause is therefore one of universal salvation. Marxism-Leninism in particular emphasized the conception of *a global struggle* or cause,[30] a call for world domination as a form of universal emancipation. Fascism too, despite common perceptions, had its sense of a universal renewal for all humanity. Much as Islamism's beacon of a renewed Islamic state was to liberate Muslims and subsequently all mankind, Mussolini's Fascism, with its core myth of imminent cultural renewal, was to herald

> the renewed flowering of the Italian creative genius which had produced the Roman Empire and the Renaissance, turning Italy into the heartland of a new type of civilization which would act as a lodestar to other modern nations of the world which found themselves so mired in crisis.[31]

The parallels of Communism with the Islamist goal of re-establishing a transnational Caliphate go in deep: in the conception of the corruption and illegitimacy of current state structures; in the illegitimacy of having any humans holding sovereignty over any other; in the need to begin by seizing power in a single state (but with the aim of ultimately destroying all states).[32] But of these features it is perhaps the emphasis on the illegitimacy and need for the dismantling of all state structures (not their reform) where the Islamist shows the strongest parallel with the Marxist revolutionary.

In the cultural field the parallels are also strong. The Soviet Union, for example, was a country based on an ideology which claimed to be a system of values and universal explanation. It had an imperative to propagate a universal "truth." Much as Islamism has an historical metanarrative to explain the unfolding of history that has led to its contemporary role, what mattered to the communist was that he felt he was part of a great historical enterprise, and his role in the revolution in world history gave him a sense of purpose and his life a meaning.[33] Most conspicuous of all, however, is the assertion common to both Islamism and Marxism-Leninism that human nature must be transformed in order to pave the way for a glorious this-worldly paradise. This was a feature that gave Marxism an air of pseudo-religiosity, and it is one that in turn makes the parallels, and even cross-fertilization, with Islamism all the more cogent.

"Re-birth" and the Anthropological Revolution

The remedy to such a crisis of failed values, of an atomized, pluralistic, and "purposeless" society, must be radical, a comprehensive cultural and ethical renewal. This renewal demands an "anthropological" as much as a political, social or intellectual revolution, through which the individual undergoes what Roger Griffith and Emilio Gentile refer to as a *palingenesis*, a "re-birth" into a new being. Only through this process can a new age begin that will restore the people to a sense of belonging, purpose, and greatness. The end result of this revolution is the emergence of a new *type* of man.

It requires the transformation of society at the levels both of society and of the individual, who is to experience a re-birth as a new type of human being. Although such a transformation should again coincide with the innate logic of things, in practice it is a process that must be forced through. As Emilio Gentile explains, it requires

the conquest of society, the homogenisation of the society formed by the governed, an anthropological revolution.[34]

For the communist this new type of being in this anthropological revolution is a formula for all humanity. For the Fascists the new *homo fascistus*, as Roger Griffin explains, is one who voluntarily lived not for himself as liberalism intended, or for the whole of humanity as communism intended, but for the greater good and higher destiny of the nation.[35]

But the new man, as he is conceived in the Islamist system, interestingly sits somewhere between these fascist and communist models: it is a being who struggles for the Nation, the *umma*, but whose struggle is for a Nation commanded and destined to reign universally supreme.

The Sacralization of the Community—the Corporate State

The two-way traffic of the language of religion and politics leads to a "sacralization" of the community and of the state, and of the person's rôle in it as part of the enfolding of a grand project. His re-birth is equally the *palingenesis* of the group, and in this new type of community the state's function is sacralised, where the individual is "raised to become a conscious member of a spiritual society" which takes on

> all the manifestations of the moral and intellectual life of man. Its functions cannot therefore be limited to those of enforcing order and keeping the peace, as the liberal doctrine had it. It is no mere mechanical device for defining the sphere within which the individual may duly exercise his supposed rights. The Fascist State is an inwardly accepted standard and rule of conduct, a discipline of the whole person.[36]

All systems that attempt to accommodate the diversity of individual Will, as under liberalism, are therefore to be repudiated. The people when rightly guided are one, and they will live the collective identity, an indivisible entity that thinks as one. One People, One Nation, One Leader. For Sayyid Qutb the nation must be liberated through a similar sacralization, through its transformation into a system that amounts to something more than a construction of man:

> This miserable state that mankind suffers from will not be alleviated by minor changes in the minutiæ of systems and conditions. Mankind will never escape it without this vast and far-reaching transformation —the transformation from the ways of the created to the way of the Creator, from the systems of men to the system of the Lord of men,

and from the commands of servants to the command of the Lord of servants.[37]

The extra refinement for the Islamists is that when they argue for the "re-sacralization" of society they claim to be able to adduce the Divinity directly into the argument. For their claim is that democracy as an expression of positive law is *a direct negation of religious truth*, and so the concept of legislation by the voice of the people therefore constitutes a false, competing *religion*.[38] It is important to resist the temptation to see this as metaphorical language. In his work *Al-Dīmuqrātiyya Dīn* (*Democracy is a Religion*),[39] the jihadist ideologue Abu Muhammad al-Maqdisi takes the reader through the logic that awakens the believer's consciousness to his unwitting *jāhiliyya* in acquiescing to pluralism and identifies the false god: Allah is the only Legislator—democracies impiously legislate by other systems in place of the shari'a as given to mankind by Allah—this means they arrogate to themselves the functions of Allah—they therefore invent and serve another "god".

Fundamentalist discourse amply supplies the language of sacralisation to the state, and replaces individualized identity with "The Nation" as a single, unchanging mass identity. The slogan of the *umma* is a mantra for this expression.[40] The generically totalitarian purpose of this, according to Emilio Gentile, is:

> to regenerate the human being and create the new man, who is dedicated in body and soul to the realisation of the revolutionary and imperialistic policies of the totalitarian party, whose ultimate goal is to create a new civilisation beyond the Nation-State.[41]

This corporate identity is most evident in the dictum that there should be no separation between private and public life. Islamists express disdain for such a separation as a hallmark of liberalism and its pandering to the rebellious nature of Mankind. The disdain is fully encapsulated in these comments by Dr. Muhammad Al Alkhuli in his work *The Need for Islam*:

> Islam is a religion, but not in the western meaning of religion. The western connotation of the term "*religion*" is something between the believer and God. Islam is a religion that organizes all aspects of life on both the individual and national levels. Islam organizes your relations with God, with yourself, with your children, with your relatives, with your neighbor, with your guest, and with other brethren. Islam

clearly establishes your duties and rights in all those relationships. Islam establishes a clear system of worship, civil rights, laws of marriage and divorce, laws of inheritance, code of behavior, what not to drink, what to wear, and what not to wear, how to worship God, how to govern, the laws of war and peace, when to go to war, when to make peace, the law of economics, and the laws of buying and selling. Islam is a complete code of life.[42]

Sayyid Qutb apparently thought that this comprehensiveness, this all-embracing demand on the life and thought of the individual was a unique badge of Islam's belief system. Indeed, the absence of this seamless spectrum of faith and the practical life, in his conception, had caused *al-fisām al-nakid*, the "hideous schizophrenia"[43] that afflicted western civilization and forced it into a permanent *jāhiliyya* that the Christian church had proved itself incapable of rectifying.

Yet the uniqueness is illusory. National Socialists and Leninists shared the disdain for the separation of public and private lives, as a hallmark of repudiated liberalism. They argued just as vehemently for their systems as constituting complete ways of life, which perforce must enter into every area of human activity. Hitler's visionary fanaticism called specifically for the *Gleichschaltung* (coordination) of every possible aspect of life in Germany, for the purpose of eliminating individualism by forcing everybody to adhere to a specific doctrine and way of thinking, and controlling as many aspects of life as possible.

Even if this core slogan of *dīn wa-dawla* ("faith and state" together) it is not considered strictly speaking to be a straight borrowing from the European ideologies—since it is an ancient mechanism—it can be demonstrated to be the typical product of reactionary, totalitarian thinking, and one that is necessarily shared with profane political ideologies. "It would accomplish nothing to remind them," writes Samir Amin,

> that their remarks reproduce, almost word for word, what European reactionaries at the beginning of the nineteenth century (such as Bonald and de Maistre) said to condemn the rupture that the Enlightenment and the French Revolution had produced in the history of the Christian West.[44]

The radical Islamist theorist Abu al-'Ala al-Maududi actually made a comparison to other totalitarian ideologies in this respect explicit, when he wrote that the shari'a-ruled state:

cannot restrict the scope of its activities, its approach is universal and all embracing... in such a state ... no one could regard any field of his affairs as personal and private. Considered from this aspect the Islamic state bears a kind of resemblance to the Fascist and Communist states.[45]

Against the criticism that atheistic communism could not be properly compared with a belief system focused on an otherworldly Creator, Jules Monnerot argued that the analogy was pertinent since it was founded upon the fact that the Qur'an was held by Muslims to constitute an indivisible religious, political and social code, and that for both Communism and Islam there was no separate entity that was entrusted with matters spiritual, such as the Church. The result of this deficit was a total conflation of the political with the sacred.[46]

Collective (not Individual) Rights

Point 24 of the *Nationalist Socialist Party Program* underlined that it "fights against the Jewish materialistic spirit within and around us and is convinced that a permanent revival of our Nation can be achieved only from within, and only on the basis of: Public Interest before Private Interest."[47] Under this system the people are conceived as a monolithic, un-individualized entity that behaves as one, and expresses the Common Will. Similarly, Benito Mussolini defined his new fascist system as one whereby the state would function as one organic whole consisting of interrelated parts that possessed value only to the extent that they contributed to the integral message of the whole. The new man in this system devotes himself, as a new de-individualised entity, and uncontaminated by selfish desires for individual rights and self-expression, exclusively to an existence as part of the renewed nation's destiny, to a fulfilment of a single creative purpose. Sayyid Qutb reproduces Mussolini's definition of the corporatist society almost to the letter, when he argues that his vision of a reformed society cannot come into existence if it does not become an active, harmonious and cooperative group, with an independent presence in itself, whose members, like the members of a human body, work together for its existence, its deep rooting, its expansion, and for the defense of its essence against all those factors which attack it, carrying this out under a leadership which is independent of the leadership of a *jāhilī* society, one that organizes its activity, marshals it and directs it efforts towards the deep rooting and expansion of its Islamic character, to combat, rise up and abolish the other, *jāhilī* entity.[48]

The leader of this society is their "interpreter", who is the voice of the un-individualized people. Needless to say democracy, in this scheme, with all it suggests of divergent, fissiparous views that harm the claimed consensus, has no place. Like the Fascists, the Jihadist antipathy to democracy is visceral:

Muslims should reject [democracy] entirely, for it is filthy; it is the rule of a tyrant, it is *Kufr* ["Disbelief"], with *Kufr* ideas, *Kufr* systems and *Kufr* laws, and has nothing to do with Islam.[49]

The Vanguard of an Elite

Political totalitarianisms provide the model for the *methodology of empowerment*—the vanguard of an élite, who alone can think for, and guide, the unenlightened masses. The "top-down" approach of empowerment as a response to the immense problem of consciousness-raising is the distinguishing badge of the totalitarian and it was in this tactical element that analysts first identified the parallels with Marxism-Leninism. Maududi's *Jama'at* is an "organizational weapon" in the Leninist tradition, devised to project the power of an ideological perspective into the political arena.[50] Sayyid Qutb gave it the same name—*talī'a* ("vanguard")—that the Leninists employed. Much as the Leninists maintained, the fact that the majority of the masses may or may not support or understand the transformation was not important:

"It is necessary that there should be a vanguard," he states, "which sets out with this determination and then keeps upon the path, passing through the vast ocean of *Jāhiliyya* striking its roots over the entire world."[51]

It was for this "vanguard"—"a waiting reality about to be materialized," Qutb stated, that his famous work *Milestones on the Way* was written.

SPECIFIC PARALLELS BETWEEN ISLAMISM AND FASCISM

From the foregoing it can be seen that the ideology of Islamism shares enough of the features of generic totalitarianism to compromise the claims made to its authenticity and uniqueness. But some of the features of the ideology parallel more specifically totalitarianisms of the fascist stamp. Moreover, these features are more closely bound in with the doctrinal fabric of the ideology and its relation to scriptural authenticity, and hence are embedded more thoroughly within the orthodox tradition. These features may be listed as:

- the call for "authenticity" and the restoration of lost vigor;
- the cult of tradition;
- cultural purity and fear of diversity;
- the conspiracy obsession;
- the hero and the permanence of the struggle.

This doctrinal fabric to Islamism's ideology, and its deep embedding within the historical legacy of Islamic thought (dominated as it is by medieval norms), adds to Islamism's resilience and presents a greater challenge to any counter ideology program that seeks to isolate the political ideology from issues of religious practice and identity. It is therefore worth examining these parallels in some more detail:

The Call for "Authenticity" and the Restoration of Lost Vigor

The "anthropological revolution" mentioned earlier is a feature common to all manifestations of Fascism and is closely tied in with the impulse towards a restoration of a pristine virtue. For the Italians it meant restoring their ancient Roman vigour. For Germany it demanded the re-Aryanization of European civilization and the purging of the tribal outsider. For Marxists, the coming New Man would be one that was devoid of the accumulated vices of modern capitalism, and devoted to building selflessly the new society.

What links this impulse to the Islamist model is the *authenticity* principle of the Islamists, among whom the *palingenesis* idea is explicitly stated in terms of a rebirth out of the prevailing *jāhiliyya* as a new, renewed, *mujāhid* Muslim. The impulse is entirely one of "re-authentication", that is, a drive towards regaining the formula that once brought Muslims their divinely ordained primacy but which now has been withdrawn from them, causing them to lose their vigor. This winning "formula" is explicitly described as the Prophetic template in all its facets: that is, the Prophet's opinions, his words, his acts and the historical emergence of the early Muslim community—since all of these are physical manifestations of God's favor and purpose.

This shadow of primordial Islam—progressing from Muhammad's preaching (*da'wā*) of the new faith in an age of ignorance (*jāhiliyya*), to his withdrawal (*hijra*) to Yathrib, to his foundation of the new Muslim state (*umma*) and its militant struggle (jihad)—permeates the consciousness of the Islamist, who will speak of his own "*jāhiliyya*" and recount his renunciation and withdrawal from its influence and his struggle for primacy over evil and all its contemporary intellectual, political and social institutions.

In jihadist militant Islamism this shadow even extends to replicating the *da'wā—hijra—* jihad template in the field. The founder of the radical movement *Takfīr wal-Hijra*, Shukri Mustafa, actively put the model into practice by forming communities in caves away from the sinful *jāhili* cities of Egypt. Bin Laden's career is conceived by *mujāhidīn* sympathisers as conforming to the pattern of *da'wā* (sermonizing repudiation of the infidel Soviets and Americans)—*hijra* (migration to Sudan and Afghanistan)— jihad (militant campaigns against Soviets and Americans), while Ayman al-Zawahiri in his work *Knights Under the Banner of the Prophet*, interprets his own curriculum vitae according to this pattern.[52]

The template for the time of vigor is provided by *al-salaf al-sālihūn* who are held to comprise the first three generations of Muslims, the companions of the Prophet Muhammad and the two succeeding generations after them (the *tābi'ūn* and the *taba'at al-tābi'īn*).[53] The ultimate authenticators are therefore these "righteous ancestors":

> who were recommended by Allāh and His Messenger for their piety and understanding of the Faith. We cherish them and those who cherished and loved them and we hate those who hated and despised them, and curse those who cursed them... Whoever attacks them is attacking the Faith, the book of Allah and the lord of the Prophets and Messengers [Muhammad]... Consequently, he who follows their way and method and holds to their understanding of the Faith is the one who is rightly guided and saved. But he who contradicts them and follows a different method and path than theirs, he will be going astray... After that comes the century of the *Tābi'īn*, and then those

who followed the *Tābi'īn*. These are the three best generations in Islam. After that, lying becomes widespread.[54]

Underpinning this is the belief that the political and cultural decline of the Islamic world is not a matter of history or politics, but a *religious* issue—the abandonment of core aspects of the faith through neglect and intellectual corruption, one that has culminated in the Enlightenment and its "desacralization" of reality. The key to reclaiming the ancient primacy is therefore to re-establish religious authenticity. This is what makes the Islamist call for reform up-ended, one where the dynamic is to take the ancient order as the starting point and adjust modernity to *its* contours.

The Cult of Tradition

There is a fascinating conflict in the Islamists' conception of tradition. On the one hand they make constant appeal to authenticity yet, as Karen Armstrong noted, they share the common fundamentalist contradiction of claiming to be restoring tradition and orthodoxy, but all the while creating a new version of an existing religion based on a mythic and romanticized past.[55] Precisely the same ambiguity affected the fascist ideologies, as Roger Griffin noted:

> Due to its peculiar modernising and palingenetic thrust, fascism is at bottom anti-traditional and hence anti-conservative... fascism is thus a radical rejection of "traditional" authority. What blurs this point in practice is that fascism often draws on traditional values and may even have recourse to religious discourse and symbology to create the "spiritual" climate it believes conducive to the new order.[56]

However, the deeper implication of the cult of tradition is that there can be no advancement of learning. Truth already has been spelled out once and for all, and we can only keep interpreting its obscure message.[57]

This feature is closely paralleled by the normative centrality among the Islamists of the Quran and the Hadith, which in their Salafist training admit of no explanatory context in their interpretation. The sounds, the phonemes, the literal renderings, all are fixed for all times, places and peoples. This untouchability of the Text—in the sense of historical or allegorical interpretation—permeates the literature and illustrates eloquently the Salafist mental cradle of the Islamist, one where the settled facts of the Text and the Law, and their pedigree, are heavily prioritized over any active speculation on theology and ethics. Radicals of all stamps seek authority to this priority in the person of Ibn Hanbal, who championed the cause of the Text with his claim that

> whoever involves themselves in any theological rhetoric is not to be counted amongst the Ahl us-Sunnah, even if by that he arrives at the Sunnah, until he abandons debating and surrenders to the texts.[58]

By contrast, the Indonesian Muslim scholar Ulil Abshar-Abdalla ridicules this logocentric universe of the Salafist whose

> theological insight which supports this "scripturalism" depends upon a rather silly assumption as follows: the more textually we comprehend God's word, the closer we are to His true will; while the more careless we are in '*ta'wīl*' or non-literal interpretation, the further we are from His true will.

Nevertheless there is an inherent and dangerous strength in this logocentric focus, for under this conception being *amoral* can be presented as an ethically superior state to being *atextual*. The case of the "scripturalist" is that while there can be no doubt about the aptness of the Text in an absolute sense, irrespective of context or purpose, a man's moral judgement is essentially a mortal's product, and therefore *a priori* flawed. The effect is to license acts that a common universalist ethics would find abhorrent. The Golden Rule is removed and instead there is a schematic gradation of the worth and legal rights of the individual. The textual argument may have ultimately dubious underpinnings, but it is a very effective means of ring-fencing the cult of tradition from challenge and protecting the moral élitism.

Cultural Purity and Fear of Diversity

Related to this is the concept of cultural purity, the rejection of the idea of foreign cultural influence as an infiltrating contaminant. For the Nazis the culprits were Jewish intellectuals and their "degenerate arts", and their goal was to create a harmonious community whose values were unsullied by differences of culture and deviant ideologies. For the Islamists the contaminant is more widespread and their blanket rejection of philosophical, historical and cultural influences from outside the Islamic tradition comes closer to a full-blown cultural autism. Taqī al-Dīn al-Nabahānī (the founder of Hizb al-Tahrīr) illustrates this instinct well. He rejected the concept promoted "by

Orientalists" of significant foreign influence, arguing that the idea that the Islamic culture was affected by non-Islamic cultures "comes from the deliberate distortion undertaken by the non-Muslims with respect to changing the meanings of things." The "core" of Islamic culture—its jurisprudence—is instead pristine and untouched:

> The Muslims themselves were not affected by any other culture, neither in terms of their way of thinking or in their understanding of Islam. The mentality of the Muslims remained a pure Islamic mentality.[59]

Here Islamists immediately come up against the record of history and project equally contradictory results. If some appeal to the essential Islamicness of all knowledge,[60] and argue for the Islamic origins of western science and the European Renaissance, others repudiate the implied intermingling. "There were some individuals affected by foreign rational disciplines," argues al-Nabahānī,

> New thoughts emerged amongst them... Muslims whose minds were confused by the study of foreign philosophies, which led them to make mistakes in understanding some of the concepts of Islam or fall into misguidance in their intellectual discussions... These are the Muslim philosophers such as Ibn Sina, al-Farabi, Ibn Rushd and their peers. [Theirs] is not considered as Islamic culture.[61]

The downgrading of the importance of rationalism is revealing. Under both the communistic and fascistic systems, the proponents of Reason were considered subversive, and constantly under suspicion of conspiratorial activity to undermine the unity, unanimity and Will of the people. For the Islamists, the threat to unity is all the stronger, since it is a challenge to the greatest of all Wills, the Will of Allah. The Rationalists, be they medieval Arabs or modern Europeans, are merely Greek intellectual interlopers.

For an Islamist such as Shaykh Samīr al-Mālikī, the lionizing of "atheist philosophers"—whether they be Avicenna, Rhazes or equally Salman Rushdie and Taslima Nasreen—is something that has to be resisted at all costs. Given that the non-religious sciences as a whole "are founded upon libertinism," the view that everything the Infidel achieve in the sciences must be learned and mastered by the Muslims is mistaken, since what is incumbent upon man is that he places all his concern in the afterlife, not in the pleasures and sciences of this world.[62]

This ideological conditioning of knowledge is a common feature of totalitarianism since the fear of analytical criticism comes from the perception of disagreement as an act of treason. Communism, for instance, even "sacralized" science, raising it to the level of an ideology and in so doing falsifying it. But actually the impulse to sacralize science is far more acute—and complicated—in the universe of the Islamist, since it conflicts with the problem of technological inferiority. The solution is vintage totalitarian doublespeak: if the study of rational sciences is "obligatory if it is a question of the means to wage war on the infidel," it should be undertaken for a specific ultimate purpose:

the modern man has to be addressed in his own language [of science and philosophy] and using his own logic ... conquered... This is the greatest striving (Jihad) of the present times... This will enable the Ummah ... to confront with all vehemence and power the onslaughts of the impostor culture.[63]

This "epistemological jihad" is to embrace a wholesale, Quixotic, enterprise to pass all rational methodologies through a corrective cultural "filter", whereby

all scientific methods are carried out in the framework of the service of Islam, so that the goal is not purely one of science ... but to link these sciences with Islam and purge them of suspicious elements.[64]

The fear of contamination leads to an outright fear of the outsider and a desire to minimize contact on any level. While Lenin expressed the dictum "we must hate, hate is the basis of communism,"[65] it is the fascist ideologies that are more characterized by this culture. In exercising this facet of the totalitarian scheme Islamists possess the advantage of a fully elaborated doctrine of al-walā' wal-barā', the practice of "Loyalty and Renunciation," mentioned earlier, that is held to mark the true believer from the hypocrite, and which draws its authority from sources deep within the orthodox tradition.[66] "If the hate at any time extinguishes from the heart," bin Laden stated, this is great apostasy! ... since battle, animosity, and hatred—directed from the Muslim to the infidel—is the foundation of our religion."[67]

Conversely, the attitude of the foe, with its religious and social tolerance is to be suspected as malevolent, since it is nothing other than a conspiracy to subvert Islam from within by lowering the Muslims' guard:

> ...for the turmoil that will ensue to their faith and [the fact that they will] absorb the habits of the polytheists' and [develop] familiarity with them which will lead in time to [ties of] affection, which Allah forbids. And their children will grow up associating with their children and pick up their many corrupt and disgusting habits.[68]

The Conspiracy Obsession

The conspiracy theme is another hallmark of totalitarianism, and has a particular place in the ideology of Fascism. "To people who feel deprived of a clear social identity," Umberto Eco explains,

> the only ones who can provide an identity to the nation are its enemies. Thus at the root of the Ur-Fascist psychology there is the obsession with a plot ... the followers must feel besieged.

The conspiracy matrix is in fact very highly developed among the militant Islamists (see appended table). At the top of the list, as we can see, are the Jews, who for the Fascists fulfilled the all-important role of the internal plotter since "they have the advantage of being at the same time inside and outside." Islamists locate the internal threat of the Jews to the very beginnings of Islam and the chequered relations of the Prophet with the Jewish tribes of Arabia that ended up with the divinely ordained massacre of the Banū al-Qurayza.[69] Taking an historical approach the parallels here, of course, with German Fascism's obsession with the Jews are at their most patent. Sayyid Qutb's highly popular work, *Our Struggle with the Jews*, lists the crimes and conspiracies in a tone familiar to readers of German tracts of the 1930s, and indeed Qutb claimed that Allah had sent Hitler to earth to "punish" the Jews for their evil deeds.

> The struggle between Islam and the Jews is still in vigor and will continue so, since the Jews will not be contented with anything other than the destruction of this faith. Since the victory of Islam they have

been fighting this faith with plots, infiltrations and the promotion of their agents in the shadows.[70]

Johannes von Leers[71], one of the most important ideologues of the Third Reich, registered his applause for what he considered to be the essential position of Islam thus:

Mohammed's hostility to the Jews had one result: Oriental Jewry was completely paralyzed... As a religion, Islam indeed performed an eternal service to the world: it prevented the threatened conquest of Arabia by the Jews and vanquished the horrible teaching of Jehovah by a pure religion.[72]

A conspiracy requires the existence of a *constant enemy*. If for Nazi Germany the role was filled by the Jews, in the case of the Islamists it is actually more than merely the Jew, it is the *ewige Kāfir*, the eternal infidel. If the "enemy" defines those with an unclear sense of their own identity in the modern multi-faith pluralist environment, Islamist ideologues make ample use of the device to force the message of an eternal plot of disbelief against Islam. Beyond Jews, Christians and imperialists luring Muslims away from the true faith, the roster of enemies expands to the more sinister, internal conspirators: these are the liberal Muslim thinkers and the secularists. The al Qaeda affiliated *al-Neda* jihadi website provides us with the list and the commentary on elements that pull Muslims away from the true faith:[73]

The Threat to Islam from Muslims
"Sometimes a hundred times worse than the hatred of the enemies of the nation, the Jews and the Christians" emanating from the leaders of Islamic countries and the clerics who serve them.

The Secular Threat
"One of the greatest threats to the hegemony of Islam and the dominance of *Shari'a* is the American secularism that will be imposed forcefully on the region... The Islamic world will change from dictatorship to democracy, which means subhuman degradation in all walks of life."

The Threat of Those Who Abandoned the Islamic Tradition
Since secularism will be rejected by a large section of Muslims, the Zionist-Crusader coalition is encouraging major spiritual groups such as the Sufis, "who are mostly infidels" and believe in monism, pantheism, and re-incarnation and observe "conscience, inspiration, and other endless falsehoods." Orders such as the Sufis "oppose *Jihad* and do not oppose the infidels."

The Threat of the Rational School
A "deadly seedling that maintains that Islam is not opposed to atheism, and that Islam must get close to the infidel and coexist with him." A school of thought, planted by British imperialism and "established by Muhammad 'Abduh and which maintains that logic takes precedence over the text [of the Quran]." This school "may become the first stepping stone to secularizing the region, because it is a mixture of secularism and Islam."

More intensive than Fascism, the plot in this case is nothing less than the machinations of Satan against the Truth, and his exploitation of the enemies of Islam *within* the Islamic world for this purpose.

The Hero and the Permanence of the Struggle

The totalitarian program is *par excellence* a call to action. There is a universal mission to act against the unsleeping forces of the conspirator. But since the fight is part of a perennial struggle there is no end to it, and the fact of the struggle becomes embedded in the very purpose of living. There is no struggle for life, but rather life is lived for struggle. The primacy of action, for Georges Sorel, was "the only possible way for men to ascend to an ethical life filled by the character of the sublime and to achieve deliverance"[74] and therefore peace is nothing less than a betrayal of values. "Fascism," according to Mussolini, as regards the future and development of humanity,

> repudiates Pacifism, which is born of a renunciation of struggle and an act of cowardice in the face of sacrifice. War alone brings up to its highest tension all human energy and puts the stamp of nobility upon the people who have the courage to meet it. All other trials are substitutes, which never really put a man in front of himself in the alternative of life and death.[75]

Expansionist jihad is a collective religious duty. If this is not carried out, the whole Islamic *umma* is sinning. Reform, according to al-Zawahiri, "can only take place through Jihad." It could be argued that the doctrine of *fard 'ayn*, the "individual duty" of the Muslim to wage jihad, implies that the life of the Muslim is conceived of as this permanent struggle. For Sayyid Qutb the struggle is certainly central to Islam:

> Jihad ... is not something accidental to the particular period which witnessed the advent of Islam. It is a permanent need, inherent in the nature of the Islamic faith."[76]

Indeed, for Qutb the Quran itself is not a "holy book" like the Christian Bible, but rather a manual for action, approached "as a soldier on the battle-field reads 'Today's Bulletin'."[77] Later, among the *mujāhidīn* fighting against the Soviets in Afghanistan, the "life as a permanent struggle" theme came to be embodied in the words of Shaykh 'Abd Allāh 'Azzām, for whom

> history does not write its lines except with blood. Glory does not build its lofty edifice except with skulls. Honour and respect cannot be established except on a foundation of cripples and corpses.[78]

Eco noted that under the fascist scheme the permanence of the struggle conflicts with the equally fascist concept of an "Armageddon complex," the final battle that ushers in the end of struggle in the final peace or Golden Age. He noted that "no fascist leader has ever succeeded in solving this predicament."[79] However, Islamist radicalism does resolve this contradiction, for the battle is indeed permanent, since it has existed since the beginning of time:

> since long before our attacks and in fact before Huntington and Fukuyama with their books on the Clash of Civilizations. This war has been going on ever since the existence of Faith and Disbelief.[80]

According to Sayyid Imam (Dr. Fadl) this struggle will continue on no less permanently, for

> [true] jihad is [a command that is] in force until Judgment Day, and jihad is not limited to any given organization... It is a law that is in force until the end of time.[81]

It is life-long, and the final battle may be enacted in each *mujāhid's* self-sacrifice, to achieve his final peace in the only true world that exists, the world after death.

The struggle, then, is the very symbol of Islam, the badge of the hero. Muhammad Farag, author of *The Missing Obligation*,[82] held that jihad was a salvific action of such central importance that Islam itself can be reduced to the question of whether or not Muslims fight. He saw jihad as a panacea for the Muslim world, and its abandonment as the principal reason for "the lowness, humiliation, division and fragmentation in which the Muslims live today." The action therefore becomes the purpose. Inflicting injury upon the enemy, al-Maqdisi asserts, "is one of the purposes and goals of life for a Muslim." The Prophet himself, he maintains, held that this was one of

the great goals for which they were created, the greatest of which are: worshipping Allāh Alone, and granting victory to His religion by inflicting injury upon the enemy. *So for this reason the Muslim is alive.*[83]

Of all the above features of totalitarianism and their parallels with Islamism, perhaps the most telling are contained in these polarities of birth and death. The totalitarian spirit is expressed in the belief in the necessity for a purifying rebirth on a pristine re-invigorating model, in the fight for primordial Truth against the conspiracies of intellectual, moral and political contamination, in a struggle that stretches to the end of Time, and where death and self-sacrifice are the culmination of the warrior's *Heldenleben*. In these respects Islamism and totalitarian political ideologies follow trajectories similar enough to make the comparison both compelling and compromising. Muslim thinkers in the Middle East have certainly recognized the validity of the analogies on this level of *intellectual mechanisms*[84] and the parallelism has been enough to convince ex-Islamists that they were indeed being indoctrinated in a modern political ideology in an Islamic dressing.[85]

IMPLICATIONS OF COMPARATIVE TOTALITARIANISM FOR COUNTER-IDEOLOGY

As the above hopes to demonstrate, the comparative approach to totalitarianism is one of the most powerful tools to fight Islamist radicalism. This approach resolves the problem of non-Muslim reticence to address the civilizational underpinning to Islamism and jihadism founded on the spurious argument that it is not their business to engage in this "internal" discussion. On the contrary, western and non-Muslim contribution to the debate is legitimate since it focuses on what these last are eminently qualified for: the discussion on the nature of western totalitarian systems of thought and their own historical experience.

It also challenges in a unique way the Islamists' claim over other Muslims to authenticity and exclusive authority, and the case which they make that there is no debate to be held. If it can be conclusively proved that the ideology of the Islamists demonstrates identical patterns of thought to man-made, infidel political ideologies of the 20th century, then the claim that their endeavors are "in God's path" is severely, if not terminally, compromised. Even if Islamists resort to the argument that the Muslim does not engage in discussions on Islam with the infidel, the discussion may just as well begin unilaterally—since a lack of response to the presentation of strong similarities compromises their position.

Comparative fundamentalism is the one method that forces Islamist radicals onto a neutral ground of discussion (since this is in the nature of a comparative exercise). Debating in this neutral arena requires the Islamists to set to one side their customary tool of textualism—of Quranic *āya* and Prophetic Hadith—and this leaves them at a disadvantage. It will require them to acquaint themselves in depth with studies on totalitarian thought and examine mindsets and motivations, instead of taking refuge in moral abdication to the letter of the scriptural Text.

Whether in terms of secular, but sacralized, political systems and their intermeshing with totalitarianisms, or in terms of comparative religious fundamentalism, the particular value of the comparative approach lies in the penetrating challenge it represents to a movement that *strenuously defines itself as authentic, uniquely Islamic and divinely sanctioned.* The comparison demolishes these pretensions by demonstrating that most of the core features of Islamism and militant jihadism are manifestations of *a commonly found deviation.* This commonality deprives the exponents of their authority, their justification and their cause.

The Enemies of the Muslims according to the Global Islamic Resistance

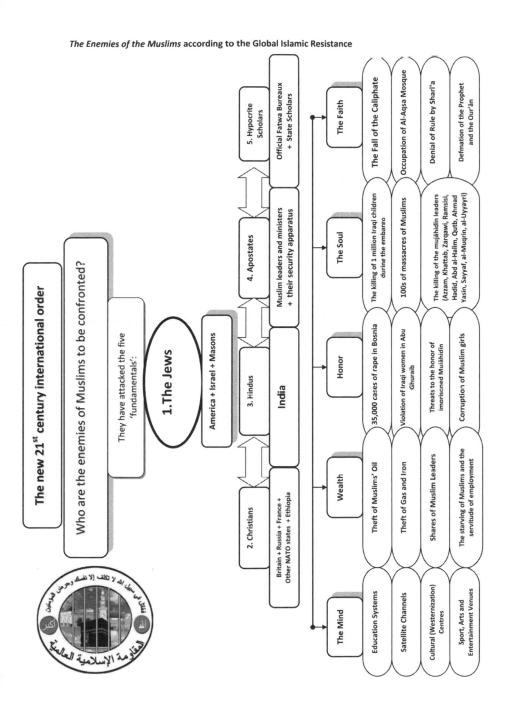

Part II

Learning from the Past

IDEOLOGY AND CENTRAL PLANNING: LESSONS FROM THE COLD WAR

John H. Moore

INTRODUCTION

The conflict with radical Islam is fundamentally a conflict of ideologies—the set of beliefs that underlie Western civilization on one side, the interpretation of Muslim beliefs that Islamists preach on the other. Ideological conflict was central in the Cold War as well, albeit within the general context of Western history and tradition. The ideological battles of the Cold War may shed light on our present day conflict. Among other things, the Cold War experience shows how difficult is it to win ideological wars even when there are seemingly objective means for settling them.

The Cold War was fought on many fronts—proxy wars, military buildups, the nuclear arms race, intelligence and counter-intelligence, projections of power, and so forth. But in important ways, the war was about ideology. Conflicting visions of the good society, or at least the kind of society that the leaders or peoples of the combatants wanted, were at its heart. Collectivism versus individualism, socialism versus capitalism, comprehensive economic planning versus the free market, the totalitarian state versus democracy and individual liberty—all of these were part of the ideological struggle. And they all converged in economic performance and economic doctrine. The principles of collectivism and the omnipotent state were those of central economic planning, which was in turn the stepchild of socialism.

On the other hand, the principles and institutions of democracy and liberty were (and are) those of free market capitalism.

The implementation of central economic planning in the Soviet Union was a central feature of its version of socialism, seen by many as the height of rationality in economic policy. The early success of the Soviet economy, together with the alleged moral superiority of socialism, won many supporters in the West. Indeed, in the 1950s and 1960s, the supporters of socialism held the upper hand in ideological debates in the West and throughout the world. Especially on academic campuses, those who favored capitalism and the free market were a distinct minority. In those days, the politically correct position had nothing to do with minority rights, multiculturalism, free speech, or any of the other issues at the center of political correctness today. At that time, the form of economic organization, and with it the role of the central government in the economy, were at the heart of campus ideological battles. This meant, of course, that economics faculties were a major battleground.

The University of Virginia's economics faculty at the time was known for being on the politically incorrect side of the ideological field of battle, as many of its members opposed socialism and the powerful central government that many others in academia favored. One of the economics professors, G. Warren Nutter, was responsible for a study that powerfully challenged the conventional wisdom about Soviet central planning. Because it was so powerful, and because it struck at the center of strongly held belief, the study and Nutter himself were subjected to harsh criticism by academic Sovietologists. In the sense that the reason for the criticism was based on ideology, the study and the reactions to it provide important insights into the workings of ideology in academia. But the ideology of socialism and central planning was held by many people, in and out of the universities, and the issue of the efficacy of the Soviet economic system went far beyond the groves of academia. The episode and its aftermath also show how dramatic real world events may—or may not—influence ideological beliefs.

BACKGROUND

The study in question was conducted under the auspices of the National Bureau of Economic Research (NBER). It was a major part of a series of studies of the Soviet economy launched by the Bureau in the early 1950s. The motivation for this undertaking was no doubt partly due to the impressive performance of the Soviet economy, especially its high reported rates of growth, at least according to official Soviet data and the estimates then prevailing in the West. It was commonly believed that Soviet industrial output was growing significantly faster than that of the United States and that the Soviet system of central economic planning was responsible. Moreover, it was believed that these high rates of growth could be sustained indefinitely.

The belief that Soviet output was growing so rapidly and sustainably had two major implications. One was very practical, in the light of the Cold War; the other was ideological, and concerned the struggle between socialism and capitalism.

The practical issue was clear. The Soviet Union's industrial output was the fuel for its ambitions for global domination, including its military power. After the devastation of World War II, the Soviet Union's economy recovered rapidly. By most estimates, 1945-1955 growth rates were at least as high as during 1928-1940, the years of the first five-year plans. Military production grew rapidly in those years; the development of nuclear and other weapons of mass destruction and the means to deliver them also was proceeding rapidly. After the war, the Red Army returned quickly to full capability. In short, the pace of industrial production raised deep concerns in the West about Soviet intentions and the threat posed by increasing productive capability.

The apparently impressive performance of the Soviet command economy also cast doubt on the relative efficiency of Western capitalism. The Soviets boasted that their economy would soon overtake the U.S. Khrushchev's famous taunt about burying the U.S. did not occur until a few years after the NBER project began, but the idea was present in Soviet propaganda years earlier. The prediction found its way into the American economics profession. Leading economics textbooks retained optimistic predictions of Soviet economic performance relative to American throughout the 1970s, including projections showing Soviet output overtaking American by the 1980s.[1]

Such beliefs about Soviet postwar performance provided powerful arguments for those in the West who favored socialism. This was so not only for Communist Party members and fellow travelers, but also for many non-communists who harbored pro-socialist views for other reasons—a belief that a free-market system is inherently chaotic, that the Great Depression had proven the instability of capitalism, that socialism was a more moral and just system, and so forth. Of course, for orthodox "scientific" Marxists, there was no argument: socialism was inevitable. But for non-Marxists who were sympathetic to socialism or simply anti-capitalist, the apparent success of the

Soviet system strengthened the belief that capitalism and the free market were obsolete relics of an irrational past. Moreover, it fit the idea that the Soviet system provided a large-scale experiment to test the idea that a socialist system, with its claims to equity, was a viable alternative to Western—particularly American—capitalism.

THE STUDY AND ITS CONTROVERSIAL RESULTS

The initial NBER plan called for studies of Soviet statistics, freight transportation, agriculture, and industry, plus a final summary volume.[2] Professor Nutter, then at Yale, was named general editor of the project. He also was to carry out the study of the industrial sector and write the summary.

Results from Nutter's industrial output study were first reported in papers delivered at the 1956 and 1957 annual meetings of the American Economic Association.[3] The complete results were presented in Nutter's book, *The Growth of Industrial Production in the Soviet Union*, which was published in 1962.[4]

That book contains a wealth of information about Soviet industrial production from the late Tsarist period (1870-1913) through 1955. It includes voluminous tables of the data that were collected and used in constructing the output indexes, as well as detailed descriptions of the construction of the indexes themselves. It contains many analyses, using different indexes, different starting and ending dates for comparisons of growth rates, and so forth. There are many conclusions and comparisons, but perhaps the most controversial were these:

- The rate of growth of Soviet industrial production was slowing.
- Soviet production in certain key industries was lagging far behind U.S. production in comparable industries and it was extremely unlikely that Soviet industrial production would ever catch up to America's.
- The best estimate of the long term growth potential in the Soviet Union was the average growth rate during the late Tsarist period, 1870–1913.

RESPONSES TO NUTTER

It should be noted at the outset that Nutter was not a member of the Soviet studies establishment. Until he undertook the NBER project, his work had been on domestic issues. His first book, published not long before he took on the Soviet project, was on monopoly in the United States.[5] The

NBER project was conceived, in part, exactly for the purpose of producing an analysis of the Soviet economy from outside the establishment.[6] But his work and conclusions came under especially sharp attack because of this. An early review[7] of the book succinctly captured this bias in its opening paragraph:

> There is—we must not conceal it—a prejudice against Mr. Nutter in the orthodox "establishment" of Soviet studies in the U.S.: he comes out of the National Bureau of Economic Research, and they in turn are an annex of Chicago; he cannot read Russian; he was driven into this field by certain high authorities in order to prove the "establishment" wrong; he believes *a priori* that capitalism is more dynamic than communism; etc., etc.[8]

Not only was Nutter an outsider subject to prejudice from the experts; his results were sharply different from the prevailing consensus. The general consensus among academic specialists at the time was that the Soviet system was capable of producing sustained high rates of growth over long periods. For example, Donald Hodgman said in 1953 that an annual rate of growth of eight percent would be "...not unreasonable as a basis for extrapolation."[9] As late as 1962, Peter Wiles published the assertion that Soviet industrial production increases at an annual rate of ten percent.[10] Nutter was the first to claim publicly[11] that the rate of growth was slowing.

This early work of Nutter's foreshadowed similar reports in the public sphere. Just a couple of years after Nutter reported his first results, Kaplan and Moorsteen[12] noted that their indexes showed slowing output growth from the first Five Year Plan (1928-32) and subsequent plan periods. They also noted that the Seven Year Plan (for 1959-65) implied lower rates of growth than in 1950-58. But they qualified this conclusion by hinting that the Seven Year Plan might be over-fulfilled, which would reverse the retardation.

By 1966, retardation was so obvious that it was the main focus of the CIA report to the Joint Economic Committee. However, the reasons given for the slowdown—exhaustion of opportunities to exploit Western technology, slowing improvements in education, slowdown in civilian investment, low operating efficiency in new plants—did not speak to the shortcomings of the Soviet planning system. Despite the acknowledgement of the slowdown, the author still concluded that "...the planned average annual increase in industrial output of 8.0-8.4 percent during 1966-70 seems cautious enough."[13]

Perhaps the most telling statement of the longstanding mistaken conviction of sustainable high rates of growth came from Senator Daniel Moynihan, who said in 1990 "...for forty years we have hugely overestimated both the size of the Soviet economy and its growth."[14]

If the finding of retardation in growth rates drew extensive criticism, the strongest objections were leveled against Nutter's comparisons with the United States. He noted that growth rates in Russia and the Soviet Union generally exceeded those in the United States over the same periods.[15] However, comparisons of economies that are at different stages of development during the same time periods tend to be misleading because growth rates typically are faster in the earlier stages of development. And the Soviet economy was generally less developed than the U.S. at any moment in time. Nutter made adjustments to compensate for these problems.

First, he compared growth rates of Soviet and American industry over periods that started and ended at roughly the same stages of development. This analysis showed that Soviet growth rates were roughly the same as American ones during periods of similar stages of development. Second, he estimated the extent to which output in a number of Soviet industries lagged behind U.S. output in corresponding industries. This analysis showed no evidence that Soviet output was catching up to America's. This was a very controversial finding, as many in the West as well as the Soviet leadership believed or claimed that production in the two countries was gradually converging.

Nutter also ran afoul of the establishment in arguing that the best predictor for long term Soviet growth was the Tsarist period, 1870-1913. According to his estimates, the growth rate during this period was higher than 1913-1955 and lower than 1928-1955, suggesting that the Tsarist record was a reasonable predictor of long run performance.

The critics pounced on his lag analyses and long-run prognosis for several reasons. First, 1913-1955 includes World War I, a tragedy for Russia, as well as War Communism and the New Economic Policy years with their internecine fighting about economic policy and structure. It also, of course, includes the Second World War. Second, while 1928-1955 avoids many of the problems associated with 1913-1955, it still includes World War II. So forecasts based on that period were rejected on the same grounds: the periods included one-time events (forced collectivization, purges, the wars, etc.) that biased the results downward. Nutter argued that the political and economic nature of the Soviet system meant that such occurrences were not singular matters but inherent in Russian and Soviet history. (Russian history during the half century since the book was published seems consistent with this position.) Consistency would suggest that such arguments be applied to the United States, in which case the Great Depression might well be excluded from growth forecasts. Doing so would, of course, increase the U.S. growth rates against which the Soviet results were compared. These arguments did not persuade the critics. In fact, as we now know, Nutter was right on all counts—actually much too optimistic about the future of the Soviet planned economy.

IDEOLOGY AND THE RESPONSE

The 1962 work consistently showed that (a) Soviet industrial output was growing less rapidly than most public estimates held; (b) the rate of growth was slowing; and (c) it was unlikely that Soviet industrial output would catch up to America's. The criticisms did not focus on the quality of Nutter's work, which was generally credited as being sound. Rather, it centered on what Nutter made of it. As Peter Wiles put it in his review, "It is the *interpretation* of Nutter's figures which must leave us, as it left the American Economic Association in 1958, gasping."[16]

Why did the interpretation leave the audience "gasping"? The simple answer is that Nutter's results and interpretations ran directly against what was at the time a generally held set of beliefs about the Soviet economy and the capacity of the Soviet system of central planning to generate high rates of growth. By implication, they also contradicted the assumptions about assessing Soviet growth that were, in essence, received doctrine about the economy. In so doing, the results and interpretations represented a frontal attack on a paradigm or, perhaps it can be said, an ideology.

The paradigm that underlay work on the Soviet economy at the time was largely due to Abram Bergson, professor of economics at Harvard and the leading figure among Soviet specialists in the postwar period. Bergson owed his pre-eminence to his 1930s work on welfare economics and his wartime and immediate postwar career in the American intelligence services. During the war, he was director of the Russian Economic Subdivision of the OSS; after the war, he led the organization and planning for studies of the Soviet economy in the newly established Central Intelligence Agency. During the course of his work, which was highly regarded in academia and the intelligence services, he developed a set of conclusions about analyzing the Soviet system that became the framework for virtually all Sovietologists at the time—a paradigm for work in the subject.

The paradigm had three main elements.[17] First, a socialist economy in which the means of production were owned by the state was held to be feasible. In this, Bergson took the side of Oskar Lange, Fred Taylor, and others in the so-called great socialist debate; the intellectual leaders on the other side were Ludwig von Mises and Friedrich Hayek. To reach this conclusion, Bergson became convinced that the incentive problems in an economic system without private property could be solved. If so, an optimal outcome could be achieved without resort to the free market of capitalism. This conclusion contains a strong anti-capitalist message and carried immense ideological content. Even if Bergson himself did not advocate a pure socialist economy in the U.S., the message resonated with many others who did favor the replacement of capitalism with some other system.

The second element of the paradigm was an extension of the first. In this, Bergson became convinced that a central planner or planning agency could actually solve the huge set of equations needed to implement such a plan in the socialist economy. It might have been true that achieving optimality in such a system was beyond the computational power then technologically available,[18] but the conclusion implied that a centrally planned (or administered) economy like that in the Soviet Union could work in practice, as well as theoretically. For measurement purposes, it meant that the prices in such an economy, as determined by the planning mechanism, could be used to combine physical output data to produce measures of aggregate economic performance such as GNP or total industrial output. These, in turn, could be used to measure rates of growth.

The third element in the paradigm concerned the data. The first official Soviet statistical abstract did not appear until 1957. Prior to that, researchers had to dig through myriad sources, including ministerial reports, statistics for individual industries, trade journals, and many more, to assemble their data sets. Whatever the source, it was widely believed that the physical output data were biased upward: by incentives at the local or enterprise level and for propaganda purposes at higher levels. Bergson and others, after much study of the biases, concluded that with the knowledge of the biases that was available, with the understanding that the biases tended to be roughly stable through time, and with proper care and adjustment, the Soviet data were usable by analysts.

These, then, were the three elements of the generally accepted paradigm in Soviet studies at the time of the NBER study. Nutter did not accept the first two elements. He was convinced that socialism could not work, that private incentives could not be aligned with the aims of a socialist system whose goals were determined by some political authority. He also did not believe that a central planning agency could cope with the enormous complexities of a modern economy. Moreover, as a matter of ideology, he rejected the authoritarianism and collectivism that a planned socialist state required. He vehemently objected to the idea that goals for society should be determined by a political authority, even a democratic one, much less a dictatorship. I think it is fair to say that he was horrified by what had occurred and was going on in the so-called socialist state of the Soviet Union, with its show trials, executions, gulags, mass starvation, and all the rest.

Nutter did, however, accept the third leg of the paradigm. Grossman's study and his own work with the Soviet data gave him enough confidence to allow himself to use them for his measurements. Of course, there was no choice; if he was to construct the measures of growth required by the NBER study, he had to use data produced in the Soviet Union. But he was fully aware of the hazards and shortcomings.

Reliance on the paradigm and, in many cases, sympathy for what many saw as a grand experiment in socialism produced the kinds of claims for Soviet performance and its future that are cited above. For academic specialists, Nutter's results struck at the heart of their conclusions and beliefs. It was not only their scientific conclusions, based on official data, that were questioned, although that was bad enough. Nutter's conclusions challenged the belief that a planned socialist economy could compete effectively with a free-market capitalist system, or even outdo it, and shattered the idealistic dream of a future socialist system. Nutter's view that catching up with the U.S. was highly improbable struck hard at this belief. Even worse was the idea that the best estimate of the long-term growth rate of the Soviet Union was the late Tsarist period. That Soviet socialism was no better than despotic Tsarism must have been unthinkable for many. No wonder people gasped.

There was another group of specialists who might *not* have gasped or who, if they did, gasped for different reasons. These were the Sovietologists who worked or had worked for the CIA and were familiar with classified work done on the economy. It appears to be a fact that internal CIA research had found retardation in Soviet growth years before Nutter's first reports on the NBER project. A National Intelligence Estimate from 1954 concluded that:

> The *rate* of growth of the Soviet Economy has declined in the past five years from the very high rates of the immediate postwar period. We estimate that during the next two years Soviet gross national product (GNP) will increase by about 6 or 7 percent, and in 1956-1959 by about 5 or 6 percent, per year.[19]

This NIE was classified Top Secret at the time; it was declassified some years later. Almost certainly, ongoing classified CIA work would have continued to produce such results. In fact, by the late 1960s, retardation was routinely reported in public reports by CIA analysts. As one example, Rush V. Greenslade published a table of annual growth rates showing a marked downward trend for industrial production in a compendium of papers published in 1972.[20] Because of his central role in the CIA's Soviet programs, Bergson must have endorsed the early reports of retardation, if he did not develop them himself.[21] Many other CIA analysts must have contributed to these results or at least been aware of them.

It is noteworthy in this respect that Bergson himself never openly criticized Nutter or the NBER project. Presumably, he could not disclose the then-secret CIA findings. So he simply remained above the fray, as might befit the most senior figure in the field. In fact, it appears that the ranks of public critics comprised academics (and unaffiliated writers) who did not have CIA links.

In Nutter's 1957 presentation to the American Economic Association, the Sovietologists with CIA links may not have been among those who gasped for the simple reason that the results did not surprise them. If they gasped, it might have been because they thought that security had been breached or were simply surprised someone on the outside, as it were, had discovered the retardation as they had, but with presumably poorer access to the data.

In the years following the publication of the NBER study, there was a slow shift in the views of establishment Sovietologists. Since the NBER study is rarely, if ever, mentioned in discussions of Soviet output and growth after the flurry of criticism,[22] it is doubtful that it was the cause of the shift. Whatever the cause, earlier conclusions about the Soviet planned economy gradually changed.

But socialism and central planning have other, deeper roots than mere macroeconomic efficiency. In part, sympathy toward or admiration of the Soviet system of central planning can be traced to a post-Enlightenment mentality that believes that human reason can and should be applied to the design and operation of an entire economic system. In 1935, less than twenty years before the NBER project, Friedrich Hayek wrote:

> ...today there is hardly a political group anywhere in the world which does not want central direction of most human activities in the service of one aim or another. It seemed so easy to improve upon the institutions of a free society which had come more and more to be considered as the result of mere accident...[23]

Such a "rationalist" view of central planning was supported by the success of wartime planning in the U.S. and elsewhere. There is little doubt that victory in the war was due in considerable measure to the mass mobilization of resources—human and physical—for the war effort. If thousands of aircraft, tanks, trucks, ships, and tons of munitions and materiel could be produced in such short order under the hand of the government, it seemed obvious to many that the same kind of direction could or would produce far better results for the postwar civilian economy than the apparent (to untrained eyes) disorganization of the free market.

Even Nutter conceded that the Soviet system had produced impressive results in industrial production. Consider this quotation from the 1962 study:

> In terms of its ability to generate sheer growth in industrial output—the questions of how much the growth has cost, what product mix has evolved, and how the products have been put to use being laid aside—the Soviet system of centralized direction has proved itself to be more or less the peer of the market economy, as exemplified by the United States.[24]

Of course, events a few decades in the future would show that this evaluation gave far too much credit to the Soviet system. But it is crucial to be careful about the statement. Nutter means, as he goes on to argue, that the Soviet system (guided by the political leaders) was focused on a relatively meager mix of products, including emphasis on investment goods and munitions.[25]

In the same vein, another expert recently characterized the Soviet economy as "structural militarization."[26] By this is meant that planners, following direction from above, focused their work on the military and its requirements. Resources were allocated in response to demands from the military sector; non-military sectors were left to compete with one another for the remaining resources. This form of planning is relatively simple, because there is a single or dominant consumer—the military—that presents well-defined requirements to the planning agency. Success in fulfilling those requirements is also relatively easy to measure, often being merely technical. It avoids the central issue of the great socialist debate—how the varying demands of a multitude of individuals can be met by producers who necessarily have limited knowledge of those demands, of the available resources, and of the technologies that might be used to produce the goods and services.

In addition to the false impression of the efficacy of planning that the war gave, the Great Depression contributed to sympathy for some form of planning or at least a much more intrusive role for the central government. It left an indelible mark in American psyches, leading many people to think that the market system was unstable, unpredictable, and unreliable. And, or so it appeared, the Soviet system was impervious to such fluctuations.[27] Indeed, after the war, such steps as the passage of the Full Employment Act of 1946 signified the appeal of a stronger government hand in the economy. It was not central economic planning of the Soviet type, but it did represent an effort to offset the invisible hand with something more visible and intentional.

The appeal of socialism lay not only in the belief that it would produce more goods and services and do it more reliably than the free market or in its appeal to post-Enlightenment rationalists. Socialism also had (and has) an emotional appeal based on what its adherents believed to be the injustices of capitalism, especially related to the distribution of incomes. This debate, even outside the borders of the capitalism/socialism divide, continues to the present day and will probably never be resolved. It should also be said that the question of the justice of income distribution is only one manifestation of fundamental philosophical differences about the nature of the good society. In the 1950s, the proponents of socialism with their perception of the good society far outnumbered those who took a different position.

Besides criticism from those who favored socialism and central direction of the economy, there was another type of criticism. This was based on the idea that a lowering of prospects for Soviet industrial production would lead to complacency about Soviet capabilities.[28] If ongoing American defense budgets were based on Soviet growth rates as officially reported or estimated by the CIA or private analysts, support would be eroded if growth rates were actually lower—and declining—as Nutter claimed. Critics on this side may have deliberately erred on the conservative side. In the atmosphere of the nuclear arms race and the aggressive posturing of the Soviets at the time, that was an understandable position. There was no way to be certain about the state of affairs, so caution was appropriate.

COLLAPSE OF A SYSTEM AND IDEOLOGICAL CONTINUITY

The NBER study represents the earliest public indication of the inherent weaknesses of Soviet socialism. But other specialists began to change their judgments. Only one year after the NBER study was published, Bergson himself had changed. In 1948, he had been persuaded that planning a social- ist economy was feasible; by 1963 he had concluded that a centrally planned economy was inferior to a market economy.[29] As years passed and the evi- dence mounted, others also came to doubt the long term superiority—or even parity—of the Soviet system.

Its total collapse, however, was shocking to nearly everybody. Although the great experiment with socialism and central planning had not produced the nirvana that some had expected, still it was believed that the system could sur- vive, albeit at a lesser level of performance than had been hoped for and expect- ed. Even Nutter, never sympathetic to anything connected with socialism, cen- tral planning, or the Soviet Union, had thought that it could survive and con- tinue to expand at rates approximating those of the late Tsarist period.[30]

But collapse it did. Did the collapse resolve the ideological conflict? Was the idea of socialism as a practical approach to the organization of an econo- my put to rest?

The former communist bloc countries swiftly abandoned their socialist systems and adopted some form of a market order.[31] The adoption of mar- ket-like systems has spread beyond Europe to South and Southeast Asia, Latin America, Africa, and some parts of the Middle East. Even communist Vietnam claims to have a market-based economy. The spectacular failure of Soviet socialism, as well as the continued success of older market-based economies, lies behind these developments.

Nevertheless, advocates of socialism persist, and their ranks are, if any- thing, growing. The recent financial collapse, of course, is a prime reason for this, reinforcing pro-socialist arguments about the instability of capitalism and even the moral arguments about the ethics of income distribution in a capitalist society. Few on the socialist side now advocate the outright abolition of private property in the means of production and the pure Marxian belief in the inevitability of socialism has largely disappeared. But what might be called "soft" socialism persists and is growing, as central governments increasingly regulate the use and restrict the exchange of property, fix prices of goods and services, and otherwise attenuate private property rights. This socialist impulse is channeled in many ways, for example in the environmental movement, the provision of health care, and restrictions on private determination of executive compensation.

If the Soviet collapse should have conclusively settled anything, it is that comprehensive central economic planning of the Soviet type is not feasible in a complex modern economy. And yet our daily political discourse is full of advocacy for economic planning. The identification of a problem (which usually means an outcome that somebody dislikes) commonly leads to calls for government to "solve" that problem. This usually means some form of government action—regulation, targeted taxation, subsidies, prohibitions of selected activities, and so forth. While not usually considered economic planning, such actions in fact have the same nature. The unfortunate result is that the accretion of thousands of such regulations, taxes, subsidies, prohibitions, and so forth creates a snarl of often conflicting laws whose overall effect is to impede economic development. Even this, and even the spectacular failure of the more comprehensive Soviet system, seems incapable of vanquishing the myth of economic planning by government.[32]

In breaking the stranglehold of conventional wisdom about Soviet economic performance, the NBER study opened the door to a widespread critique of socialism and socialist central planning that, in turn, played an important role in the demise of the Soviet Union. However, the resurgence of public policies that embody many of the characteristics of socialism illustrates how powerful ideological positions can be.

REFERENCES

Central Intelligence Agency, "Soviet Capabilities and Probable Causes of Action Through Mid-1959," National Intelligence Estimate 11-4-54.
"How Russia Has Grown," *The Economist*, July 7, 1962.

Rush V. Greenslade, "Industrial Production Statistics in the USSR," Vladimir Treml and John P. Hardt, *Soviet Economic Statistics* (Durham, N.C.: Duke University Press, 1972), pp. 155-194.

Rush V. Greenslade and Phyllis A. Wallace, "Industrial Growth in the Soviet Union: Comment," *American Economic Review*, Vol. 49, No. 4, 1959, pp. 687-695.

Gregory Grossman, *Soviet Statistics of Physical Output of Industrial Commodities: Their Composition and Quality* (Princeton, N.J.: Princeton University Press, 1960).

Friedrich A. Hayek, "Socialist Calculation I: The Nature and History of the Problem," 1935; republished in Friedrich A. Hayek, *Individualism and Economic Order* (Chicago: Regnery, 1948), pp. 119-147.

D.R. Hodgman, "Industrial Growth," Abram Bergson (ed.), *Soviet Economic Growth* (White Plains, N.Y.: Row, Peterson, 1953).

N.M. Kaplan and R.H. Moorsteen, "An Index of Soviet Industrial Output," *American Economic Review*, Vol. 40, No. 3, 1960, pp. 295-318.

Jerzy Karcz, "Review," *American Statistical Association Journal*, June 1963, pp. 572-575.

David M. Levy and Sandra J. Peart, "Soviet Growth and American Textbooks: An Endogenous Past," *Journal of Economic Behavior and Organization*, Vol. 78, 2011, pp. 110-125.

Daniel P. Moynihan, "The Soviet Economy: Boy, Were We Wrong," *Washington Post*, July 11, 1990.

James H. Noren, "Soviet Industry Trends in Output, Inputs, and Productivity," U.S. Congress, Joint Economic Committee, *New Directions in the Soviet Economy*, Part II-A, 1966, pp. 271-326.

G. Warren Nutter, *The Extent of Enterprise Monopoly in the United States* (Chicago: University of Chicago Press, 1951).

G. Warren Nutter, *The Growth of Industrial Production in the Soviet Union* (Princeton, N.J.: Princeton University Press, 1962).

G. Warren Nutter, "Industrial Growth in the Soviet Union," *American Economic Review*, Vol. 48, No. 2, 1958, pp. 398-411.

G. Warren Nutter, "On Measuring Economic Growth," *Journal of Political Economy*, Vol. 65, No. 1, 1957, pp. 31-63.

G. Warren Nutter, "Some Observations on Soviet Industrial Growth," *American Economic Review*, Vol. 47, No. 2, 1957, pp. 618-630.

G. Ofer, "Soviet Economic Growth, 1928-1985," *Journal of Economic Literature*, Vol. 25, No. 4, 1987, pp. 1767-1833.

Svetozar Pejovich, *Law, Informal Rules and Economic Performance* (Northampton, MA: Edward Elgar, 2008).

Steven Rosefielde, *Russia in the 21st Century: The Prodigal Superpower* (New York: Cambridge University Press, 2005).

Steven Rosefielde, "Tea Leaves, and Productivity: Bergsonian Norms for Gauging the Soviet Future," *Comparative Economic Studies*, Vol. 47, No. 2, 2005, pp. 259-273. (Text page references are to the manuscript.)

Thomas Sowell, *A Conflict of Visions* (New York: Basic Books, 2002).

Statistical Abstract of Industrial Output in the Soviet Union, National Bureau of Economic Research, New York, 1956.

Judith G. Thornton, "Review," *Journal of Economic History*, Vol. 23, No. 2, 1963, pp. 253-257.

TsSU, *Industry of the USSR (Promyshlennost' SSSR)*, Moscow, 1957.

Peter Wiles, "Sinews of Soviet Strength," *Challenge*, July 1962.

Ernest Williams, *Freight Transportation in the Soviet Union: A Comparison with the United States*, National Bureau of Economic Research, New York, 1959.

Eugene Zaleski, *Planning for Economic Growth in the Soviet Union, 1918-1932* (Chapel Hill, N.C.: University of North Carolina Press, 1962).

Eugene Zaleski, *Stalinist Planning for Economic Growth, 1933-1952* (Chapel Hill, N.C. and London: University of North Carolina Press and Macmillan, 1980).

Political-Ideological Warfare in Integrated Strategy, and its Basis in an Assessment of Soviet Reality[1]

John Lenczowski

At the heart of the Reagan policy toward the USSR was a strategy to address squarely and ultimately eliminate the causes of tension between East and West. Despite little consensus in the American foreign policy establishment about these causes, the Reagan Administration proceeded from an unambiguous interpretation of what they were: nothing less than the nature of the Soviet regime. From this view, it followed that U.S. policy had to find a way to change that nature, and do so, if possible, without risking total war.

Whereas in previous Administrations, U.S. policy toward Moscow was principally reactive and defensive, the Reagan strategy proceeded from a fundamentally offensively-oriented premise: the identification of the principal weaknesses of our adversary. To identify weaknesses required a proper understanding of the nature of the Soviet system—again, a matter over which there was no consensus among experts in the field. Once these were identified, the Administration set forth a multifaceted strategy whose ultimate goal was to bring about regime change from within.

IDENTIFYING THE SOURCES OF EAST-WEST CONFLICT

The Reagan strategy was based on the premise that the source of the conflict between the two powers was neither the existence of nuclear weapons— if it were, then we should also have had cold wars and arms control negotiations with other nuclear powers such as Britain, France, China, and Israel—nor economic rivalry, nor any other material factor. Such elements were not causes of the conflict; they were its symptoms. The Cold War, rather, was political in nature, and it would not end until its political causes were addressed.

So what were the political causes? From the American perspective, they had to do with the USSR's domestic policies—particularly its treatment of its own people—and its aggressive, subversive, and expansionistic foreign policies. And what was the foundation of these policies? It was the political system of the Soviet state that had been established by its founding ideology of communism. If the ideological nature of the Soviet system could be changed, then the source of tensions could be eliminated.

Similarly, from the Soviet view, their concerns were not so much with capitalism, which their propaganda could more easily attack, as with the nature of Western democratic republicanism and its founding philosophy of consent of the governed—a philosophy, which, if ignited in the minds of the peoples of the Soviet empire, threatened the seemingly unchangeable monopoly of Communist Party rule.

THE ASSUMPTIONS UNDERLYING PREVIOUS U.S. POLICIES TOWARD THE USSR

The absence of consensus about these matters within the U.S. foreign policy community—both in government as well as in the academic and research communities—lay at the root of the inability of the United States to conduct a coherent, long-term U.S. policy to resist Soviet expansionism. After years of consensus that underlay the policy of containment, large swaths of the foreign policy community had come to believe that the nature of the Soviet regime had changed at one time or another. Some believed that its fundamental genetic code changed with the death of Stalin and with Soviet Communist Party chief Nikita Khrushchev's "secret speech" at the 20th party Congress in 1956 on the "crimes of Stalin." This initiated a gradual rejection by the American Sovietological community of the "totalitarian model" as an accurate description of the nature of the Soviet regime.

By the late 1960's and early 1970's, the new conventional wisdom held that the USSR was moving in a more liberalized direction, as some authorities began to describe it as an "authoritarian welfare state" and an "administered society." Some scholars like Jerry Hough of Duke University and the

Brookings Institution went so far as to describe the Soviet Union as a "pluralist" society. The logic behind this analysis was that there existed "interest groups" in the USSR, each competing for its own influence and resources.[2] Not everyone agreed with this assessment, however. Indeed, after the collapse of the Soviet Union in 1991, the new President of post-Soviet Russia, Boris Yeltsin, declared that the USSR *under Soviet Party chief, Mikhail Gorbachev,* was none other than a "totalitarian" system. What then could it have been twenty years earlier under the leadership of Leonid Brezhnev? If Brezhnev's USSR was a "pluralist" society, then the same could be said for every political system in human history, including that of the Pharaoh, Genghis Khan, and even Adolf Hitler, under all of whom existed "interest groups" as defined by the Sovietologists who rejected the totalitarian model.

The corollary to the rejection of the totalitarian model and the subscription to one of the more optimistic interpretations of the nature of the Soviet system was a general acceptance of the unspoken but nevertheless operational assumption that the underlying ideology of the Soviet system was in such a state of decay that hardly anybody—even among the ruling Soviet elite—believed in it anymore, and thus that ideology could no longer be operational within the system, except as an atavistic window dressing. In effect, this assumption led to a subsequent assumption that the Soviet system had thereby changed to such an extent that it no longer necessarily possessed the attributes of a "communist" system, especially those attributes which, as a matter of genetic necessity, required it to maintain unlimited global strategic objectives. And what were those objectives? They were to transform the world into as much of its own image as necessary for that world to recognize the Soviet regime as a legitimate regime. Once this assumption had taken root, two conclusions became possible:

1. that Soviet goals were now limited, and in contrast to the unlimited goals that prevailed before, they could be at least partially accommodated. Hence, it became possible to believe that a "spheres of influence" policy could be shared with Moscow, and that other arrangements of ostensibly mutual interest could be realized, such as arms control agreements with which both sides complied.

2. that Moscow's intentions might indeed have changed significantly enough that the West no longer needed to be concerned about the putative Soviet "threat" and there may even have been no need to worry about containing any expansionism.

During the 1970s, U.S. policy toward the USSR operated to one degree or another based on these assumptions. Presidents Richard Nixon and Gerald Ford insisted on a policy of "détente" that was premised on the possibility of long-term peaceful coexistence with the Soviet system. President Jimmy Carter epitomized the regnant assumptions underlying detente when he castigated many Americans' "inordinate fear of communism."

THE ASSUMPTIONS UNDERLYING THE REAGAN POLICY

With the election of President Reagan, U.S. policy could change based on new assumptions—principally that the Soviets still were communists and that their policies proceeded from this central fact. Underlying this analysis was the assessment, shared by many on his team (but by no means all), that, however much the Marxist-Leninist ideology may have been in a state of decay, and however fewer people in the USSR accepted all its tenets, it still remained operational in the Soviet system and thus remained as both a guide and a constraint to policy.

It was this assessment alone that could explain the persistence of political tensions between East and West. But how could a decaying ideology still be operational, especially if fewer and fewer people even in the Party could accept all its dogmas? How could it still impel the Soviet regime to pursue tyranny at home and aggression abroad? And what difference did all this make for U.S. policy?

The answer to these questions lay in a proper understanding of the role of Marxist-Leninist ideology within the Soviet system. That ideology originally served as the animating force that brought together the Bolsheviks to prosecute their coup d'état against the weak, democratic, Provisional Government in post-Tsarist Russia. It served as a guiding theory of knowledge, of history and historical change, of economics, of politics, and of society. Less understood was the fact that it also served as a theory of the use of power, which included maxims of how to advance, remain steady, or retreat, as dictated by a "scientific" measurement of the "correlation of forces."[3] Vladimir Lenin also used the ideology as an instrument to enforce conformity of thought among the revolutionaries, as this ensured conformity in the realm of action, which, in turn, was the only way by which a minority could seize power over an unorganized majority. Once in power, Lenin used this strategy to address the principal weakness that his Bolshevik government suffered: its internal security problem, which fast became the most important fact of political life in the new USSR and which dogged it throughout its existence. This internal security problem was the central weakness that the Reagan strategy first identified and then succeeded in exploiting.

The internal security problem derived from one essential reality: the lack of legitimacy of the regime. The Bolsheviks knew that if the peoples of the new Soviet Union were free to give their consent as to who governed them, they would not choose the Bolsheviks. This fact was made manifest with the loss by the Bolsheviks to the non-communist Socialist Revolutionary Party in the first post-revolution elections to the Constituent Assembly. The Bolshevik reaction to this loss was summarily to execute the various delegates who assumed their seats in elected office.

The extent of the internal security problem can be usefully measured by the actions the Communist Party of the Soviet Union (CPSU) took to address it. These can be briefly summarized as follows:

- the Party's monopoly of information and communications, including its vast propaganda system, its monopoly of printing, copying, paper, newspapers, radio, television, etc.;
- its jamming of foreign radio broadcasts;
- its monopoly of education;
- its monopoly of entertainment and culture: books, music, art, film, theater, etc.;
- its monopoly of economic power and its control over: employment, promotion, job transfer, production and distribution, and the enforcement of "parasitism" laws;
- the KGB and its various structures and methods, such as block committees, forced recruitment of citizens to be informants, and pervasive surveillance;
- the various other organizations with police-type functions that would monitor the lives of individuals and enforce Party policy throughout society, including local Party organizations, "trade union" organizations (which were Party-controlled bodies that had nothing in common with trade unions as understood in the West), the internal security *militsiia*, the armed forces, etc.;
- the Gulag Archipelago, its slave labor camps, its death camps, and its "psychiatric clinics" as well as various lesser punishments;
- the Party's control over and penetration of religion;
- its arbitrary use of the legal system to serve its political ends;

- its control over all internal travel, through the internal passport system and other required documents;
- its control of the borders and all external travel;
- its penetration of all organized social bodies—including clubs, fraternal organizations, hobby groups, sports organizations, and even the family—to prevent them from becoming fronts for organized opposition;
- creating such an atmosphere of distrust (due to the pervasive coercive cooptation of people as secret police informants) that it produced the atomization of society—i.e., the separation of each individual from all others so that he or she was isolated and incapable of organizing with others in resistance to the regime; and finally,
- the use of the ideology and the attendant use of foreign expansionism. This deserves further explanation, for even after all our historical experience with communist rule, it is still little understood how the ideology was not only the prescription for how to achieve the radiant future and a guide to the exercise of power, but also, arguably, the most important element of the internal security system.

First and foremost, the Party promoted Marxist-Leninist ideas, and discredited competing ideas, particularly those having to do with democratic republicanism and those philosophical and religious ideas that posit the existence of a transcendent, objective, universal moral order that exists independently of the will of those (here, the Communist party) who would use force to impose their ideas of moral order upon society. The metaphysical (or even theological) element of this ideological strategy was key: if there exists an authority higher than the Party—say, for example, God—then those whose primary allegiance is to God represented a threat to Party control. Such people were, from the very beginning, non-conformists upon whom the Party could count for neither loyalty nor submission. This explains the pervasive, intensive, and necessary focus on atheistic propaganda and why the existence of 700,000 churches in pre-revolutionary Russia was reduced to 7,000 by the Gorbachev era.

At a less profound level, the ideology had to demonstrate the legitimacy of the regime by showing that there was a practical, rational, or moral reason why the Communist Party deserved to be in power. This was the first step in creating a psychological attitude of public acceptance of the regime. The Marxist doctrine of the worldwide inevitability of communism then served to bolster this attitude. If the laws of history were inexorable, if no act of human will could stop the march of history toward the final establishment of communism, then any attempt to exercise such will was futile. Thus, the ideology served to induce among the people not just acceptance of the regime but a sense of "futile resignation"—a fatalistic attitude that resistance to Communist rule was impossible.

How exactly did the ideology justify the Communist Party in power? It did so by a doctrine that was summarized by the Marxist axiom, "freedom is comprehended necessity." As the Party argued, one frees oneself from the consequences of phenomena in nature by understanding the laws of nature. Hence, by knowing that dark clouds portend a rain storm, one can free oneself from the consequences of the storm by seeking shelter and then, through this knowledge, harness the power of flowing water to run a mill or generate electricity. Similarly, by understanding the "laws of history," the Party can free itself from the consequences of historical developments—such as suffering oppression at the hands of the ruling class—and then harness the forces of history in order to help guide it to its "inevitable" goal. This is the meaning of Marx's explanation of the role of "true philosophy": "Philosophers have hitherto only interpreted the world in various ways; the point is to change it."[4] In other words, since philosophical theory without the test of praxis is useless and unverifiable, that philosophy which is true is that which, having properly understood the "laws of history," verifies its validity by the praxis of working to change the world in the direction of communism. The Party, thus, justified itself in power because it understood the laws of history better than anyone else. With this special knowledge, it could help guide the force of history by serving as the "vanguard" of a working class that was too ignorant of its own oppression to be able to do anything about it.

This ideological justification of the Party's rule was simply another form of Gnosticism: "we possess unique, esoteric knowledge and therefore we have earned the privilege of ruling society and ultimately the world."

Just as the ideology was used as a method to establish a "Party Line" to which the Bolshevik revolutionaries had to conform in order to overthrow the *ancien regime*, so was it used as an instrument to enforce conformity of thought and action throughout the Soviet system.

Internal security was achieved in this way because ideological conformity served as an analog to a drum beating for soldiers marching: it set the standard against which deviationism could be measured. Among its most effective methods was to insist that everyone—from Party member to ordinary subject of the regime—repeat falsehoods that were a key element of the Party

Line. In many respects, it was easier to establish conformity with a falsehood than with the truth, which could have different shades of valid meaning.

This system was analogous to Hans Christian Andersen's story of "The Emperor's New Clothes"; everyone in the court had to proclaim that the naked emperor was wearing beautiful clothes, and they did so either out of loyalty or out of fear. Anyone who stated the truth could be immediately identified as a deviationist and the threat to the established regime that he in fact was.

The Lie of the clothed emperor in the USSR could be understood in several ways. At one level, it could be understood as the steady stream of misrepresentations of daily and past realities.

But on a more profound level, the Lie lay at the root of the ideological foundations of the regime. At this level, the Lie could be understood as the central premise of Soviet socialism: that there is no transcendent universal moral order in the world, and that what moral standards exist are determined entirely by man, specifically by his personal preferences, and more specifically by those with the greatest power, will, and ruthlessness to enforce those preferences. In dialectical materialist terms, this idea was expressed by Lenin when he denied the existence of objective moral standards and posited instead that whatever aids the revolution is good whereas whatever hinders it is evil.[5] Although this theory is said to mean that "history makes right," the fact is that the making of history—and whether it moves in the direction of revolution or not—is under the control of willful men. Thus, all moral standards are established by man and not by any transcendent source, whether it be nature or God. As a practical matter, this means that society determines moral standards by power struggle: whoever has the greatest number of votes or, when things get serious, the biggest guns and the greatest will to use them, determines the morals of society. This is nothing less than the doctrine of "might makes right." So, whatever the Party said is just was just, and there was no independent justice—no natural moral law—to which dissidents could appeal to seek redress in the case of arbitrary and capricious administration of man-made "law." In other words, there was no basis upon which to claim that a law might be unjust.

The Lie also took a corollary form: that man's capacity to do good or evil is determined by his material environment and not by individual moral choice. According to this vision, rooted in 18th-century thought, man is an empty vessel with no permanent human nature and thus the capacity to be molded and perfected into the "new Soviet man" as his sculptors saw fit.

Thus, according to the communist vision, the human person has no transcendent dignity, and he or she can be manipulated, used, experimented with, degraded, and destroyed according to the needs of the revolution, which, as a practical matter, meant the needs of the Party.

Ultimately, the Lie held that the regime was legitimate and should be recognized as such by everyone both inside and outside the empire.

In the USSR, the ideological Lie served many purposes:

- It was a test of loyalty (or submission) to the regime.
- It concealed the ruthless methods used by the state.
- It created "enemies" that were used to justify repressive measures.
- It concealed policy failures.
- It concealed evidence which challenged the ideology and thus the legitimacy of the regime.
- Together with the KGB's system of forced recruitment of informants, it destroyed trust between individuals and among the people as a whole.
- It forced people to live in what Alain Besancon has called a "pseudo-reality" whereby the individual would have to pretend he was living in a society of fully realized socialism and thus adopt an attitude of gratitude and appreciation toward those who had bestowed this "benefit" upon him.[6]
- It served the goals of political socialization and mass mobilization for the purpose of creating the "new man."
- Its pervasive coerciveness then served, in the words of Leszek Kolakowski, "to remind the people who had the gun."[7]

When combined with the historical determinism of the ideology that said: "It is futile to resist the forces of history," the Lie thus served to disarm and demoralize the people.

As Solzhenitsyn explained, the Lie penetrated to the depths of men's souls:

In our country, the lie has been incorporated into the state system as the vital link holding everything together, with billions of tiny fasteners, several dozen to each man. This is precisely why we find life so oppressive.... When oppression is not accompanied by the lie, liberation demands political measures. But when the lie has fastened its claws on us, it is no longer a matter of politics! It is an invasion of man's moral world and our straightening up and refusing to lie is also not political, but simply a retrieval of our human dignity.[8]

The Cold War, then, as President Reagan saw it, was not only a conflict between East and West, it was in essence a moral conflict—even within the Soviet empire and within the West—which, at its heart, took the form of *a war between truth and falsehood.*

Soviet foreign policy was designed to serve the security interests of the regime, the most important of which was the internal security interest. Foreign policy had to demonstrate that the ideology was correct, so that it could continue to serve as the accepted instrument of establishing the legitimacy of Party authority. So long as Soviet foreign policy could help advance the spread of communism worldwide, the ideology could be plausibly presented as correct. And so long as communism advanced, Moscow could show that Soviet power was unstoppable, that it could not be resisted even by U.S. military might, and that therefore it was futile for anyone within the empire even to consider resisting communist rule.

A key element of the Soviet regime's foreign policy was its ability to use nuclear blackmail, intimidation, and manipulation of the atmospherics of tension in East-West relations to demoralize its subject peoples. This was achieved by intimidating the West into silence, thus precluding the possibility of external moral-political resistance to communism. And if external resistance was impossible, then how could internal resistance succeed?

If Western leaders wanted to avoid a barrage of Soviet threats and an atmosphere of Cold War tension that could harm their domestic political fortunes, they had to censor themselves. This was the Soviet price for maintaining peace and quiet. Soviet foreign policy used intimidation and manipulated the truth to compel other states to accept their version of the "truth" as a sign of either loyalty or submission. This was nothing more than the Emperor's New Clothes on an international scale. If the Kremlin could not compel everyone in the "court" to utter the Lie, it demanded, at minimum, that the "courtiers" stand silent. This is what is called "Finlandization," with all due respect to the Finns, who have a proud tradition of resisting totalitarian aggression. The reality of Finlandization was that the shadow of Soviet power was so great that it compelled even such courageous people as the Finns to censor themselves.

Western silence and self-censorship, of course, were seen by the peoples of the Soviet empire as a sign of weakness in the face of Soviet power. If the

American President was too frightened to tell the full truth about Soviet human rights violations at home and Soviet aggression, espionage, and subversion abroad, if he was too "prudent" in his management of East-West relations that he could not counter the lies of Soviet disinformation and propaganda with plain truth, then how could the peoples of the Soviet empire even contemplate telling the truth, even about the smallest things? As the empire's subject peoples saw it, if Soviet power was so great that the American President would not publicly reveal the truth about Soviet arms control treaty violations, then, as a practical matter, Soviet power could compel those violations to "vanish" as if they never existed.

The Soviets knew that military and economic strength alone were insufficient to determine the outcome of any conflict. They knew that we lost the Vietnam War, not because of either military or economic weakness, but because of moral-political weakness and vulnerability to North Vietnamese and Soviet propaganda—i.e., vulnerability to the Lie (see, for example, the almost completely ignored testimony to this effect by the victorious North Vietnamese generals).[9] Perceiving such weakness in the moral-political realm, and the consequent inability of the United States to resist the advance of communism, the Kremlin could minimize its internal security threat. This assessment of American weakness in the Soviet calculation of the "correlation of forces" (the systematic measurement of the relative strengths and weaknesses of both sides in the Cold War) prompted Moscow to believe that it could make strategic advances throughout the 1970s in Somalia, then in Ethiopia, South Yemen, and simultaneously with Cuban help in Mozambique, Angola, Namibia, Central and South America, Grenada and other islands of the Caribbean, and finally in Afghanistan.[10]

Ideological warfare was an essential part of Soviet foreign policy. It was based, first, on a recognition that all socio-political order derived from the material, or economic, "basis" of society, which, in turn, produced class struggle.[11] In the international arena, this took the form of a "struggle between the two social systems"—socialism and capitalism—and a consequent struggle between two worldviews, and thus two concepts of international relations, international law, and world order.

Soviet foreign policy was thus devoted to promoting a "new form of international relations": "proletarian internationalism." This concept described relations that would no longer be conducted between "states"—since the state, according to Marxism-Leninism, was the instrument of the oppressor class—but rather between "peoples." (Why the Soviet state continued to exist as late as the 1960s rather than "withering away" once the bourgeoisie had been smashed was the subject of considerable ideological contortions during the Khrushchev and Brezhnev eras. The upshot of these exertions was the formulation of a new concept: the "state of the whole people" whose existence was justified by the fact that it was surrounded by threatening "imperialist" states.) *Mezhdunarodnaya otnosheniia*, which is conventionally translated as "international relations," is, in fact, literally translated as "relations between peoples." As a practical matter, for the Soviets, this meant relations between the proper representatives of the people: the communist parties. Hence, the Soviet relations with a communist satellite country such as Cuba were not conducted by the Soviet Foreign Ministry, but rather by the Bloc Relations Department of the Central Committee of the CPSU. Similarly, "genuine" inter-people relations between the USSR and the U.S. were conducted between the CPSU Central Committee's International Department and the Communist Party USA. Diplomatic relations with non-communist countries conducted by the Soviet Foreign Ministry were merely a temporary arrangement, designed largely to deceive the West into believing that the USSR was a conventional and not a revolutionary state and thereby into treating it accordingly.

The International Department was the modern successor to the erstwhile Moscow-directed Communist International ("Comintern") and the subsequent Communist Information Bureau ("Cominform"). Its goal was to bring about the revolutionary transformation of non-communist states to the Soviet model of communism. These new communist states would then recognize the Soviet Party-state as a legitimate regime, thus ending their potential ideological threat to Soviet rule.

The ongoing attempt to promote communist takeovers required a massive investment in ideological warfare. This consisted of:

- promoting Marxist-Leninist ideology worldwide;
- assistance to various Marxist-oriented revolutionary movements (including education in political ideology, political action, and irregular warfare, as well as assistance in propaganda, communications, intelligence, armaments, and other logistical matters);
- the vilification and subversion of enemy regimes, institutions, and cultures; and
- the isolation of anti-Soviet countries, political parties, organizations, and individuals.

The incremental erosion of the Free World and the addition of new revolutionary states to the Soviet column would thus gradually bring about a new world order. The groundwork for this order would also be laid by continuing Soviet efforts to replace "bourgeois international law" with communist international (or, more properly, inter-people) law. Part of this effort involved matters of a moral tactical nature, such as attempting to rewrite the international laws of war in such a way as to legalize terrorist activity and irregular warfare. And part of it involved a grand strategic effort to establish new "rules of the game" in international relations by creating a psycho-political environment that would define the parameters of legitimate conduct by the respective protagonists in the "struggle between the two social systems."

The latter strategic effort first involved dividing the world into two zones much in the same way that Islam does: the "war zone"—the non-communist world—and the "peace zone"—the communist world (otherwise known as the "socialist community of states").[12] The first derived its appellation from the Leninist theory that the cause of war was "imperialism"—the highest stage of capitalism—wherein advanced capitalist countries resort to war in their rapacious struggle amongst themselves for new markets abroad. The second derived its name from the theory that true "peace" prevails where capitalism has been vanquished and can no longer cause any more war. The new rules (inter-people laws) that derive from this conceptual framework require that anything within the "peace zone" is off limits to the scrutiny of any non-communist state or international organization, while anything within the "war zone" is fair game for any international scrutiny, criticism, interference, and intervention. Thus, to make an analogy with American football, a scrimmage line was drawn, and no one in the West could cross that line. Instead, it was the Kremlin, its allies, and its proxies who would possess the ball, determine the timing of the next play, choose whether to run or to pass, go left or right, shallow or deep, and keep the West psychologically, strategically, and tactically on the defensive and in a reactive frame of mind. Any violation of this scrimmage line would face a threat of nuclear war.[13]

To a remarkable degree, American foreign policy during large parts of the Cold War accepted this conceptual framework. The United States did not want to risk crossing the communist scrimmage line:

- to achieve victory in the Korean war;
- to help the Hungarians in their uprising and their defense against the ensuing Soviet invasion in 1956;
- to stop the construction of the Berlin Wall;

- to achieve victory in Vietnam; or
- to help defend the Czechoslovaks against the Soviet invasion in response to the "Prague Spring" in 1968.

The corollary to this demarcation of the larger battlefield was the systemic effort to define the terms of international political discourse. Here the Soviets made massive investments in semantic warfare. Every imaginable political term with normative connotations was subject to ideological manipulation. In addition to its definition of "peace," the Kremlin worked overtime to ensure that such prominent terms of international discourse were endowed with their own unique communist definitions:

- "peaceful coexistence"—a form of struggle between the two social systems where all forms of struggle are permitted except all-out armed struggle;
- "freedom"—freedom from capitalist exploitation: i.e., those conditions that pertain under communist rule;
- "security"—security from imperialist aggression: i.e., again, those conditions that are enjoyed under communism;
- "democracy"—rule by the people: i.e., rule by the people's true representatives, the Communist Party;
- "cooperation"—agreeing with the Soviet position in international negotiations;
- "arms race"—the policy of arms buildup conducted solely by imperialist powers (in other words, it was only the U.S. and its allies that did any "racing," and never the USSR);
- etc.[14]

The semantic effort was manifested constantly in Soviet official rhetoric as well as in selected theaters of ideological combat. An example was the cataloging system in the library of the United Nations. Here Soviet agents of influence engineered the entire subject catalog of the UN library to conform to Soviet terminology and concepts. A search literature on "imperialism" or "colonialism" would reveal books solely on Western imperialism both genuine and alleged, with no references to Soviet/Russian imperialism, whether in the Caucasus, the Baltic states, Central Asia, or elsewhere in the extended system of communist states.[15]

Pursuant to these ideological semantic efforts came policies such as the Soviet proxy efforts by Cuba to raise U.S. "imperialism" in Puerto Rico before the U.N. Decolonization Committee—this, in spite of the fact that regular referenda in Puerto Rico revealed that 49 percent of the people wanted to maintain the existing "commonwealth" status, 49 percent wanted Puerto Rico to become a full state of the United States, and only 2 percent sought national independence.

Soviet ideological warfare initiatives found their way into every imaginable theater of potential subversion, whether by direct Soviet agents or their socialist or "New Left" "fellow travelers"—i.e., those with similar or shared ideological roots:

- efforts to indoctrinate, alienate, and coopt ethnic and religious minorities within the West;[16]
- efforts to subvert religion, not only among the churches within the communist realm but throughout the non-communist world. This included the promulgation of "liberation theology" among Christian churches worldwide;[17]
- efforts to promote sexual libertinism and narcotics usage to undermine traditional mores and to substitute license for liberty;[18]
- insertion of agents of influence in the media, philanthropic foundations, the film industry, and the literary and artistic communities of non-communist countries;[19]
- infiltration of and promotion of ideological propaganda in schools, colleges, and universities, and their various educational materials. Included in this effort was the lowering of educational standards and the rewriting of history, with heavy emphasis on: promotion of "class-based" perspectives on social history, emphasis on the victimhood of oppressed groups within the capitalist world, distortion of diplomatic history so as to put the blame for the Cold War on the West, etc.;
- infiltration and cooptation of the labor movement in the West;
- cooptation of Western business leaders to serve Soviet interests, and in some cases, the use of business leaders, such as Occidental Petroleum Chairman Armand Hammer, as agents of influence;[20]
- etc.[21]

THE RESULTANT POLICY: DEMONSTRATING THE FALSITY OF THE IDEOLOGY, THE ILLEGITIMACY OF THE REGIME, THE POSSIBILITY OF SUCCESSFUL RESISTANCE, AND THE BANKRUPTCY OF THE SOVIET WORLDVIEW

The overall strategy to "contain and reverse Soviet expansionism" and to "weaken the sources of Soviet imperialism" became codified in National

Security Decision Directive 75 (NSDD-75), on "U.S. Relations with the USSR" and several other Presidential directives. NSDD-75 began by observing that "Soviet aggressiveness has deep roots in the internal system" and therefore U.S. policy must "promote ... the process of change in the Soviet Union toward a more pluralistic political and economic system in which the power of the privileged ruling elite is gradually reduced."[22] The NSDD contained a specific section on Political Action (later in the text described as a "major political/ideological offensive"), which prescribed the necessity of "an ideological thrust which clearly affirms the superiority of U.S. and Western values of individual dignity and freedom, a free press, free trade unions, free enterprise, and political democracy over the repressive features of Soviet Communism." It then directed U.S. policy to: 1) support democratic forces within the Soviet Union; 2) highlight Soviet human rights violations; 3) strengthen U.S. broadcasting to the Soviet Union; 4) expose the double standards used by the Kremlin in dealing with its own domain and the capitalist world (the treatment of labor, policies toward ethnic minorities, the use of chemical weapons, etc.); and 5) prevent the Soviet propaganda machine from seizing the semantic high-ground in the battle of ideas through the appropriation of such terms as "peace."[23]

A key element of the NSDD was its directive to exploit weaknesses within the Soviet empire, including efforts to "encourage Soviet allies to distance themselves from Moscow in foreign policy and move toward democratization domestically."[24] This meant "loosening Moscow's hold" on Eastern Europe and putting greater pressure on the Soviet occupation of Afghanistan and Soviet-Cuban designs in the Western Hemisphere and Africa.

As a practical matter, following the directive to weaken the sources of Soviet imperialism by promoting the process of change within the USSR toward a pluralistic political-economic system in such a way that diminished the power of the ruling elite meant that U.S. policy had to counter all those methods by which the Soviet regime and its satellites prevented internal political competition and resistance to their rule. This required undermining the Marxist-Leninist ideology, its ability to provide plausible legitimacy for the regime, and ultimately the ability of the regime to induce that sense of "futile resignation" among the peoples of the Soviet empire. To do this, U.S. policy had not only to prove that the ideology was false, but to show the peoples of the Soviet empire that resistance was indeed possible. The strategy to achieve these objectives had both material and non-material components.

The Material Dimension: How It Had Strategic Effects in the Political-Ideological War

The material elements of the Reagan strategy were designed first to discredit the Party's claims that "scientific socialism" was the most advanced form of social-political-economic organization. Since the Bolshevik revolution, the Party had maintained that the communist system would produce the greatest wealth for the greatest benefit of society as a whole. Khrushchev, for one, predicted that the Soviet economy would outrank that of the U.S. by the 1980s. In response, the Reagan policy set out to put strains on the Soviet economy that would undermine both these ideological claims and also the ability of the Soviet economy to maintain military competitiveness.

The inability of the Soviet economy to be innovative meant that for decades it depended on the purchase or theft of Western technology. The Reagan policy of technology security and export controls made it increasingly hard for Soviet industries to produce modern goods, particularly military equipment. The Reagan strategy of sabotaging the technology that it permitted Moscow to purchase or steal exacerbated this situation.

The Reagan arms buildup put increasing pressure on the Soviet military economy to maintain military competitiveness. The creation of revolutionary new technologies, such as the computer systems that enabled President Reagan to propose the Strategic Defense Initiative, demonstrated a sprint capability in the West that was a lethal challenge to the Soviet military economy. The dual strategy of stopping the Soviet gas pipeline to Europe and cooperating with the Saudis to increase oil production and lower world oil prices deprived Moscow of its ability to earn hard currency that could enable it to purchase foreign goods in general and Western technology in particular.

The Soviet civilian economy began its ongoing crisis in 1917. Soviet consumer goods production always lagged far behind the immense output of Western economies. For years, the peoples of the USSR made enormous sacrifices in hopes that the radiant future of socialist prosperity would be just around the corner. The failure of the Party to overcome the permanent systemic crisis became clear during the Brezhnev era—the "era of stagnation"— and it was at this time that even the loyal Soviet intelligentsia began its gradual slide toward alienation from Soviet socialism. By the time of the Andropov and Chernenko Administrations, each of which was subjected to the pressures of the Reagan economic strategy, that alienation was virtually complete.

In effect, that alienation was an enormous internal symptom of a crisis over the very legitimacy of Communist Party rule. If the Soviet economy could not produce the benefits to society as a whole that Marxist-Leninist ideology promised, then perhaps the ideology was wrong. And if the ideology was wrong, then how could the regime justify itself in power?

A similar purpose was served by the Reagan military buildup and the policies of technology denial, technology sabotage, and economic warfare (e.g., stopping the Yamal gas pipeline and lowering world oil prices to deprive Moscow of hard currency)—all of which struck major blows to the Soviet military economy and thus Soviet military competitiveness. These policies prevented Moscow from advancing the communist cause worldwide with impunity. They prevented the Kremlin from issuing such threats that could amount to nuclear blackmail. They undermined the ability of the Soviets to use military power and threats to show that communism was the wave of the future, that it was able to overcome all foreign "imperialist" resistance, and that it was an inexorable force propelled forward by nothing less that the "laws of history." If the advance of communism could be stopped by human will—in the form of Ronald Reagan's defiance of the accommodative policies of détente—then, once again, perhaps Marxism-Leninism was wrong and there was no plausible ideological basis for Soviet Communist Party legitimacy.

Stopping the advance of communism was the central tenet of the long-time policy of "containment." And while the essence of that policy was sound as a method of undermining the claims of Soviet ideology, Moscow could avoid a crisis of legitimacy by setting the parameters of the worldwide "struggle between the two social systems" in a timeframe of sufficient length. Thus, with a strategy of "protracted conflict," Soviet theoreticians could argue that the march of history always has a dialectical nature, takes unexpected turns, and thus can been seen as a process of "two steps forward, one step back."[25]

In the face of such logic, the Reagan strategy had an answer: the "Reagan Doctrine" of support for anti-communist resistance movements. This policy, pursued in theaters throughout the world, put further strain on the Soviet system. While, on the one hand, it put pressure on Soviet "imperial overstretch," on the other hand, it showed that the "forces of history" could be reversed and that, once again, the claims of the ideology were false.

The Reagan Doctrine had a further logic to it: it was designed to demonstrate to the peoples of the extended Soviet empire that resistance to communist rule was not futile, that, on the contrary, it was very possible indeed. If

Nicaraguan *campesinos* could stop the consolidation of communist rule in Managua on their own and without the intervention of the U.S. military, if Afghan *mujāhidīn* could drive out the Red Army and its *spetsnaz* troops, if Angolan guerrillas could resist a communist regime in Luanda that was supported by Cuban troops and Soviet bloc counterintelligence, then perhaps the peoples of the East-Central European satellite states and the Soviet peoples themselves could eventually cast off the communist yoke as well.

The Non-Material Dimension

The Reagan Doctrine reached its zenith in the case of Poland. But here, for all the material support given to the Solidarity movement, the non-material support may well have been more strategically decisive than any other element of the Reagan strategy. This dimension of the Reagan Doctrine took the form of public diplomacy, "political warfare" and "ideological warfare"— tools that had been utterly neglected by the foreign policy establishment, both in its official incarnation and in the academic and think tank communities. It was these arts of statecraft, targeting the publics of East-Central Europe and the inner Soviet empire, that spurred the chain of revolts against Soviet rule that would prove decisive.

Before examining the specific case of Poland, it is necessary to review the entire scope of the public diplomatic effort and its centrality to President Reagan's strategy. While methods of information policy and strategic communications were essential, the President recognized that the content and spirit behind the messages he wished to convey lay at the heart of his overall strategy:

> While America's military strength is important, let me add here that I've always maintained that the struggle now going on for the world will never be decided by bombs or rockets, by armies or military might. The real crisis we face today is a spiritual one; at root, it is a test of moral will and faith.
>
> Whittaker Chambers, the man whose own religious conversion made him a witness to one of the terrible traumas of our time, the Hiss-Chambers case, wrote that the crisis of the Western World exists to the degree in which the West is indifferent to God, the degree to which it collaborates in communism's attempt to make man stand alone without God. And then he said, for Marxism-Leninism is actu-

ally the second oldest faith, first proclaimed in the Garden of Eden with the words of temptation, "Ye shall be as gods."

"The Western World can answer this challenge," he wrote, "but only provided that its faith in God and the freedom He enjoins is as great as communism's faith in Man."

I believe we shall rise to the challenge. I believe that communism is another sad, bizarre chapter in human history whose last pages even now are being written. I believe this because the source of our strength in the quest for human freedom is not material, but spiritual. And because it knows no limitation, it must terrify and ultimately triumph over those who would enslave their fellow man.[26]

The Reagan strategy in the non-material realm proceeded further from the President's recognition that the political-spiritual heart of the Cold War had just undergone a strategic turning point: the election of a Polish pope, John Paul II, whose election and subsequent visit to Poland galvanized the Polish people as had few other developments in their thousand-year history. It was thanks to his witness to the truth and his use of the words of Jesus to inspire and encourage his Christian countrymen to "Be not afraid" that made possible the poetic justice of a workers' movement in the "workers' paradise." His electrifying appearances brought literally millions to the streets and to public celebrations of the Mass in a new spirit of hope for both earthly deliverance and spiritual salvation.

Building on what he knew was a revived movement for freedom, President Reagan adopted a public diplomacy strategy that amounted to a war of ideas resting, above all, on moral witness and conviction. It first took shape in his own rhetoric and was then supported by various programs in public diplomacy and political warfare which, in coordination with the other elements of the President's integrated strategy, were designed to connect with the peoples of the Soviet Empire to show them that they were not alone; combat the falsehoods of Soviet propaganda, discredit communist ideology, totalitarianism and aggression; promote a positive alternative set of ideas and political solutions; and assist the efforts of individuals, groups, and movements that were adopting these ideas and resisting Soviet and communist rule.

Presidential Rhetoric

The rhetorical dimension of the President's role in the war of ideas involved using the spoken word to combat the Lie and all its effects by telling the truth—i.e., giving the peoples of the Soviet empire that for which they hungered even more than food. Telling the truth was a sign of moral resistance to the fear-laced system of enforced conformity—a system that pertained not only domestically within the Soviet empire, but internationally as well. The man who had the impertinence and the nerve to buck not only the Party line as enforced by Moscow, but the "party line" of self-censorship dictated by the foreign policy and media elites of the West, demonstrated his moral courage not only to those elites but also to the ordinary people in both East and West. From the beginning, alongside Pope John Paul II, Ronald Reagan proved to be one of two Little Boys in the Emperor's Court.

Presidential rhetoric was not something done either spontaneously or without design; it was carefully crafted for strategic purposes. As a memorandum to the President requested by National Security Advisor William P. Clark and composed by this author in early 1983 noted:

> The Soviet system depends for its survival on the systematic suppression of the truth... The key element in Soviet assessment is the adversary's strength of moral-political conviction—i.e., his will to use force if necessary to defend his vital interests. In practice, as the Soviets see it, this means the willingness of their opponent to speak plainly about the nature and goals of communism... The key feature of "Finlandization" is for the target country to censor itself—if not to lie outright, then at least to remain silent... As the Soviets see it, to tell the truth about the USSR is to risk igniting their internal security threat—the threat of mass popular resistance to the ideology, as in Poland. When stating that the Soviets will "lie," "cheat," and "commit any crime" to further their goals, you lifted a partial veil of self-censorship we had imposed on ourselves for some 15 years. Thus, by simply telling the truth, you incalculably strengthened the credibility of our military deterrent.[27]

The President emphasized the spiritual dimension of the "twilight struggle" and how truth was the critical element:

> We in the West must do more than merely decry attacks on human freedom. The nature of this struggle is ultimately one that will be decided not by military might, but by spiritual resolve and confidence in the future of freedom, especially in the face of the decaying and crumbling dreams of Marxism-Leninism. Lenin advocated resorting

to all sorts of stratagems, artifices, maneuvers, illegal methods, evasions and subterfuges. Well, we in the West have at our command weapons far more potent than deceit and subterfuge. We have the power of truth—truth that can reach past the stone and steel walls of the police state and create campaigns for freedom and coalitions for peace in Communist countries.[28]

The power of truth and moral witness was effective for three major reasons: 1) it comported with the natural sense of justice of oppressed peoples; 2) it respected and elevated their human dignity; and 3) it formed a natural bond with people who possessed the same fundamental moral sense that underlay the founding of all free societies—that virtue, and therefore self-control, is the prerequisite for a people to be self-governing and, therefore, ultimately free.

The President recognized that the Cold War was going on within the Soviet empire itself, between those whose souls were enslaved—those who had developed moral calluses and who had successfully suppressed over time their inner voice of conscience for purposes of personal gain—and those whose enslavement was only external as they possessed an "inner freedom." This inner freedom consisted of a refusal to submit to the false moral standards imposed by the regime—constantly shifting standards that did not comport with the Natural Moral Law—the "Law of Decent Behavior" that is written on the human heart and that endows the human being with a transcendent dignity. Those possessed of this inner freedom never lost sight of the fundamental injustice inherent in the violation of their natural rights by the Communist state—rights endowed not by man but by their Creator. That inner freedom, then, was the continued possession of the conviction that there is such a thing as justice no matter what the laws of the communist system said—because there exists a transcendent, objective, universal moral order in the world by which they would live no matter what external injustices were imposed upon them.

The task of this central moral dimension of the President's Cold War strategy was to connect with those people who had not sold their souls, to connect with them at the most profound level of human existence—the spiritual. It meant helping them reclaim their human dignity through such moral witness as could be inspired by spiritual solidarity from abroad.

Presidential Press Conference

At his first press conference, President Reagan shocked the world by telling a truth that the world had long since decided to suppress: that the Soviets had a different morality than ours. He then added that according to that morality, Soviet leaders reserved the right "to commit any crime, to lie, to cheat to further the goals of communism."[29] The President, of course, was exactly, clinically, correct. Communist morality *is* different, as was made amply clear in the classic statement of that morality in Lenin's speech to the Youth Leagues in 1920 cited earlier—a speech that was required reading for every Soviet school child.[30]

What did the President's statement accomplish?

1. It told the world that there was an elephant in the room that nobody saw or wanted to see.
2. It combated the main theme of Soviet disinformation and propaganda: i.e., that "We, the Soviets, are not communist anymore."[31]

This deceptive theme was designed to induce, and then sustain, the very analysis that had taken hold in American Sovietology: the idea that the USSR had changed to such an extent that its ideology was: either no longer believed and thus no longer operational in the Soviet system; or believed only by retrograde Stalinist "hawks" who were gradually being overshadowed in Kremlin politics by "moderate, pragmatic, doves" who had long since rejected doctrinaire Marxism-Leninism. Of course, if the Soviets could persuade us that they—or at least the most important of their officeholders—were no longer communist, then, by definition, their goals would no longer be unlimited and revolutionary, and thus we in the West could let down our guard. In the face of the many ways Moscow was conveying this theme, the President reminded the world of the truth of the matter.[32]

3. The President's statement was the first step in reconnecting America with the millions of people suffering under communism—people whom the West had for all practical purposes abandoned for two decades.

Project Truth

Initially, this "project" began without being so named. It first consisted of a stream of Presidential speeches, radio addresses, proclamations (such as those for Captive Nations Week), reports, and public statements telling truths about the Soviet empire that had been suppressed for years.

One of its earliest products was the El Salvador White Paper issued by the State Department. This described the extension of Soviet-Cuban subversion from Nicaragua to El Salvador and communist support of the Farabundo Marti Liberation Front guerrillas in that country. (Although it successfully convinced larger numbers of Americans that it was merely a party of agrarian reformers committed to setting up day-care centers in the countryside, the FMLN was in fact a communist movement named after the founder of the Salvadoran Communist Party.)[33]

Another major initiative was the publication of an annual report by the Defense Department: *Soviet Military Power*. This annual book-length report was filled with declassified military intelligence on Soviet military capabilities and included photographs and "intelligence art" depicting Soviet weapons systems.[34]

This publication was followed the next year by the President's televised speech to the nation on the enormous Soviet military buildup.[35] His various statements about this buildup had the strategic effect of mobilizing a domestic consensus in support of his own program of rearmament.

A related product was the unprecedented public revelation of Soviet arms control treaty violations. The first of these reports was issued by the Administration's General Advisory Commission on Arms Control and Disarmament (GAC). This report was designed to alert the public to the dangers of neglecting compliance with arms control treaties and to minimize the political warfare and strategic benefits that the Soviets could reap from concluding treaties and violating them without compunction.[36] The arms control industry both in and out of government had long manifested such a strict self-censorship and willful blindness with regard to such violations that ignorance about Soviet purposes underlying these violations was pandemic in the larger foreign policy community. As a result, most people in official positions relating to arms control negotiations were unaware: that Moscow had a strategy to violate arms treaties; that it would plan such violations even before signing a treaty; that violations were designed not only to secure incremental strategic advantages but also to gain intelligence and the transfer of technology, and to achieve counterintelligence objectives.[37] The Administration's reports on these violations were the first step in a process of educating not only the public but also the larger foreign policy community about Soviet violations. Given the Soviet negotiating tactic of accusing the U.S. of not being serious about arms control as a way of mobilizing the peace movement in the West to pressure the U.S. into making concessions to Moscow, these reports helped level the playing field by putting the Kremlin slightly more on the defensive than it was accustomed.

If the reader is curious as to why the arms control industry suffered from willful blindness and self-censorship concerning treaty violations, it can be explained as follows. Self-censorship served an important diplomatic purpose that derived from the prevailing understanding about Cold War tensions. This understanding, in contrast to that of President Reagan and those in his Administration who shared his perspective, maintained that the USSR would be a permanent feature of the international political landscape, and thus, it was incumbent on the United States to learn to get along with it. The policy of détente followed from this assessment. If anyone were to make a public issue of Soviet treaty violations, such an individual would be ostracized from respectable society (and from any serious participation in the arms control policy-making process) on the grounds that he was destroying arms control. When, in response, one asks: who is destroying arms control: the violator or the person who points out the violations, the arms control industry's answer is the latter. Why? Because if one follows the recommendations of the accuser, namely, to eschew any new treaties until the Soviets comply with existing ones, the arms control *process* must necessarily be suspended. According to the logic of the "arms controllers," if the *process* does not continue, then the chances for peace diminish severely. The process itself was the highest diplomatic priority. "Peace," according to this logic, has nothing to do with the substance of agreements—specifically, the mutual honoring of arms limitations—or the reduction of political concerns that produce Cold War tensions; rather it is understood to be the sustaining of dialogue, which is better than war. Needless to say, those who had a different understanding of the sources of tension, the prospects of change in the Soviet Union, and the formula for true peace did not share this assessment.

Increased publicity for Soviet human rights violations was another essential element of Project Truth. This took the form of public statements, Presidential radio addresses, increased focus on such violations in the State Department's annual reports on human rights, and editorials and news reports on U.S. international broadcasting stations such as the Voice of America and Radio Free Europe/Radio Liberty.[38] An example was a statement on Soviet human rights violations by the President in October 1983:

> Barely a month after attending an international conference in Madrid
> and joining 34 nations in a commitment to respect human rights, the

Soviet Union has gone back on its word, launching a new campaign of repression against human rights activists...

Putting a human face on the phenomenon, he then raised an alarm about the arrests of specific victims such as Soviet Jewish refusenik Joseph Begun, Father Sigitas Tamkevicius, a Lithuanian Catholic priest active on behalf of religious freedom, and Oleg Radzinskiy, a member of the unofficial Soviet peace organization, Group to Establish Trust Between the U.S. and USSR.

He then issued the following condemnation, typical of statements in solidarity with such victims:

> Soviet policy toward Jewish emigration and dissident movements has sunk to a new low of brutality and repression. Antisemitism has escalated dramatically, as has harassment of other human rights defenders... The inability of Soviet authorities to tolerate any activities by those who are not members of their government-controlled, "captive" peace groups illustrates the hypocrisy of their statements. There is a night and day contrast between aggressive Soviet efforts to encourage peace demonstrations in the West and their brutal arrests and exile of peace activists in the East. We condemn these illegal and inhumane acts. We hold the Soviet Union accountable for its violations of numerous international agreements and accords on human rights to which it is a party. We call upon the Soviets to reverse their inhumane policies and to prove to the world they will back up their words with action and start living up to their agreements.[39]

Project Truth became institutionalized within the U.S. International Communication Agency (USICA, later renamed the U.S. Information Agency, USIA) under the vigorous leadership of Charles Wick. The agency launched a stream of publications widely distributed abroad and designed to compete with Moscow for people's hearts and minds both within the Soviet empire and worldwide. Among these were reports on Soviet-Cuban support for subversion and guerrilla war in Central America, the Afghan people's struggle against the Soviet occupation, and the efforts of the Solidarity Movement to challenge communist rule in Poland.[40]

In the face of the Soviet-induced imposition of martial law by the Polish communist government in December 1981, President Reagan spoke to the nation expressing his and America's moral support for the Solidarity movement that was being suppressed in Poland. He called on the Polish communist government to lift the martial law or risk suffering economic sanctions. In the wake of this, USICA/USIA Director Wick launched a special initiative: a television program to be broadcast globally called "Let Poland Be Poland." In this program, he mobilized the prime ministers of Canada, the UK, France, West Germany, Luxembourg, Japan, Norway, and Turkey as well as prominent celebrities such as Henry Fonda, Charlton Heston, Bob Hope, Glenda Jackson, Paul McCartney, Frank Sinatra, Max von Sydow, and Orson Welles, each to speak in support of the Poles and in condemnation of the Polish puppet government's repression. The program was broadcast worldwide by satellite as well as in audio versions over the Voice of America and Radio Free Europe/Radio Liberty. It had a powerful impact in calling global attention to the plight of the Poles and putting Moscow and its Polish puppets on the defensive.

Counterpropaganda and Counter-Active Measures

A huge part of the Soviet effort in the Cold War consisted of communist propaganda targeting audiences both within the larger empire and everywhere else in the world. Soviet bloc domestic propaganda, as mentioned earlier, was a major element of the internal security system, designed to shape domestic perceptions and induce a psychology of fatalistic acceptance of the regime.

Soviet propaganda was also designed to discredit the West, blacken its reputation, and demonstrate its "internal contradictions," which were leading to its "inevitable" demise. America was portrayed as a rapacious, exploitative, imperialistic, and aggressive power that harmed both its own people and countless millions abroad. Special efforts were made to target minority groups within the United States and the West to aggravate any grievances they harbored and alienate them as much as possible from the system of representative government, rule of law, and political-economic liberty.

Oftentimes, the propaganda crossed into the realm of the fantastic. The United States was accused of developing the AIDS virus as a weapon to use against third-world peoples. It was similarly charged with developing an "ethnic weapon" specially designed to kill black and brown-skinned people. Americans were also accused of arranging the killing of Latin American babies to harvest their body parts for organ transplants.[41] And if the reader is tempted to question the usefulness of such absurd accusations, the target of such propaganda was not the educated peoples of Western democracies, but rather the peoples of the third world—particularly those in regions that were host to intensive ideological and proxy wars.

When it came into office, the Reagan Administration was well aware that such propaganda was being undertaken by the Kremlin. But it discovered that for years, almost no information on such Soviet activities had been collected by the government. Administration officials thus worked to modify the information collection taskings for both the intelligence and diplomatic communities to raise the priority of this subject. Early on, the Administration had the benefit of the testimony of a former KGB official, Stanislav Levchenko, who had been in charge of Soviet "active measures" operations in Tokyo. As a result, larger numbers of executive branch officials were introduced to the existence of such "active measures"—a KGB term of art to describe disinformation, forgeries, and covert political influence operations.

In response to the cascade of intelligence information collected on such active measures, the Administration formed an interagency group dedicated to analyzing and declassifying this intelligence, disseminating the analysis publicly, and dispatching "truth squads" to brief foreign governments and media organs about these Soviet activities. The very act of exposing these operations had the effect of discrediting the Soviet government and its information sources.

Meanwhile, Moscow and its international communist network, connected by the various institutions and mechanisms of the old Comintern—now run by the International Department of the Soviet Communist Party's Central Committee—organized and ran the various campaigns of the "peace movement" as part of Moscow's arms control strategy.[42] This movement was designed to instill fear in Western and foreign publics so as to put constant pressure on the United States to limit its arms acquisitions and deployments. Moscow saw the entire arms control process not as an arena of mutual compromise but as a theater of political warfare where one side would win and the other would lose. But the field of battle was uneven: because the Kremlin could target Western publics, which could pressure their governments on arms acquisitions, while the reciprocal pressure on the Soviet public was effectively useless, since it had no effect on Soviet government policies.

A major battle in the arms control propaganda war took place in Europe over the matter of the deployment of intermediate-range (or "theater") nuclear forces (TNF, and later INF). In the late 1970s, European members of NATO lost confidence in the credibility of the U.S. nuclear guarantee of their security. Given the obsolescence of U.S. theater forces, mainly the FB-

111 fighter-bomber, as compared to Soviet intermediate-range ballistic missiles, the Europeans perceived that several rungs were missing on the ladder of escalation options. Hence, they did not believe that Washington would launch its ICBMs against the USSR in retaliation for a Soviet attack on Western Europe: for such a retaliatory salvo risked a Soviet attack on the United States itself.

If the U.S. would not deploy modern, credible intermediate-range nuclear weapons to restore the credibility of the U.S. deterrent in Europe, then individual allies of the U.S. would feel compelled to split from NATO and reach their own security accommodations with Moscow. Based on this scenario, which many NATO countries saw as completely plausible, the Europeans requested Washington to deploy the necessary deterrent forces. In response, the U.S. developed Pershing-2 ballistic missiles and both ground-launched and air-launched cruise missiles (GCLMs and ALCMs).

In anticipation of the deployment of these missiles in Europe, Moscow launched an estimated $100 million propaganda campaign in Europe to stop the deployment. The campaign was designed to persuade European publics that the deployment was an American imperialist initiative that was increasing the danger of Europe becoming a nuclear battlefield. The campaign was so effective that public opinion polls revealed that referenda or parliamentary votes in several countries would veto the deployment.

The Reagan response to this constituted one of the most effective counterpropaganda efforts in modern American history. In the Department of State, it was led by Deputy Assistant Secretary Mark Palmer, who formed a path-breaking interagency group entitled "Shaping European Attitudes." The group was the forerunner of a series of public diplomacy interagency groups on various subjects that mobilized, for the first time in three decades, an effective, "whole of government" approach to the wars of information and ideas. On the ground in Europe, the counterpropaganda campaign was led by Ambassador Peter Dailey, with the active mobilization of USICA/USIA. Individual European countries were targeted and major efforts were made to disabuse their publics and parliaments of the Soviet disinformation.

This information effort was accompanied by a major diplomatic initiative: the proposal by the United States that both the U.S. and the USSR eliminate the most modern of these INFs—the Pershings and cruise missiles on the American side, and the newly deployed SS-20 intermediate-range ballistic missiles. This negotiating ploy assisted the U.S. information effort by showing the Europeans that the U.S. would not be interested in any such deployments if it were not for the enhanced Soviet missile threat to the continent. Armed with this negotiating position, the American counterpropaganda effort succeeded in one country after another and the political groundwork was laid for the eventual deployment of the necessary missiles.

The Modernization of the Freedom Radios and the President's Direct Communication to the Peoples of the Soviet Empire

Radio Free Europe (broadcasting to the satellite states of East-Central Europe), Radio Liberty (broadcasting to the various major national groups within the Soviet Union), and the Voice of America (VOA) were arguably the most powerful weapons wielded in the political war against Soviet communism. The importance of the radios to the liberation of the peoples of the Soviet empire, which remains misunderstood and underestimated by American observers to this day, was fully recognized by the most prominent representatives of anti-communist resistance within the bloc.

In 1980, Nobel laureate Aleksandr Solzhenitsyn described the radios as "the mightiest weapon that the United States possesses to create mutual understanding (or even an alliance) between America and the oppressed Russian people." But, referring to the détente period of the 1970s, he blasted the U.S. government for failing miserably to utilize these strategic assets properly. Specifically, he charged the VOA with ineptitude, self-censorship (in the interest of avoiding offense to the Kremlin), and broadcasting "frivolous," "worthless, and irrelevant twaddle" that served to repel and alienate the sympathies of the thoughtful Russian listener.[43] He concluded by recommending that Washington "open a propaganda offensive as powerful and effective as that conducted against your country by the communists for the last sixty years," especially by harnessing "the mighty non-military force which resides in the airwaves and whose kindling power in the midst of communist darkness cannot even be grasped by the Western imagination."[44]

President Reagan and key members of his team recognized this power and voiced a commitment to strengthening them during the 1980 presidential campaign. In early 1982, in response to the crackdown on the Solidarity Union in Poland—a crackdown that came under threat of a Soviet invasion—the President launched a new policy intimately related to his strategy of truth. This was the modernization of Radio Free Europe/Radio Liberty (RFE/RL) and the VOA. The logic underlying this initiative and its timing was that a way had to be found to sanction the Polish communist regime— and the Soviet regime that had pressured it into this repression—without harming the oppressed people, and indeed, by *helping* the people.

In one sense, these radios were arguably the greatest threat to Soviet rule. Why?

First, they were the most prominent method of connecting with the peoples of the Soviet empire and showing them that they were not alone in their struggle against communist oppression. The VOA would disabuse the captive peoples of the illusions about America and the West that had been inculcated into their minds by Soviet propaganda. Meanwhile, RFE/RL served as a "surrogate domestic free press" supplying people with information about their own countries. They transmitted the truth and unfiltered information directly to millions of people. This included: domestic news; alternative ideas; their own country's true history that had been eviscerated and revised as a way of destroying each nation's identity; religious programs; and even music. They exposed the misrule of the communist authorities and the falsity of communist ideas. Among the alternative ideas they promoted were those of representative government and the institutions of civil society necessary to sustain it.

All this enabled millions of secret listeners to share with one another their special secret: their knowledge of the truth. Sometimes the mere whistling of a song that could be heard only over Radio Free Europe was a public, yet "secret" signal to others that you were a listener. And when others joined you in whistling the song, or discussing forbidden information, *something of decisive strategic importance occurred*:

- people reconnected to one another;
- trust was restored; and
- political organization in defiance of the regime began or was immeasurably enhanced.
- In other words, the radios, as vehicles of the truth, undermined one of the linchpins of the internal security system: the atomization of society.

One aspect of the radios was particularly threatening to the internal security system of the state: they transmitted information *instantaneously*—which confounded the regime's ability to suppress dissent and civil disturbances.

The usual way by which communist regimes suppressed civil disturbances—demonstrations, strikes, riots—was by isolating them and cutting off all communications to the affected area. If the rest of the country learned about the event a few weeks later, it mattered little to the regime: the news was that the unrest was successfully suppressed and contained.

When a cell of internal resistance realized that it could communicate with millions of fellow countrymen, a vital new strategic tool became possible: it could develop underground lines of communication to the freedom radios and thus to their own people.

This is what happened with the Solidarity Union when it went on strike at the Lenin shipyard in Gdansk. As usual, the regime cut off communications to the city, claiming that "high winds" knocked down telephone lines. But through underground lines of communication, Radio Free Europe learned of the strike and transmitted the news within hours to millions of Poles. The strike was contagious. Within a matter of days, Solidarity had hundreds of thousands of new members. And within weeks, it had 10 million members: practically the entire working-age population of the country. This was "solidarity" at work: the ability of millions to join the movement before it could be crushed and while it was still alive.

The radios and the messages they conveyed thus served as an expression of U.S. solidarity with the millions suffering under communism. By showing them that they were no longer alone, the radios and their message of truth *helped embolden resistance to the regime.*

In subsequent years, President Reagan would use the radios to communicate directly to the peoples of the empire. In 1985, in an interview over RFE/RL, the President explained his strategy of emboldening resistance:[45]

I believe that the principal thing that we in the U.S. and the Western democracies can do to overcome this artificial division of Europe is to stand for the principles of freedom, democracy, rule of law, unconditional individual human rights and governmental legitimacy by the consent of the governed. By standing firmly for these principles and holding our ground both morally and strategically around the globe, we can demonstrate that communism is in fact not the wave of the future, that it can be resisted. By doing so, we show the captive nations that resisting totalitarianism is possible.

We should learn the lesson that Vladimir Bukovsky, the Russian human rights activist, taught us: he said that each time the USSR commits an act of aggression abroad, it is sending a message to its own people:

"Look, peoples of the communist world, we can invade Afghanistan, shoot down airliners and deliver arms to Nicaragua under the nose of Uncle Sam and not even the greatest imperialist power on earth can resist us. So how can you people even contemplate resisting us?"

But, if we understand this lesson and succeed in preventing the further expansion of communism, the captive peoples will know that there is hope. What the peoples of East Europe choose to do to achieve their freedom, of course, is their own decision. But it is almost impossible to resist oppression without having access to the truth and without being able to communicate with your fellow man. Radio Free Europe and Radio Liberty can help the people of Eastern Europe and the Soviet Union overcome these problems. They are indispensable—the closest thing to a domestic free press that outsiders can provide for them.

In that interview, the President also explained how real peace can be achieved and how it requires both telling and facing the truth:

Totalitarian states do not have the built-in mechanism of popular pressure which compels the governing elite to behave responsibly and to abide by international agreements which their people avidly support. This mechanism of popular pressure, of course, is one of the greatest conflict-resolution mechanisms ever devised by the mind of man and, indeed, if everyone were to comply with the Helsinki Accords and respect the human rights provisions, we would have the prospect of long-term peace in Europe.

This is because true peace and human rights are not two separate issues. In fact, peace and human rights are indivisible; they are one issue. Because so long as people are not free to speak, worship, or think as they please, they cannot be free to restrain their own rulers from warlike behavior...

We greatly appreciate the enormous sacrifices the peoples of the East made in the struggle against Nazism. But the great hopes for post-war peace proved so illusory because they were based on an unrealistic understanding of what it took to create real peace. People somehow forgot that real peace is indivisible from respect for human rights. Those hopes were also illusory because people were not realistic about the nature of the forces which occupied Eastern Europe at the end of the war.

There has been a constant tendency for people in the West to indulge in wishful thinking when viewing unpleasant realities of the world. Sometimes we don't like to admit that these realities exist. But the consequences of not facing up to these realities can be as grave as any visited upon mankind. Because when we fail to look at the world realistically, we can fail to understand the strategic ambitions of aggressors.

Because of the threat posed by the radios, the Soviets did their best to confound their effectiveness. In February 1981, the Munich headquarters of RFE/RL were bombed in an operation that involved the cooperation of several Soviet proxies: the East German, Hungarian, and Romanian intelligence services.[46] Moscow and its proxies would use terrorism as a method to silence the radios. RFE/RL employees were threatened and one, RFE Bulgarian Service broadcaster Georgi Markov, was assassinated. Soviet bloc agents of influence infiltrated the various language services of VOA, RFE, and RL to provoke internal conflict within the individual language services, including inter-ethnic, inter-religious, and partisan political conflicts. Such agents also worked to broadcast programs that would echo Soviet propaganda and thus demoralize listeners, who would often risk severe punishment for listening to Western broadcasts.

Perhaps the most effective Soviet bloc response to U.S. broadcasts was jamming. Moscow had some two thousand 500,000-watt jamming stations—ten times the power of the most potent U.S. clear-channel AM stations. Ground-wave jamming made it impossible for people in cities to hear the broadcasts. Sky-wave jamming, designed to interfere with broadcasts over large swaths of territory, were effective most of the time. However, there were times when this form of jamming could not work—the periods of "twilight immunity," which afforded listeners a window of an hour or two of uninterrupted broadcasts.

In response to these various measures, President Reagan's plan for the radios involved first and foremost devoting national strategic attention to instruments that had been systematically neglected for over a decade. During that period, not only had the radios been broadcasting the self-censored "twaddle" to avoid irritating Moscow; they had also become technologically weaker because of obsolescent equipment, the absence of spare parts, and the debilitation of their transmitter facilities. Efforts by such figures as Senator J. William Fulbright, Senator George McGovern, President Lyndon Johnson, and Secretary of State Henry Kissinger had been made to change the names of RFE and RL, to deprive them of their trademark, to move their headquarters to the United States from Munich, where they enjoyed proximity to their target areas, and even to close them down altogether in the spirit of "detente."[47] Budgets had been systematically cut, with fewer resources for adequate reporting, program development, or equipment maintenance and modernization. The radios were operating with 1940s vacuum tube technology, rusting transmitter towers, and spare parts that, due to their unavailability, had to be custom built by hand.

The Reagan program would reverse all this. It put new leadership in the various broadcast services—individuals who had the will and intellectual capacity to challenge Soviet communism on the moral and ideological plane. It secured the appropriation of $2.5 billion to modernize the headquarters, the studios, and the technology of all three radio stations and to purchase new transmitters and secure new transmitter sites in various countries surrounding the Soviet bloc. These new sites would help overcome the jamming (this included the newly discovered technique of utilizing a period of "north-south immunity"), and would enable broadcasts for the first time to reach Soviet territories east of the Urals. The latter project involved a major diplomatic effort with several friendly countries in the Middle East and South Asia. What was noteworthy about this effort was that most of the countries the Administration approached—*even those who already had U.S. military facilities located on their territory*—recognized (in stark contrast to the American foreign policy establishment) that the strategic influence of the radios was a matter of such sensitivity and offensiveness to Moscow that they refused our requests.

Notwithstanding the failure to secure transmitter sites for signals east of the Urals, the effects of this overall effort were powerful indeed. As Polish President (and former Solidarity union leader) Lech Walesa testified after the collapse of the empire, Radio Free Europe "was our radio station. But not only a radio station. Presenting works that were 'on the red censorship list,' it was our ministry of culture. Exposing absurd economic policies, it was our ministry of economics. Reacting to events promptly and pertinently, but above all, truthfully, it was our ministry of information."[48] When asked at a press conference in Washington about the importance of the radios to the rise and sustenance of the Solidarity movement, he replied: "Would there be life [on earth] without the sun?"[49] And when Czechoslovak dissident and later President Vaclav Havel visited Washington, D.C., he made a pilgrimage to the Voice of America to thank its staff for keeping his national flame alive for half a century.[50]

Support for Anti-Communist and Pro-Freedom Groups

Another early Administration initiative was its support of various organizations that could conduct research, analysis, information programs, cultural programs, and political action in opposition to Soviet power both at home and abroad. Some of this was conducted by the Office of Private Sector Programs at USICA/USIA. Among the groups receiving its support were the AFL-CIO, the Claremont Institute (which conducted specialized democracy education programs), and the National Strategy Information Center. The CIA also lent covert support to various organizations.

The Administration, occasionally through the State Department and more often through the National Security Council, supported various national heritage organizations representing the various captive nations of the inner Soviet empire, and resistance groups fighting communist regimes in the outer empire, in such places as Nicaragua, Angola, Mozambique, Ethiopia, and Vietnam.

The array of these groups was rich and variegated. Some of these groups were composed of, or led by, émigrés. Others, such as the Congress of Russian Americans, comprised and were led by Americans whose families had been in our country for several generations. Rarely before in American history had the White House given such regular and enthusiastic welcome to organizations such as the Joint Baltic American Committee, the Polish American Congress, the U.S. Ukraine Foundation, and the Ukrainian Congress Committee of America, and similar groups of Czechoslovak-Americans, Bulgarian-Americans, Hungarian-Americans, Romanian-Americans, etc. Indeed, such groups had never found support in official Washington since the early 1960s. Under President Reagan, their representatives were constantly invited for briefings and discussions with NSC staff members about policy issues relating to the nation of their concern. They were inspired by the annual White House statements on Captive Nations Day. They and their constituents were recipients of encouraging messages transmitted from the White House's Office of Presidential Correspondence.

The inclusion of these groups in such briefings, policy deliberations, special events, and White House correspondence inspired their leaders and members to take action in support of the people in their countries of origin that would not have taken place in the absence of such a supportive administration—actions that would have been seen as less effective, if not futile, under other circumstances.

The Administration also lent moral and tangible support to various international resistance groups that were either born or revived during the Reagan years. One of these was Resistance International, led by the courageous Russian dissident Vladimir Bukovsky, one of the most effective political warriors of the Cold War. This group was a consortium of anti-communist resistance organizations in each of the countries with active and organized resistance movements. Prominent among these were the Nicaraguan resistance and UNITA in Angola. Another group that received sympathy and support was the Anti-Bolshevik Bloc of Nations.

Finally, given the President's recognition of the spiritual character of the Cold War, the Administration demonstrated its support of religious groups and their advocacy of human rights and religious liberty. The Union of Councils of Soviet Jewry was one such group, which sought support for the rights of Soviet Jews, including the right of "refuseniks" to emigrate. Other groups, not always formally organized, also received support. Lithuanian nuns, who took enormous risks to smuggle reports on the plight of the Catholic Church in Lithuania to the U.S. embassy, found help from Edmund McWilliams, the courageous human rights officer who had support from the White House for his intrepid activities on behalf of dissidents and human rights activists. As part of this overall effort, the Voice of America and RFE/RL broadcast religious programs, including full religious services, to adherents of various faiths throughout the Soviet empire. It should be noted that none of these uses of religion as instruments of public diplomacy and ideological warfare constituted a violation of the Constitutional prohibition against establishing a state religion within the United States.

The question naturally arises: how effective were these various groups? Did they make any difference? While it is admittedly difficult to measure their effectiveness, one can say that the knowledge within the extended Soviet empire of their very existence, of the fact that these groups were of concern to the Kremlin and its satellite regimes, and of the moral and tangible support that they were receiving from the United States could not but have been encouraging to the various internal resistance movements: those resistance forces were not alone.

Speech to the British Parliament

In 1982, in his historic speech to the British parliament, President Reagan shifted the terms of the entire East-West conflict. Instead of mere containment or detente, he proposed a policy of peaceful political change in the Soviet empire. The concept of this speech, developed by a Reagan cell in the Department of State, was based on a strategy of fighting communist tyranny not solely with anti-communism, but also with a positive alternative: freedom, democracy, human rights, and hope for a better life. Instead of reacting to Soviet initiatives that pointed to the ultimate goals of world communism, the United States should propose its own vision and political goals that it would like to see achieved—a world of free peoples living according to the consent of the governed. This is what President Reagan set forth in this speech. Instead of tacitly accepting the legitimacy of the Soviet regime as had his predecessors, he challenged it at its very core:

> We cannot ignore the fact that even without our encouragement there has been and will continue to be repeated explosions against repression and dictatorships. The Soviet Union itself is not immune to this reality. Any system is inherently unstable that has no peaceful means to legitimize its leaders. In such cases, the very repressiveness of the state ultimately drives people to resist it, if necessary, by force.
>
> While we must be cautious about forcing the pace of change, we must not hesitate to declare our ultimate objectives and to take concrete actions to move toward them. We must be staunch in our conviction that freedom is not the sole prerogative of a lucky few, but the inalienable and universal right of all human beings. So states the United Nations Universal Declaration of Human Rights, which, among other things, guarantees free elections.
>
> The objective I propose is quite simple to state: to foster the infrastructure of democracy, the system of a free press, unions, political parties, universities, which allow a people to choose their own way to develop their own culture, to reconcile their own differences through peaceful means...
>
> What I am describing now is a plan and a hope for the long term—the march of freedom and democracy which will leave Marxism-Leninism on the ash-heap of history as it has left other tyrannies which stifle the freedom and muzzle the self-expression of the people."[51]

By challenging the legitimacy of the Soviet regime, once again the President emboldened the peoples of the Soviet empire to resist.

Establishment of the National Endowment for Democracy

The outgrowth of the Westminster address was the proposal, again from the small Reagan cell in the State Department, to found the National Endowment for Democracy (NED) and its four subsidiary organizations: the Republican Party's National Republican Institute for International Affairs (now called the International Republican Institute), the Democratic Party's National Democratic Institute for International Affairs (now called the National Democratic Institute), the U.S. Chamber of Commerce's Center for International Private Enterprise, and the AFL-CIO's American Institute for Free Labor Development (now, having been merged with other AFL-CIO subsidiaries, called the American Center for International Labor Solidarity).

Modeled partly after the German political party foundations, the NED and its subsidiary organizations conducted democratic institution-building programs and made grants to various domestic and foreign organizations for the same purpose. Among the recipients of such grants were various pro-democracy and human rights groups in the Soviet bloc, particularly Solidarity-affiliated organizations in Poland. These included: The Solidarity Coordination Office in Brussels (via AFL-CIO); the Polish American Congress; OKNO; Helsinki Committee; the Aurora Foundation; Freedom House; The Institute for Democracy in Eastern Europe; and The Polish Institute of Arts and Sciences in America.[52] Early NED efforts also funded the "East European Democracy Project," which published books and materials that were smuggled into Poland, along with grants to political prisoners and their families. In Czechoslovakia, the Charter 77 Foundation received NED funds to support dissidents and encourage free speech and communication, while another organization was aided in setting up a communications system that would allow several Soviet-bloc countries to produce and share anti-communist material with each other.[53] Part of the logic behind NED supplying such aid was that it was overt and, therefore, not subject to being stained and discredited by association with covert intelligence operations. Furthermore, such aid was not directly tied to official U.S. government policy, as the NED organizations were all independent of Executive Branch policy direction. Thus, where appropriate, the United States could proudly demonstrate its solidarity with the cause of freedom in the Soviet empire and encourage forces of resistance that they were not alone.

Speech to the National Association of Evangelicals

Perhaps the culmination of President Reagan's rhetorical campaign was his speech to the National Association of Evangelicals in the spring of 1983 (quoted above). After frankly discussing America's own legacy of evil (passages about which almost no one knows), he then noted that "the glory of this land has been its capacity for transcending the moral evils of our past." Then he branded the USSR as an "evil empire" and the "focus of evil in the modern world."

The speech was received with shock by the establishment. But it was greeted with joy by the oppressed millions of the East.

As a policy advisor to the President and as an internal participant in, and witness to, the formulation of U.S. policy toward the Soviet Union, I personally had ambivalent feelings about the use of the term "evil empire." On the one hand, I was glad that the President had told the unvarnished truth. But on the other hand, I had forebodings that by using incendiary adjectives he was leaving himself vulnerable to Soviet propaganda and therefore political pressure. How?

Soviet strategy in general was to achieve conquest without war—or, to put it more precisely, the transformation of its adversaries' political systems without war. This eventually required disarming the U.S. physically, but first intellectually, morally, and psychologically. Part of this strategy involved isolating the U.S. in the world, and then isolating anti-communists, such as President Reagan, within the United States. A key part of this strategy— which was the Number One Tactical Objective of Soviet Foreign Policy— was to compel President Reagan to silence himself, to censor himself, and thus to Finlandize America. This was done by a ceaseless Soviet campaign, conducted, among others, by a stream of Soviet visitors to the United States, to get the President to "tone down his rhetoric in the interests of peace." A critical element of this campaign was the constant and massive drumbeat of threats and warnings of "unpredictable consequences" that could come from the President's "reckless policies" and rhetoric.

The Soviet-sponsored "peace" movement portrayed the President as a "warmonger" and a "nuclear cowboy." It organized massive demonstrations against the President and U.S. policy. One of these, organized principally by the Communist Party USA and various Soviet front groups, mobilized a quarter of a million people in New York on the occasion of the UN's Special Session on Disarmament in 1982. By such activities, Moscow put enormous pressure on our allies and on various constituencies within the U.S. to pressure the President to reverse course.

Because of its massive propaganda and political influence apparatus, Moscow had the power to modulate the entire tone of East-West relations. If we spoke the truth, thus mobilizing a pro-defense consensus in the West as well as internal resistance to Soviet rule, Moscow would turn up the atmospherics of tension. If we censored ourselves, we would be rewarded with summit meetings, agreements, a peaceful atmosphere, sweetness and light. To repeat: self-censorship was the Soviet price for peace and quiet.

By using the term "evil empire," President Reagan accomplished one goal, but left himself vulnerable to being accused of gratuitous name-calling and aggravating tensions. It was now easier for Moscow and its fellow-travelers to call the President a warmonger. In fact, Soviet propaganda to this effect did have an adverse impact on the unity of the Administration on Soviet policy, not to mention the support the President enjoyed in Congress. Efforts were made to have the President deliver another kind of speech—one in which he would demonstrate clinically and dispassionately the entire record of the Kremlin's behavior at home and abroad. This speech would have had the President present the world with the facts of the entire case, and the global audience could then attach its own adjectives to Soviet conduct. Such a speech would have insulated the President from being accused of recklessness by the members of the "peace" movement both at home and abroad. In the end, suggestions that he make such a speech were not successful.

The effectiveness of the evil empire rhetoric, however, could not be denied. Not only were dissidents behind the iron curtain encouraged and inspired by this moral witness, but the Kremlin was alarmed.

Promoting an Ideological Alternative

In the face of the ideological lie that served as the foundation of Soviet power, the President led an ideological counterattack. In the face of the communist denial of a transcendent, objective moral order—standards of justice that are universal and thus the prerequisite of any inalienable rights—he slammed the Kremlin's "end-justifies-the-means" morality and regularly invoked the founding principles of America as reflected in the Declaration of Independence: that the inalienable rights endowed by the Creator to all men apply not just to Americans but to everyone. As he told his audience at Moscow State University:

Go into any schoolroom [in America], and there you will see children being taught the Declaration of Independence, that they are endowed by their Creator with certain unalienable rights—among them life, liberty, and the pursuit of happiness—that no government can justly deny...[54]

In the face of the communist rejection of the transcendent dignity of the human person, the President constantly reaffirmed that dignity with his repeated invocation of the Declaration's principle of the right to life. In the face of Soviet concepts of arbitrary justice, he invoked an independent judiciary. In the face of Soviet concepts of thought and speech control, he invoked American ideas of freedom of speech and conscience.[55]

Altogether, the various ideas of freedom, democracy, human rights, moral order, and the dignity of the human person were promoted not only by the President's rhetoric and personal moral witness but by the Administration as a whole in numerous forms: in VOA editorials, in RFE/RL broadcasts, in articles in USIA-published magazines targeted at Soviet bloc populations (e.g. the Russian language magazine, *Amerika*), on the USIA-run billboard on the sidewalk outside the U.S. embassy in Moscow[56], in American diplomats' addresses at various international fora, in the distribution of books to Soviet bloc audiences and U.S. libraries abroad, in films distributed abroad, etc.

Splitting the Peace Movement

Another tactic that the Administration supported was an effort to split the "peace" movement. Most of this movement was composed of innocent citizens concerned about nuclear war and not committed to the communist ideological agenda. But the majority of these people were naïve about the degree to which their movement had been infiltrated, influenced, and at times, directed by communists and the leaders of Soviet front organizations. One way of reducing the ability of the communist and communist-front leaders to manipulate the larger movement was to expose their radical ideological agenda and diminish their credibility in the eyes of the non-communist membership.

One initiative to achieve this objective was undertaken in Los Angeles County by Soviet dissident Vladimir Bukovsky and Los Angeles lawyer and human rights activist William Pearl, with the Administration's support. This initiative involved putting a referendum measure on the June 1984 ballot for approval by County voters. What was noteworthy about the choice of Los Angeles County is that, at the time, its population was larger than that of some 35 states of the union, and thus, any referendum passed there would have a larger than usual political significance. The measure read:

> Shall the Los Angeles County Board of Supervisors transmit to the leaders of the United States and the Soviet Union a communication stating that the risk of nuclear war between the United States and the Soviet Union can be reduced if all people have the ability to express their opinions freely and without fear on world issues, including a nation's arms policies; therefore the people of Los Angeles County urge all nations that signed the Helsinki International Accords on Human Rights to observe the Accords' provisions of freedom of speech, religion, press, assembly and emigration for all their citizens?

The results of the final vote affirmed the ballot initiative. However, during the campaign in advance of the final vote, the communist and Soviet front leadership of the peace movement opposed the referendum initiative, because it called for freedom of speech in the Soviet Union, while the ordinary membership supported it. Seeing this opposition to freedom of speech, many ordinary, non-communist members of the peace movement found it strange and repellent that their movement's leaders would oppose something as basic as free speech. This ultimately raised many people's consciousness about the radical political agenda of the peace movement's leadership.[57]

The Covert Dimension

Covert Assistance to Poland and Other Central European States

A major element of the subversion of the Soviet system was the program of covert support for the resistance movements within the Soviet bloc. The rise of the Solidarity trade union movement in Poland and its suppression by the Soviet-induced state of martial law in December 1981 was the catalyst for this effort. A Presidential Directive, NSDD-32, supplied the official authority for these actions.[58]

Solidarity was not an ordinary union movement, nor did it comport in any way with the existing official trade union structures within the Soviet bloc. Those official trade unions were completely controlled by the communist parties of the various bloc states, and were institutionalized fictions designed to give the West the impression that there existed organizations within those states that represented the interests of the working class. In contrast, Solidarity arose as a union fully independent of Communist Party or state control. Its goals were to advocate for the rights of workers, which, as a practical matter, could be realized only by promoting change in the very genetic code of the communist political system. Given the pretensions of Marxist-Leninist states to represent, in their very essence, the interests of the working class, the rise of a workers' movement in the "workers' state" was a matter of poetic justice and the highest historic irony.

The covert action program initiated by Director of Central Intelligence William J. Casey had four elements:

- providing cash and equipment to help the movement—particularly to sustain its media operations, from newsletters to radio broadcasts;
- supplying advanced communications equipment to enable Solidarity members to communicate with each other even under conditions of martial law—a complete C^3I system. This initially included basic printing equipment and portable radio transmitters. Later, it involved fax machines, computers, and advanced printing equipment. Most of the funds were funneled through the Provisional Coordinating Committee (TKK) which linked conspiratorial networks in various regions of the country. Among the most prominent recipients of media assistance were the underground publishing house, NOW-a, which, from 37 secret locations, published the 50,000-circulation newspaper *Tygodnik Mazowsze*, and Radio Solidarity. Eventually, the underground movement would publish thousands of newspapers, newsletters, books, and monographs on an annual basis;
- training selected Solidarity members in the use of that equipment;
- sharing intelligence information with the movement.[59]

According to former Chairman of the President's Foreign Intelligence Advisory Board, Glenn Campbell, the funding reached a peak of $8 million per year.[60] The transfer required the creation of a complex structure of financial institutions and instruments to maintain the security of the operation. While the Vatican had the capability to transfer such funds, it kept its distance from covert operations of this sort. Instead, Director Casey used various entities in Europe, including several European companies, one of which even established a separate account to accommodate these fund transfers.[61]

The program utilized the good offices of the AFL-CIO, which had been supplying its own financial assistance to Solidarity since 1980. Other mechanisms of support included:

- the assistance of the French intelligence service, the SDECE (Service de Documentation Extérieure et de Contre-Espionage), in exfiltrating Solidarity activists;
- the assistance of the Israeli intelligence service, the Mossad, in establishing a covert communications channel into Poland;
- the assistance of the Vatican, despite its refusal to be involved in covert operations, in identifying reliable contacts within Poland, as well as supplying reliable information about conditions there;
- the use of the Voice of America to relay information through code words, phrases, songs, and other devices to Solidarity activists;
- the use of Polish Americans to make contact with Solidarity activists to learn precisely how the United States could best help the movement;
- the use of a Swedish shipping route to transfer communications equipment under several guises, including machine tools for agricultural equipment;
- the establishment of an intensified intelligence collection effort against the Communist Polish government to supply warning of impending actions it was planning to take against the movement;
- providing support for émigré groups in Europe that were assisting the overall effort, among other things by debriefing immigrants from the East bloc; and
- training of Solidarity activists in intelligence, operational security and counterintelligence so that they could set up an intelligence organizations (the "Bureau of Hygiene and Safety") to protect the movement from the many efforts to penetrate it by the Polish secret services.[62]

The operation continued unabated in spite of various penetrations of the movement by Communist agents and the leaking of the Swedish equipment smuggling route by an official in Sweden who was eventually unmasked and discreetly transferred by Swedish counterintelligence. It was accompanied by a sustained program of economic sanctions that severely curtailed Polish trade with the West. Whereas in 1980, the volume of that trade had been $7.5 billion, in 1986, it had sunk to $1 billion. Similarly, Poland's ability to secure credit from the West had mostly dried up. Whereas Warsaw had been able to borrow as much as $8 billion before 1980, the amount it could borrow by 1985 was reduced to $300 million.

Under this economic pressure, the Polish Communist regime was forced to submit to American demands: first, to release the many political prisoners it had incarcerated; second, to begin a process of national reconciliation through dialogue with opposition groups; and third, to begin a dialogue with the Polish Catholic Church. On July 22, 1986, a general amnesty was called and most of the imprisoned members of the underground were released. U.S. covert support to the Polish resistance would continue until 1989, when the first, partially free, national elections were held.[63]

While Director Casey was supervising these operations, he also was looking for opportunities to support other resistance groups elsewhere in East-Central Europe and, if possible, within the Soviet Union itself. The opportunity first presented itself in Czechoslovakia, where dissident groups had been in contact along the Polish-Czechoslovak border with members of the Polish resistance who were dedicated to spreading their opposition movement throughout the Soviet bloc.[64] Some of these contacts were made and backpacks were exchanged at the summit of the Tatra Mountains between Polish and Czech dissidents who doubled as mountain climbers.[65] In view of these reports, the CIA asked friendly diplomats in the Vatican, among others, if they had any reliable contacts among dissidents in Czechoslovakia. Eventually, the CIA identified groups in Czechoslovakia that merited support.[66] These mostly included small groups of intellectuals and human rights activists such as those in Charter 77 and lay Catholic activists. Then, with the help of Czechoslovak expatriates in the West, it established a pipeline to funnel support to the Czechoslovak underground.

Although considerably more modest in scope than the support to Solidarity, these efforts to support the Czechoslovak resistance were eventually followed by similar efforts to funnel support to Hungarian resistance organizations. Together, these efforts produced a force-multiplying effect, as the spirit of Solidarity spread throughout the Soviet bloc. It reached a critical point in October 1986, when 122 dissidents in four countries—Poland, Czechoslovakia, Hungary, and East Germany—issued, with U.S. help, a joint protest letter.[67] Joint action of this type was one of the Kremlin's biggest nightmares.

Covert Action Inside the USSR

Finally, the Reagan Administration's program to undermine Soviet rule involved a covert plan to bring the Soviet war in Afghanistan to the USSR itself. This began with a discussion between William Casey and King Fahd of Saudi Arabia, who had been funneling significant financial support to *mujāhidīn* guerrillas fighting the Soviet army in Afghanistan. Initially, Casey had the idea of inciting nationalist-religious passions among the populace of the Islamic regions of Soviet Central Asia—an idea for which Fahd expressed some interest.[68] Subsequently, Casey secured the cooperation of Pakistani President Zia ul-Haq and his Foreign Minister, Yaqub Khan, and proposed further that literature be smuggled into Soviet Central Asia to stir up dissent, as well as arms that could be used as part of local insurrections.[69]

With this support lined up, guerrilla operations were launched inside the Soviet Union by Afghan irregulars based in Iran. These involved laying mines, attacking isolated military outposts, and ambushing Soviet border patrols in Turkmenistan.[70] To incite Uzbek dissent, the CIA bought Qur'ans and other books containing accounts of Soviet atrocities against Uzbeks for smuggling into Soviet Uzbekistan.[71] Towards the end of 1984, the CIA launched a major covert campaign to incite dissent in Soviet Central Asia. Working with Pakistan, Turkey, and China, the campaign smuggled literature and broadcasting equipment into the USSR while also operating clandestine radio broadcasts.[72] Over the next couple of years, Afghan *mujāhidīn* escalated their attacks within the Soviet Union. Trained by the Pakistani intelligence service and equipped by the CIA, they attacked electric power lines, power stations, and airfields, while ambushing Soviet forces using rocket-propelled grenades, machine guns, and antitank mines.[73]

The efforts to incite dissent within Soviet Central Asia contributed to the rise of nationalistic and religious rebellion against Soviet rule. Early manifestations of this rebellion occurred in Kazakhstan on the eve of the Soviet withdrawal from Afghanistan.[74] They reached full bloom in 1989-1990 when "peoples' fronts" were established in most of the USSR's "union republics" and the world witnessed huge anti-Soviet demonstrations in provincial capitals such as Alma Ata, Tashkent, Dushanbe, and Bishkek.

WHAT FINALLY PRECIPITATED THE SOVIET COLLAPSE?

The final collapse of the Soviet regime in December 1991 was the result of a confluence of internal crises that were aggravated by the many "straws" placed on the Soviet "camel's back" by the Reagan Administration. Here is a brief summary of those internal and external factors.

There were three simultaneous internal crises that put enormous pressure on the Kremlin to change its policies.[75]

The first was a crisis of legitimacy. The Marxist-Leninist justification for why the CPSU deserved to be in power was no longer commanding widespread respect. The Party's special knowledge of the "laws of history" had become a joke. The laws of history were simply not working out as the Party's ideologists had predicted. Socialism was not producing benefits for the entire society. The classless society had not emerged. The "new class," as explained by Yugoslav communist Milovan Djilas, had established itself as the new *nomenklatura* elite and was enjoying greater privileges than any putative capitalist "exploiters."[76] The state, established as the instrument of the oppression of the capitalist ruling class over the proletariat, had not "withered away" as it was supposed to do, according to dialectical materialism. Meanwhile, the auxiliary method of legitimation, the CPSU's embrace of the Soviet victory over Nazism during World War II, was getting less and less credible. The notion that the "indispensable defenders of the fatherland" deserved to be in power, as they were the only ones capable of sustaining this defense, was straining credulity. The result was the growing alienation of the Soviet intelligentsia from the entire socialist cause.

The second crisis was that of the Soviet military economy. Contrary to the conventional understanding of this realm, the Soviet economic problem was not a crisis of the civilian economy: that sector had been in crisis—as understood in Western terms—since 1917. The part of the Soviet economy that had worked reasonably well throughout Soviet history was the military economy, on which the Politburo had placed the highest priority. It was this sector that started facing serious crisis owing to the revolution in military affairs in the United States: the application of modern digital technologies to the use of arms. The Reagan military buildup—with its demonstrated sprint capability not only in computer technologies but also in such things as stealth technology—had aggravated the lack of competitiveness of the Soviet military. This situation was exacerbated further by the Administration's technology denial program as well as its other economic warfare efforts such as reducing the Kremlin's capacity to earn hard currency.

These externally-generated economic pressures accentuated the normal pattern of Soviet politics, as brilliantly described by French Sovietologist Alain Besancon. This pattern was one of "freeze and thaw"—of enforced conformity with socialist norms alternating with periods of relaxation of that enforcement. This pattern can be best understood by recognizing the parasitical relationship the Party had with society at large. The Party was a completely unproductive class: creating no wealth, but rather sapping the production of society while acting as prefects and "back seat drivers" for their productive counterparts in the government apparatus who actually operated the state economic enterprises. The prefects would ensure that the managers were faithfully executing the policies of the Party.

As a parasite sucks the blood of its host—society at large—the host gets sick and becomes ever less productive. This was what happened when the Party taxed the peasants at 100 percent as it "requisitioned" the harvest during the period of War Communism. Society (the 95 percent agricultural economy) grew weak as its sustenance was sucked away. It rebelled by refusing to sow and even went so far as to burn its crops. The parasite had to retreat and let the agricultural economy resuscitate itself: after the "freeze," this was the "thaw"—the New Economic Policy (NEP), which restored limited private property, the selling of crops in the marketplace, and the restoration of a progressive income tax so that people could keep some share of the fruits of their labors.

But just as the freeze could last only so long without threatening the power of the Party, the thaw could last only so long. Too much power restored to society risked jeopardizing the power of the Party on the other side of the continuum. The NEP had to be stopped, and by 1928 it was: Stalin imposed a second round of collectivization on Soviet agriculture.[77]

By 1985, the Party was faced with a terrible choice: to reform its domestic economy to such an extent that it could efficiently develop modern technologies independently; or to keep the economy frozen according to socialist norms and rely ever more on acquiring technologies (and financial resources in general) from the West.

The first option necessarily meant decentralizing economic decision-making—which threatened the Party's ability to maintain military production as the highest priority, and which threatened pressures for the decentralization of political decision-making, which, in turn would jeopardize the Party's monopoly of power. Gorbachev tried every method in the Soviet repertoire to enhance economic growth short of permitting private property and genuine economic decentralization. He tried exhortations to meet the five-year plan. He tried the restoration of Stalin-style labor discipline, which meant the resumption of collective punishment of work collectives even when poor performance was manifested by only a single worker. He tried the anti-alcohol campaign. Then he adopted his famous policy of *perestroika* (restructuring). This involved, among other things, an attempt to achieve profitability by implementing "cost accounting" in state enterprises. But this did not work because enterprises could not control any costs beyond payroll costs (what it did accomplish was to create greater job insecurity). He then tried land leasing—in hopes that having a lease would be treated by the renter as bestowing the same incentives as property ownership. He would not dare trying private property. None of it worked.

As a last resort, Gorbachev needed a bailout from the West. But to get the loans and technology that his military economy needed, he could not give the West the impression that he continued to be an unreconstructed communist and an enemy of the United States. As a result, he began a détente policy and a charm offensive to achieve as much psychological disarmament in the West as possible. This involved such things as a cultural diplomacy campaign, a series of pageant-like summit meetings with President Reagan, and the signing of new arms control agreements (notwithstanding the fact that Moscow was continuing to violate every agreement it had previously signed).[78] It also involved portraying his policy of *perestroika* as a fundamental change in the very nature of Soviet communism. The goal of all this, as described by one of Gorbachev's top theoreticians, Fedor Burlatsky, was "to destroy the enemy image … still haunting Soviet-American relations" so that the U.S. would have no more justification for its military buildup, and thus relieve the Soviet military economy of its main external pressure.[79] Gorbachev made this point himself: "Our *perestroika*, with all its international consequences, is eliminating the fear of the 'Soviet threat', with [U.S.] militarism losing its political justification."[80]

The third crisis was that of the Party. By late 1982, when former KGB chief, Yuri Andropov, became CPSU General Secretary, he and a number of his colleagues in the Politburo had become convinced that the Party had become bloated, bureaucratized, undisciplined, ineffective, and corrupt. Andropov initiated efforts to reform it, but died before he could implement all the desired measures.

After the brief tour of anti-reformer Konstantin Chernenko, Mikhail Gorbachev, who shared Andropov's concerns about the Party, came to power. He believed that the Party crisis was due to several influences that needed to be purged from the system. The most prominent was the existence of the vast underground economy. Successive generations of Soviet leaders had to tolerate this economy, as it was the only vehicle ensuring the efficient distribution of goods and services to areas of acute shortages (because it was the only instrument to distribute goods and services according to price, i.e., according to supply and demand, as opposed to central planning or Party privilege). Thus, it served as the only method to ensure the physical survival of the labor force. The problem was that for this economy to function, its participants had to bribe Communist Party officials to avert their gaze from prohibited commercial transactions. In due course, many of those officials not only took bribes but also invested in underground enterprises. This meant developing forms of self-interest that were at variance with the Party's interest. This problem, called a lack of *partiinost'* (Party-mindedness), was the source of huge corruption and lack of Party discipline.

Gorbachev's solution to this corruption and lack of discipline was threefold: 1) the imposition of an ideological purification campaign within the Party to ensure ideological conformity; 2) an unprecedented attack on the underground economy, during which over 800,000 underground entrepreneurs were arrested or fled their jobs for fear of arrest; and 3) a purge of the Party's ranks, whereby some 250,000 members of the Party and managerial elite were arrested and prosecuted.

The original vehicle for the Party purge was *glasnost'*. This campaign, which came to be defined, inaccurately, by the Western media as "openness," was originally designed as a method of encouraging ordinary citizens (insofar as they could be called so) to tattle on corrupt Party and government officials. (This explains why the definition of *glasnost'* in Soviet political lexicons refers to "revolutionary vigilance.")[81] Gorbachev also used *glasnost'* as a means to improve the credibility of the Soviet propaganda apparatus: Soviet media had become so predictable and without credibility that the desirable effects of propaganda could no longer be achieved: namely the defining of the frame of reference by which people would understand reality. *Glasnost'* involved injecting more truth into the mixture of truth and falsehood that makes propaganda effective. Thus, Gorbachev used the *glasnost'* campaign as a vehicle to effect a literary thaw of the kind that Khrushchev had implemented in the 1950s as a method to attract the intelligentsia back to greater loyalty to socialism.

Finally, when the West started to view *glasnost'* as a de facto "freedom of speech" type of reform, the campaign became an indispensable instrument to persuade the West that the USSR had reformed so much that it was not really a Marxist-Leninist state anymore. (It should be noted that the first post-Soviet President of Russia and former Soviet Politburo member, Boris Yeltsin, called Gorbachev's USSR a "totalitarian state.") Gorbachev's exploitation of this Western perception of a new Soviet policy of "freedom of speech" was taken to special heights in his "military *glasnost'*" campaign, which involved giving American delegations access to ostensibly sensitive Soviet military facilities to show that military secrecy was no longer a Soviet priority and that therefore the Soviet Union was no longer a threat to the West.[82] All this served psychologically to disarm the West.

The problem that the Party faced, however, was that *glasnost'* was seized upon by many members of society as a method to criticize not just corrupt members of the *nomenklatura* but also the entire Soviet system. Dissidents, knowing that, thanks to American public diplomacy, they were not alone, emboldened by the rise of Solidarity in Poland, encouraged by the successful resistance of anti-communist movements from Nicaragua to Afghanistan, and sensing that the Party was trapped in a box with no good options, started to speak out. One, Sergei Grigoryants, established *Glasnost'* magazine. In response to its extraordinary articles, KGB thugs would smash its office and printing equipment, but they could not send Grigoryants to the Gulag: to do so would restore the "enemy image" that Gorbachev was working so assiduously to eliminate from American consciousness. And even though Gorbachev's forces used poison gas on demonstrators in Tbilisi (and slaughtered many of them with sharpened military shovels), invaded Vilnius and Baku[83], and cracked down on various other demonstrations throughout the USSR, he was forced by the pressures from all sides to refrain from restoring full-fledged repression through violence lest his entire strategy of saving the military economy should collapse.

The first demonstrations of massive people power in the Soviet bloc took place in East-Central Europe in 1989. Some, and possibly all of them, were stimulated by the Soviets themselves as mechanisms to replace many of the Brezhnev-style Communist bosses with Gorbachev clones: figures with greater public relations ability to appeal to the West. The purpose behind these efforts was to ensure that, as Western European nations were poised to turn inwardly for their international trade as the planned 1992 integration of the European Union loomed ahead, more palatable leaders in East-Central Europe could encourage the continuation of trade with the East, and thus preserve a technology and financing pipeline to Moscow.

With the collapse of the Berlin Wall, so many people within the extended USSR had become so emboldened that Moscow and other major cities witnessed massive demonstrations. In Moscow alone, demonstrations of hundreds of thousands—some possibly close to one million—took place. People were ready to risk the possibility of violence or Gulag to make their voices heard. But the courage to take to the streets was the essential element. This courage did not come from consumer goods shortages, from knowledge of the superiority of Western goods, from rock and roll, or from any material factor. It was a matter of the spirit. It was a matter of inspiration. And this came from the contagious moral witness to truth that lay at the heart of the war of ideas.

The final collapse came with the defection of Boris Yeltsin, a leader with the courage to call upon the Soviet armed forces to refrain from shooting at their fellow citizens and to stand up against the Party that had denounced him Stalin-style just months beforehand. The man who had demonstrated that one could break with the Party without fear put the final dollops of courage into the hearts of millions of ordinary people so that they could do the same. People who had been kept in a cage for three quarters of a century, and who did not know the full meaning of freedom, could not easily define what that freedom would look like. The main thing they wanted was to lead what so many of them described as "a normal life"—something that was the opposite of the abnormal life to which they knew instinctively they had been subjected.

The denouement that came in December of 1991 was thus the result of the combination of external pressure, external inspiration, internal resistance and the impossible dilemma faced by Gorbachev: whether to liberalize, thereby unleashing political forces beyond his control, or to crack down on those forces, thereby jeopardizing the external economic bailout and the psychological disarmament of the West. It was a combination that could not have been achieved without a profound connection by the Reagan Administration with the peoples of the Soviet empire. That connection was made possible by the courage of a President who understood the critical moral dimension of the Cold War and his mobilization of the mechanisms of public diplomacy the substance of which touched the depths of the human heart.

Public Diplomacy in an Age of Global Terrorism: Lessons from the Past

Robert R. Reilly

"We are losing the war of ideas because we are not in the arena the way we were in the Cold War ... just at the moment when there is this ferment for democracy breaking out." So said Secretary of State Hillary Clinton in her recent testimony before the United States Congress. It is worth quoting her at greater length. "We invested so much money and effort over so many decades to get behind the Iron Curtain, to talk about what democracy was, to keep the flag of freedom unfurled in people's hearts, to get our messages in through every means of short wave radio and smuggling Bibles, and we did all kinds of things just to give people a sense that they weren't alone, and that maybe their ideas about the human spirit were not subversive. Well, we don't have those messages going out."

Why don't we have those messages going out anymore? Have we lost the ideas behind them? Or have we lost the means to transmit them? To answer the latter question first, we should recall that in 1999, under President Bill Clinton, the United States Information Agency, the principal institution for the conduct of our side in any war of ideas, was eliminated. This was purportedly done as part of the peace dividend at the end of the Cold War. In other words, the war of ideas was over or, to put it in Francis Fukuyama's words, the "end of history" had arrived. He meant by this that the model of a democratic constitutional regime with a free market economy stood undisputed and uncontested in moral terms throughout the world. This model would be implemented globally in a faster or slower manner, depending upon local conditions, but there stood no competing ideology to its moral claims. The logical conclusion to such a view would be the dismantlement of the organizational apparatus for the conveyance of these ideas. The agency was eliminated because it had lost its mission. I recall the congressional testimony of Dr. Joseph Duffy, USIA's last director. When queried over the mission of the Voice of America, he answered. "I'm not sure we should be broadcasting to the world. We should be listening to the world."

However, history had not ended. Or perhaps one should say that others envisaged a different end of history than that of Mr. Fukuyama. In his "End of History" article, Salman al-Awdah, one of bin Laden's spiritual mentors, spelled out an alternative version that culminates with the destruction of the U.S. He said, "The oppressors are the swords of Allah on earth. First Allah takes his revenge by them, and then against them. The same as Allah has used, in Islamist eyes, the United States in order to destroy the Soviet Union, so he will take revenge against the Americans by destroying them." This version of the end of history was delivered at our doorsteps on 9/11 at the cost of some 3,000 lives. History had apparently resumed or, to those less under the influence of Hegel, it had simply continued.

However, the resumption of history found the United States bereft of the institutions with which to fight a new war of ideas. Let us consider for a moment what is missing from the days of the Cold War. At the height of the Cold War, USIA had some 10,000 employees (including foreign nationals) and a $1 billion budget. In 1999, USIA's functions were dispersed to the State Department and the Broadcasting Board of Governors. The most senior official in the war of ideas became the new Under Secretary for Public Diplomacy and Public Affairs, a third-tier State Department officer, whose status speaks volumes about the severity of the demotion that "war of ideas" issues suffered. Within the State Department, public diplomacy functions were further dispersed to regional and other bureaus, making coordination and control a major problem.

The State Department should not have been expected to do both diplomacy and public diplomacy, as they sometimes conflict. Public diplomacy attempts to reach the peoples of other nations directly over the heads of their governments. This can make the State Department's job more difficult, as its responsibility is to work with the heads of those same governments and maintain good relations with them. The two missions should not reside in the same institution. Public diplomacy has suffered as a result. In short, since the dismantling of USIA, there has been no central U.S. government institution within which policy, personnel, and budget could be deployed coherently to implement a multifaceted strategy to win the war of ideas over an extended period of time. As a result, as Secretary Clinton said, the U.S. is largely absent from the field.

On its part, the Broadcasting Board of Governors (BBG) inherited all non-defense government broadcasting, including the Voice of America. The BBG became a stand-alone agency run by part-time board members, most of whom have had no experience in foreign policy or public diplomacy. The eight Board members exercise executive power, to the extent that eight CEOs can, and are not directly accountable to anyone. Since the professional backgrounds of the governors have been mainly in American mass media, they have sought to replicate that media in government broadcasting by refashioning much of it with American pop culture—Radio Sawa being the primary example. Over the past decade, the BBG has seen fit to eliminate VOA's services to Brazil in Portuguese, to Russia, to India in Hindi, to the Arabic world, and now to China in both Mandarin and Cantonese. There seems to be a perverse logic at work here, in which the BBG has abandoned attempts to reach the most important audiences in terms of our national strategic interests about who we are, what we are doing, and why.

In the Arab world, the VOA 12-hour, content-rich Arabic service was replaced with a 24-hour pop music station featuring the likes of Britney Spears, J-Lo, and Eminem. The intellectual premise of this effort, as explained to me by the chairman of the board when I served as the director of VOA, was that "MTV brought down the Berlin Wall." Radio Sawa has been proclaimed a success in attracting large youth audiences. However, as the dean of journalism in Jordan informed me, "Radio Sawa is fun, but it is irrelevant." In a war of ideas, performing a lobotomy on your enemy might be a good move. It is almost unheard of to perform a lobotomy on yourself, and then to declare it a success. How would you like to have a superpower adolescent in your neighborhood?

We might pause here to reflect more accurately upon what exactly it was that did bring down the Berlin Wall as, actually, MTV broadcasts did not reach into eastern Germany. We are so far into the global war on terrorism that the conflict that defined most of the century that preceded it has almost receded from view, along with the role ideas played in bringing it to an end. As a foot soldier in the Cold War, I did not think I would live to see its conclusion. I vividly remember the day in 1990 when I read a statement in the

Soviet press by Alexander Yakovlev, the Politburo chief of Soviet ideology, that he had come to understand that Leninism was based upon class struggle and hatred, and that this was "evil." The chief of Soviet ideology had used the exact same word to describe the Soviet system as had President Ronald Reagan. Excitedly, I faxed his remark around Washington. Yakovlev's words meant the end of the Cold War and the Soviet empire. The actual deeds of its dissolution soon came in their wake.

Words and the restoration of their relationship to reality were critical to the Communist collapse. This was no small thing since, for many in the West, words had lost their meaning. Therefore, the huge lie about humanity in communism remained undetected by them. A recovery of meaning was essential before a real challenge could be presented to the East. No single individuals did more for this restoration than John Paul II and Ronald Reagan, who insisted upon calling things by their proper names. Naming communism for what it was required, first of all, the refutation of modern nominalism and radical skepticism. You cannot use "evil" as an adjective until you know it as a noun.

Everyone now celebrates "our" victory over communism, conveniently forgetting that the struggle was not only with communism, but within the West as to what communism meant. The anti-anti-communists in the West were frightened by the Pope's and Reagan's vocabulary for the Soviet Union because they feared it might lead to war, but also because the use of the word "evil" had implications for themselves with which they were extremely uncomfortable. As English writer Christopher Derrick once said, the only real iron curtain runs through the soul of each one of us. If we can know what "evil" is, how then does that apply to our own lives? Rather than face up to the answer to that question, many preferred to attack the people using it and to explain the Cold War away as just another variation of power politics and realpolitik. Communism was simply a mask for traditional Russian imperial expansionism and could be dealt with similarly. Power dealing with power can reach an understanding.

So long as this view was regnant in the West, communism was a form of absolutism fighting a form of relativism. As such, communism had the clear advantage, and gained it on the field with stunning geographic advances in Central Asia, Africa, and Central America, and strategic advances in both conventional and non-conventional weaponry. So great was the progress of the Soviet Union in the 1970s that anyone looking at these factors alone would have expected it to win. Those expectations were defeated by a factor outside of those calculations.

Reagan was the first political leader to use the moral vocabulary of "evil" to describe the Soviet empire in the recent era. The reaction was hysterical. How reckless could Reagan be? Yet the President calmly responded that he wanted them, the Soviets, to know that he knew. This acknowledgment inspired great hope behind the Iron Curtain. Then, finally, the Soviets used the term about themselves. Once the proper vocabulary was employed, it was over. Semantic unanimity brought the end not in the much-feared bang, but in a whimper. Truth turned out to be the most effective weapon in the Cold War. Truth set free the imprisoned peoples of the evil empire.

Part of that truth was expressed religiously. The religious alliance against the Soviet Empire could be broad because the contest was between atheism and religion of any kind. The U.S. Cold War strategy used religion to undermine the Soviet bloc—Jews in Russia, Muslims in Afghanistan, and Christians in Poland, for example. Who could imagine during the Cold War that religion could be turned *against* the United States, not so much within it, as in alienating Muslims in large parts of the Islamic world key to U.S. strategic interests? Unlike the Cold War, the contest with Islam is in terms of one kind of religion against something else, either secularism or another religion, or, in Islamic terms, between belief and unbelief.

It is essential in a war of ideas to understand the ideas one is at war with. This includes an understanding of how we are seen from the Islamist side. What is it about United States or the West that so repels the Islamists that they are driven to destroy it? Read the following statement and then guess who said it. "This great America: What is its worth in the scale of human values? And what does it add to the moral account of humanity? And, by journey's end, what will its contribution be? I fear that a balance may not exist between America's material greatness and the quality of its people. And I fear that the wheel of life will have turned and the book of time will have closed and America will have added nothing, or next to nothing, to the account of morals that distinguishes man from object, and indeed, mankind from animals."

When I was recently lecturing to a group of mid-career American officers, one of them guessed it was Winston Churchill. Wrong. The answer is Sayyid Qutb, the chief Egyptian ideologue of the radical Islamist movement the Muslim Brotherhood, which seeks our destruction. In Arabic, *qutb* means the pole around which the world revolves on its axis. The entire Islamist world revolves around the thinking of this man, who was hanged by Nasser in 1966, but whose thought has spread from the Philippines and Indonesia to Morocco. You can be sure to find his writings at the foundation of any radical Muslim group today, including al Qaeda.

The value of Qutb's quote is that it so clearly illustrates the *moral* judgment on America that is behind the Islamist movement. This is such an important point that it deserves another example. One member of the team that carried out the first attack on the World Trade Center in 1993, Mahmoud Abouhalima, had this to say in an interview: "The soul, the soul of religion, that is what is missing." The 17 years he had lived in the West, Abouhalima said, "is a fair amount of time to understand what the hell is going on in the United States and in Europe about secularism or people, you know, who have no religion. I lived in their life, but they didn't live my life, so they will never understand the way I live or the way I think." Abouhalima compared a life without religion to a pen without ink. "An ink pen, a pen worth $2000, gold and everything in it, it's useless if there's no ink in it. That's the thing that gives life, the life in this pen ... the soul. The soul, the religion, you know, that's the thing that's revived the whole life. Secularism has none, they have none, you have none."

Statements like these are easy to find and appear almost daily in the Muslim media. Notice that these critiques do not addresses any *policy* problems. Those who insist that America's public diplomacy nightmare in the Middle East is due only to its policies mistake the fundamentally moral nature of the attack. In fact, there is no policy the U.S. could change in the Middle East that would reverse this moral condemnation, including the abandonment of Israel. When Qutb wrote his statement in "The America I Have Seen" in the early 1950s, Israel was not the major issue it is today, nor were we seen as the sponsors of the autocracies in the region.

Why, then, have we ended up in this situation? Most of us do not see ourselves as immoral and materialistic; why do others? The United States has failed to present its true self and the problem has only gotten worse with the spread of American pop culture through globalization. Instead of using public diplomacy and its powerful broadcasting tools, like the Voice of America, to counter the impression of America that pop culture creates, the United States, as I have mentioned, has chosen to reinforce this impression by officially embracing it.

The first thing the United States needs to do is address the moral critique of America as a godless, secular, sex-obsessed society immersed in materialism. Just when the moral basis of American life may be eroding, it is precisely this basis that it most needs to present to the Muslim world if it is to defuse the contempt and anger American popular culture provokes. In other words, an essential part of the war of ideas is our own self-recovery. Absent that, the United States will be seen, as it is now largely seen, as a purveyor of its will through brute force.

How will we raise the standard in this new war of ideas? In his inaugural address, President Obama said that "our security emanates from the justness of our cause." However, security can emanate from the justness of a cause only if others share the same conception of justice. That, after all, is the substance of what wars of ideas are about. How, then, is President Obama conveying that sense of justness, particularly to the Muslim world?

Obama's initial Muslim outreach effort came in his June, 2009, speech in Cairo. It followed and should be contrasted to the speech he gave in Accra, Ghana immediately prior to it. In Accra, the president spoke some hard truths about what is required for sustainable democratic governance and how African countries had failed in the past. He did not flinch in his denunciations of African strongmen or widespread corruption. These hard truths were absent from his Cairo speech. In other words, he spoke powerfully to the poor (Ghana) and meekly to the powerful (Egypt), or truth to the poor and fantasy to the powerful. The differences were pronounced. Why?

The only rhetorical strategy that can make sense of the Cairo speech is: instead of confronting the unreality of the world in which most Arabs live (which would have generated resentment), Obama decided to embrace it, enter into it, and then try to change it from within by changing the meaning of some words. As Egyptian writer Tareq Heggy said in reaction to the speech, "it is as if he (Obama) is a magician." This magical approach produced Obama's absurd claim that al-Azhar, instead of being an intellectual backwater retarding Muslims' ability to enter the modern world, was a light to the world and laid the foundations of the European Renaissance and Enlightenment. There were other such gaffes, including his praise of Muslim tolerance in "Andalusia and Cordoba during the Inquisition." However, the Muslim presence in Spain and the period of the Inquisition did not historically overlap, making the comparison ludicrous. Even some American history was distorted to serve this view. President Obama said that "it was not violence that won full and equal rights" for the black people in America, but "a peaceful and determined insistence upon the ideals at the center of America's founding." Somewhere in there the Civil War got lost. Also, President Obama said that, while Turkey, Pakistan, Bangladesh, and Indonesia have elected women heads of state, "The struggle for women's equality continues in many aspects of American life."

In addition, the president proclaimed that "in ancient times and in our times, Muslim communities have been at the forefront of innovation and education." If one is speaking of the ninth century in Abbasid Baghdad, this was certainly true. However, according to the UN Arab Human Development Reports, written by Arabs themselves, the level of education in the Arab world is the worst in the world but for that of sub-Saharan Africa. These distortions and fantasies were received with understandable enthusiasm by the audience.

However, despite the absurdities of some of the remarks, obviously delivered in obsequiescence to the Arab world, the president did try to express and advance the principles of equality and democracy within the Muslim world. The problem is that such attempts are bound to fail when they do not address the principal obstacles to their acceptance. In fact, none of these obstacles was mentioned except in the most general way, and never as being in any way Islamic. It is, after all, "the dignity of all human beings," which Obama vigorously espoused, that *is* at question in Islam according to its own revelation and legal doctrines, which are inimical to the proposition that all people are created equal. Why not simply say this?

Perhaps President Obama did not say this because he thinks that not saying it makes it no longer so. Rather than conforming his words to reality, he tends to think that reality will conform itself to his words. He also sees the source of the problems in the Middle East, as elsewhere in the world, in the United States itself. This would explain his propensity to apologize (we are the victimizer; you are the victims), and then to pretend—or rationalize. Pretend, for instance, that the problem in Iran is nuclear weapons instead of the nature of the Iranian regime. Perhaps it was the hostility of the United States that provoked them to seek nuclear weapons. Therefore, let us reassure them of our peaceful intentions. Look away when the Iranian people are in the streets demonstrating against a stolen election in the hopes that the regime will, out of gratitude, reach an acceptable nuclear compromise. In other words, the nature of the Iranian regime is irrelevant so long as it does not possess nuclear weapons. This ignores the fact that it is the nature of the Iranian regime that makes its possession of nuclear weapons a problem.

Pretend that Syria is not subverting Iraq, your ally, and implicit in killing American soldiers in that country, and demurely turn away in hopes that by doing so Syria will give you a deal to stabilize Iraq and Lebanon. Pretend that

Syrian President Bashar Assad is a reformer, and perhaps he will become one. This mistaken mission of giving Arabs a new vision of themselves from within their own delusional world was reflected in Secretary of State Hillary Clinton's extraordinary remark about President Assad that what "we have tried to do with him is to give him an alternative vision of himself." Apparently, he has not embraced his doppelganger and is perfectly content with his old self, which he maintains in power at the cost of hundreds of Syrian lives.

Magic does not work in foreign policy. It is, in fact, simply another version of realpolitik, disguised in a self-abasing form of false humility. The infamous phrase that the Obama Administration is "leading from behind" means that it will advance American principles only when they are thrust upon it by external events—in other words, when it is realpolitik to do so. Otherwise, it is most content as a power, although a weakened one, dealing with other powers. Obama's Middle Eastern strategy has reflected his rhetorical approach to Ghana and Egypt. Speak powerfully to the weak or weakened—demanding that Mubarak and Gaddafi leave office—and meekly to the powerful—not making such demands on Bashar Assad or Ahmadinejad.

In May, 2011, President Obama made his next major outreach speech to the Middle East. In it, he seemed to abandon the realpolitik of the Cairo speech. In the spirit of "leading from behind," he belatedly endorsed the Arab revolutions and finally delivered a form of his Ghana tough love speech. He directly addressed the problems of Arab tyrannies and corruption. He also generally intimated that the Arab Spring had made the late Osama bin Laden and his ideology obsolescent. It is true that bin Laden's name was not chanted during any of the uprisings. However, neither was the United States', nor were there any statues of liberty constructed, as was famously the case in Tiananmen Square in 1989. In fact, a case could be made that the Arab Spring demonstrated the irrelevance of the United States more than it did al Qaeda's. Obama's "leading from behind" did not impress Fares Braizat of the Arab Center for Research and Policy Studies in Qatar. He said, "He should have said something from the very beginning, but we've been waiting... Most people have realized that what the U.S. does or does not do is no longer important, because people took matters into their own hands and decided their own future. So why should people care what he says? America is no longer an issue."

President Obama also failed to notice that these uprisings have come close to achieving one of al Qaeda's principal goals—the elimination of the apostate authoritarian regimes in the Middle East and North Africa. What is to replace them is still very much up in the air. That is why bin Laden, in his posthumously broadcast audiotape, saw in the Arab Spring such potential for the achievement of al Qaeda's aims. That this might be the case did not seem to occur to the president, other than by his saying that the changes made may not be to the immediate tactical advantage of the United States, which would nevertheless accept them if they were produced democratically. This is confusing process for substance.

Obama characterized the uprisings as democratically inspired and therefore deserving of American support. What will happen, however, will very much depend on how Islam is understood in the respective countries of the Arab Spring. Curiously, though, the word "Islam" did not appear once in President Obama's lengthy speech. It is the dominant interpretation of Islam that will determine whether any of the vaunted democratic goals he enunciated can be achieved. Obama said that this is "a chance to pursue the world as it should be," rather than as it is. But what the world "should" be is exactly what is at issue within Islam itself. The president's speech assumed that Egyptian aspirations are identical to our own. This is a somewhat bipartisan view. James Glassman, President George W. Bush's last Under Secretary of State for Public Diplomacy, wrote in the *Wall Street Journal* on May 19th that "Muslims deserve and desire freedom as much as everyone else." This statement is very appealing, and there is certainly an element of truth in it. However, one must ask whether the desired freedom is truly based upon the proposition that *all* people are created equal. How many Egyptians actually believe that Copts and Muslims, men and women, believers and nonbelievers are equal—to say nothing of Jews and Muslims? Where is the underlying support in their culture for the truth of this proposition? If it is not there, it will be freedom for some and oppression for others. How many share the view of Osama's former body guard (now resident in Yemen), Abu Jandal, that politics is illegitimate because "when you accept the other as he is then you are in agreement with his infidelity and lowliness"?

Pretending that this is not so does not make the problem magically go away. Assuming that the Arab Spring was a rejection of bin Laden does not necessarily make it one. In fact, Dr. Tawfik Hamid's analysis of several thousand readers' comments on the Al Jazeera and al Arabiya websites in response to the death of bin Laden showed: "67% support for bin Laden, 19% against bin Laden, and Unclear answers 14%." Bin Laden, after all, was just another product of the Muslim Brotherhood, whose spiritual leader, Sheik Yusuf al-Qaradawi, addressed crowds of several million Egyptians in Tahrir Square at a victory rally on February 18th. He praised the "youth of the revolution," as *the new partisans of God.*" It is the Muslim Brotherhood that is currently positioned to take maximum advantage of the Arab Spring, bringing the Islamist dreams of Sayyid Qutb one giant step closer to reality. Speaking of current events in Egypt, Naguib Sawiris, one of the founders of the Free Egyptians Party, which promotes liberal and secular policies, lamented that, "they have substituted the dictatorship of the Mubarak with the dictatorship of the Muslim Brotherhood. That's where Egypt is going now." What does Obama propose to do to prevent this from happening?

He proposes some economic programs. These are not to be gainsaid, as the doubling in the price of wheat over the past year could by itself imperil a democratic transition in Egypt. However, one wonders why President Obama did not choose to remind Egyptians of some of their own history. After some 60 years of British presence in Egypt, Egyptians were left with a constitutional monarchy in which the basic human freedoms were enshrined, along with the rule of law, a functioning parliament, a relatively free press, and an independent judiciary. In a military coup in 1962, Gamal Nasser overthrew the constitutional monarchy and changed the constitution. His successor, Anwar Sadat, amended the constitution, enshrining shari'a as the main source of legislation, and Hosni Mubarak amended it again. The end result was a one-party, authoritarian state. Imperial powers did not do this to Egypt; Egyptians did it to themselves. Through another military coup, it appears that Egyptians may have the opportunity to choose again. It would not have been amiss to remind them of the criteria by which to make a choice that can lead them out of this sad history and back to the freedoms that they once enjoyed—not as a legacy of the British, but as their own. This would require more than the litany of specific human rights that Obama enumerated in the speech. It would require a natural theology to undergird them, and a sincere examination of whether that natural theology is compatible with Islamic revelation. It is not, of course, for a non-Muslim to answer the question as to whether it is or not, but it is perfectly appropriate, indeed, vitally necessary, to pose it.

Muslim writer Irshad Manji, author of *The Trouble with Islam Today*, writes that "bin Laden and his followers represent a real interpretation of Islam that begs to be challenged relentlessly and visibly." Obama chooses not to do this, preferring to pretend that it has gone away. He seems to believe that speaking of it brings it into, or at least sustains its existence, while not speaking of it denies its existence. This nominalist, or magical, approach is reflected in the tortured rhetoric the Obama Administration uses to portray the current conflict in order to avoid any mention of its nature. Consider the verbal gymnastics engaged in by the Secretary for Homeland Security, Janet Napolitano, in her description of a terrorist attack as a "man-caused disaster" or of war as an "overseas contingency operation." The President's counterterrorism advisor, John Brennan, said that jihad, rather than presenting a moral problem, "is a holy struggle, an effort to purify for a legitimate purpose." (Conceding legitimacy to your enemy in a war of ideas is not a good move.) On February 10th, Director of National Intelligence James Clapper told a congressional committee that the Islamic Brotherhood is a "largely secular" organization. Muslims could not care less what Brennan or any other non-Muslim thinks jihad is. And they would be, at least, bemused by the secular description given to an explicitly religious organization such as the Muslim Brotherhood. The only people Brennan, Clapper, Napolitano and Obama are confusing is the American people.

Why the semantic obfuscation? Self-delusion is one problem and ignorance is another. Many in the secular West find it hard to believe that anyone takes religion seriously anymore. Since they have lost their faith, they don't have the ability to comprehend the terms of faith in anyone else's life. In fact, their incomprehension, their obliviousness to the sacred, is one of the things that inflames Islam against the West. President Obama's National Security Strategy defines America's opponents as "a loose network of violent extremists." Whereas the Obama Administration is reluctant to speak of a "war against terrorism" (which is, admittedly, a misnomer itself), it is apparently at ease in defining the opponent as "violence." What about non-violent extremists? Do they present a problem? The Obama Administration now supports a role for the Muslim Brotherhood in a reformed Egyptian government on condition that it "rejects violence and recognizes democratic goals." If the Muslim Brotherhood's defined aim of creating a shari'a state in Egypt is achieved peacefully, is it any less inimical to U.S. strategic interests than if it were reached violently?

Confusion over these matters are sure signs that the United States is suffering from the same kind of conflict within itself over the nature of the threat that it is facing that it suffered from during the Cold War. There exists the same reluctance to name things for what they are and therefore to do the things that are necessary. One reason for this reluctance resides in President Obama's relativism. In his book, *The Audacity of Hope*, he discussed the U.S.

Constitution and the Declaration of Independence. He wrote, "Implicit in [the Constitution's] structure, in the very idea of ordered liberty, was a rejection of absolute truth, the infallibility of any idea or ideology or theology or 'ism,' and any tyrannical consistency that might block future generations into a single, unalterable course, or drive both majorities and minorities into the cruelties of the Inquisition..." In other words, truth leads to tyranny. Truth does not set you free; it imprisons. This statement would have amazed the American Founders, including John Adams, who, when reflecting back upon the principles of the American Founding, claimed that "those principles of liberty are as unalterable as human nature. And I could safely say consistently with all my then and present information that I believe they would never make discoveries in contradiction to these general principles."

How do you fashion a public diplomacy strategy based upon the belief that the United States does not represent any permanent truths? As was mentioned earlier regarding the Cold War, a form of absolutism fighting a form of relativism always has the upper hand. Who wants to die to prove that nothing is absolutely true? How exactly is one supposed to promote this idea? By playing pop music, and hoping that the walls come tumbling down?

In the current war of ideas, we have lost the means and we have lost the message. We won the Cold War because we developed the means, and we recovered the message. If we still have something to tell the world, if we still stand upon the embrace of a universal truth as the foundation of the "justness of our cause," then we will be impelled to find the means to reach others with this truth. If not, we will have lost ourselves for reasons having nothing to do with the challenge of Islam. Public diplomacy should aim for a new Yakovlev moment of semantic unanimity—a point at which the moral illegitimacy of the radical Islamist vision is self-confessed, a point at which its adherents admit that its central tenets are "evil." We cannot expect them to use this vocabulary if we do not.

Part III

Winning the Ideological War

The Jihadist States

Thomas Joscelyn

Summary

In early 1981, the Central Intelligence Agency (CIA) was asked to write an assessment of the Soviet Union's sponsorship of left-wing terrorism. Top Soviet analysts at Langley dismissed out-of-hand the possibility that the Soviets were behind much of international terrorism. The CIA was forced to admit that the Communist bloc did dabble in terrorism only after an intense bureaucratic battle. But even then the CIA downplayed the Soviets' role, arguing that Marxist terrorist groups received little assistance from Communist states. After the Soviet Union fell, archival evidence made it clear that the CIA had badly misjudged the Soviets' hand in left-wing terrorism.

During the 1990s, the U.S. intelligence community once again assumed that terrorism was largely "stateless." Al Qaeda and its allies were viewed as rogue transnational actors, loosely affiliated with one another and lacking any significant state sponsorship. Once again, America's intelligence analysts got it wrong. Al Qaeda has sought and received assistance from several jihadist states, or at least the military and intelligence components of those states.

This paper highlights how intelligence analysts missed the mark on al Qaeda's rise in the 1990s and continue to miss the mark today. Even though Osama bin Laden has been killed, the assumption that al Qaeda and its affiliates are "stateless" continues to be a dangerous one. Evidence included in the 9/11 Commission's final report and hundreds of leaked Joint Task Force Guantanamo threat assessments is cited throughout to show that the jihadist states sponsor al Qaeda in various ways.

Recognizing the role played by these jihadist states is an essential component of any winning strategy in the long-term fight against Islamist terrorists and their allies. During the Cold War, the Soviet Bloc sponsored anti-Western terrorism as a form of asymmetric warfare. Although the U.S. and its allies successfully implemented a strategy of deterrence against large-scale warfare, the failure to recognize the Soviets' key role in sponsoring left-wing terror networks meant that a similar strategy of deterrence was never applied to smaller-scale acts of provocation. Therefore, Soviet sponsorship of terrorism continued unabated.

This failure is even more problematic in the long war against Islamist terrorism, as the scale and breadth of terrorist attacks has greatly outpaced anything that occurred during the Cold War. Indeed, whereas terrorism was just one tool employed by the Soviets in their efforts to destabilize the West, terrorism is the principle weapon employed by the jihadist states against their enemies. An explicit message of deterrence is necessary to dissuade the jihadist states from allowing or sponsoring further terrorist attacks against the West. Such a message should become a critical part of what has been coined the "new deterrence."

A COLD WAR ANALOGY

During the Cold War, the United States and its Western allies were confronted by dozens of Marxist and radical Leftist terrorist groups. Some, like the Red Army Faction (or RAF, also known as the "Baader-Meinhof Gang"), were based in the heart of Europe. Others, such as the Popular Front for the Liberation of Palestine (PFLP), were headquartered in the Middle East but threatened Jewish and Western targets in Europe and elsewhere. While none of these groups was ever able to execute anything as devastating as al Qaeda's September 11, 2001, attack, they did wreak havoc across the globe. Like al Qaeda, the Marxist-Leftist terrorist groups placed little value on human life, especially the lives of those opposed to their ideology.

The Western bourgeois states and Israel could not be defeated, the terrorists believed, unless extreme violence was used to overthrow the ruling class. Hijackings, kidnappings, bombings, and shooting sprees were the norm.

These organizations were particularly fond of striking American military personnel and installations. Terrorist attacks against military assets were seen as an easy way to destabilize U.S. interests. So, for example, the RAF detonated a car bomb at the Ramstein Air Force Base in West Germany on August 31, 1981. No one was killed, fortunately, but seventeen people were injured in the attack. Other RAF terrorist attacks succeeded in killing American servicemen, as well as civilians.

In addition to their unflinching use of violence and unwavering Marxist ideology, the left-wing terrorist groups that routinely attacked the West in the 1970s and 1980s had something else in common: they were sponsored by the Soviet Union and their client states.

You would not know that, however, if you talked to the CIA's top Soviet analysts in early 1981. Soon after President Ronald Reagan took office, members of his Administration asked the CIA for an assessment of the Soviets' role in international terrorism. The bureaucratic fight that ensued between then Director of Central Intelligence William J. Casey and Langley's Soviet analysts is somewhat legendary. Former Secretary of Defense Robert Gates, who was Casey's chief of staff at the time, colorfully describes it in his book, *From the Shadows: The Ultimate Insider's Story of Five Presidents and How They Won the Cold War.*[1]

As Gates tells it, Secretary of State Alexander Haig asked for an interagency assessment after he had already "asserted publicly that the Soviets were behind much of international terrorism."[2] The CIA's analysts did not care for that characterization because they had already concluded it was not in the Soviets' interest to sponsor terrorism. Thus, Gates writes, the "first draft by the analysts proved beyond a shadow of a doubt that Haig had exaggerated the Soviet role—that the Soviets did not organize or direct international terrorism."[3] The CIA's analysts argued that "the Soviets disapproved of terrorism, discouraged the killing of innocents by groups they trained and supported, and did not support" Third World terrorist groups or "nihilistic terrorist groups" such as the RAF.[4]

If the Agency's analysts had their way, the story would have ended there. But Casey would not abide. Casey observed that the CIA did not regularly analyze the Soviets' so-called "active measures"—the "seamier side of Soviet activities around the world," as Gates describes it—including sponsorship of terrorism.[5] It was not until the end of 1981, after Casey forced it upon them, that the CIA's analysts began to regularly report on such behavior. Furthermore, Gates says that Casey challenged the analysts' "intellectual rigor," as well as the evidentiary standards they employed. Incredibly, the analysts put much stock in the Soviets' official disavowals. They ignored the commonsense observation that the Soviets had every incentive to say one thing while doing another. The analysts demanded a level of "proof" from the available evidence that would normally be reserved for court proceedings—i.e., proof beyond a "reasonable doubt." Casey dismissed the CIA's initial draft as having "the air of a lawyer's plea."[6] And he observed that "the practical judgments on which policy is based in the real world do not require that standard of proof, which is frequently just not available."[7]

An alternative to the CIA's assessment was prepared by the Defense Intelligence Agency (DIA). After much interagency bickering, a compromise analysis was agreed upon. Gates summarizes the new estimate, entitled "The Soviet Role in Revolutionary Violence," in detail. Gates explains: "It acknowledged that the Soviets were deeply engaged in support of 'revolutionary violence' worldwide in an effort to weaken unfriendly societies, destabilize hostile regimes, and advance Soviet interests."[8] The estimate cited "conclusive evidence" showing that the Soviets "directly or indirectly supported a large number of national insurgencies and some separatist-irridentist groups, many of which carried out terrorist activities as part of their larger program of revolutionary violence."[9] Many of these groups "did not accept Soviet control and direction."[10] With "respect to the nihilistic, purely terrorist groups," such as the RAF, the "estimate said the evidence was thin and contradictory but noted that some individuals in such groups had been trained by Soviet friends and allies that also provided them with weapons and safe transit."[11]

Gates says the new estimate "wasn't too bad," but it still downplayed the Soviet role to a large extent, especially when it came to groups like the RAF.[12] Then, with the fall of the Soviet Union and the dissolution of the Eastern bloc, the Communist archives were made available. It turns out Casey "had been more right than the others."[13] Gates writes, "For all the blood on the floor at the end, and for all of the careful compromise drafting to get the damn estimate out, we would learn a decade later that it had been too cautious."[14] The East German Stasi, for example, "supplied the West German Red Army Faction with weapons, training, false documentation, and money."[15] The RAF used the "training and weapons" in the 1981 car bomb attack against Ramstein Air Force Base. "It was inconceivable that the Soviets, and especially the KGB, which had these governments thoroughly penetrated, did not know and allow (if not encourage) these activities to continue," Gates concludes.[16]

The Soviet bloc's sponsorship of terrorism was not confined to Europe. Archival evidence summarized by historian Christopher Andrew in his book, *The World Was Going Our Way: The KGB and the Battle for the Third World*, shows a strong relationship between the KGB and the PFLP (Popular Front for the Liberation of Palestine).[17] The relationship was managed through Dr. Wadi Haddad, the head of the PFLP's foreign operations. In 1970, KGB spymaster Yuri Andropov wrote:

> The nature of our relations with W. Haddad enables us to control the external operations of the PFLP to a certain degree, to exert influence in a manner favourable to the Soviet Union, and also to carry out active measures in support of our interests through the organization's assets while observing the necessary conspiratorial secrecy.[18]

The KGB armed the PFLP and remained in touch with Haddad "during the spate of PFLP hijackings and attacks on Jewish targets in European capitals," even giving advice on specific operations.[19] The KGB also used the PFLP in a number of attacks against the Israeli Mossad and CIA, including an aborted operation to kidnap the CIA's deputy station chief in Lebanon.[20] In other words, not only was the KGB sponsoring terrorist organizations; it was also using them directly against the CIA.

We should pause here to reflect on the fundamental irony of this situation. At roughly the same time the KGB was sponsoring terrorism directly against the CIA, the CIA's Soviet analysts were pretending that the Soviets had little to no involvement in terrorism whatsoever. This may seem like ancient history. And you may be wondering: What does the CIA's bungling of Soviet-sponsored terrorism have to do with modern Islamist terrorist organizations, including al Qaeda? During the Cold War, the West relied on deterrence to prevent a "hot" war from breaking out. The logic of Mutually Assured Destruction ("MAD") meant that if the Soviets were to launch a massive nuclear attack, the West would respond in kind, thereby ensuring the destruction of both parties. The West employed a range of tactics that were intended to deter Soviet aggression in other ways as well. However, because the Soviets' sponsorship of terrorism was never explicitly recognized, the deterrence strategy was never applied to the left-wing terror network. As a result, the Soviet Bloc continued to train, arm, in some cases direct, and provide safe haven for various terrorist groups that targeted the West. Because no message of deterrence was delivered, and therefore no retribution for these acts was promised, the Soviets' sponsorship of terrorism continued unabated.

Only with the fall of the Soviet Union did the Marxist-Leftist terror network cease to threaten the West in a significant way.

The lack of a cohesive deterrence strategy with respect to the jihadist states is potentially an even graver problem, as Islamist terrorists have launched attacks on America itself—something the Soviet-sponsored terrorists never did. As we shall see, there is compelling evidence that multiple states have sponsored al Qaeda and like-minded terrorist groups in various ways. Ultimately, it is these states—in particular, Pakistan and Iran—that, at a minimum, allow the jihadist terror network to operate. But first we must recognize this role if we are to craft a convincing message of deterrence.

AN INCOHERENT PARADIGM: "STATELESS" AL QAEDA

History does not typically repeat itself—not precisely, anyway. But it does, as the saying goes, rhyme. Thus, in the 1990s, many U.S. counterterrorism officials and intelligence analysts made the same assumption about Islamist or jihadist terrorism that the CIA's Soviet analysts made about Marxist and Leftist terrorism. That is, they simply assumed that al Qaeda and related terrorist organizations were "stateless." This assumption has led to a crucial blind spot in America's counterterrorism policy. Osama bin Laden and his al Qaeda were never beholden to any one state. Bin Laden's objective, ultimately made impossible by a team of elite Navy Seals, was to acquire power for himself in the Middle East, Central and South Asia, and beyond. But in seeking to make his desire a reality, bin Laden sought and received the support of several jihadist-sponsoring states.

Al Qaeda and similar terrorist organizations need territory to operate. Without it, they are severely limited, operationally speaking. Most of the significant terrorist plots in recent years can be traced to al Qaeda and its allies in Pakistan and Yemen.[21] For example, the failed Christmas Day 2009 terrorist attack and the attempted Times Square bombing in May 2010 were both launched by jihadist recruits who traveled half a world away to receive terrorist training. At a minimum, then, states provide jihadist terrorist groups the space to operate. States can do this either by explicitly granting terrorist organizations turf, or by refusing to take turf away from them. The latter is true in Pakistan, where the military has consciously decided not to launch a sustained offensive against the jihadist hydra operating along the Afghanistan-Pakistan border. Instead of clearing and holding this territory, the Pakistani military has cut a series of peace deals with terrorist groups, claiming that the costs of intervention are too high. The Pakistani military has sustained significant casualties, but the truth is, as discussed more fully below, much of the Pakistani military-intelligence establishment remains deeply in bed with the jihadists.

The necessity of safe haven for Islamist terrorists is plain to see. Consider that Osama bin Laden was killed in his house in Abbottabad, Pakistan, where he had reportedly resided since 2005. As many have noted, the equivalent of Pakistan's West Point is just down the road. The identity of bin Laden's Pakistani benefactors remains the subject of widespread speculation, but it is inconceivable that someone of prominence within the Pakistani military-intelligence establishment did not know that he was there.

Consider, too, that bin Laden's interim replacement spent nine years in Iran after the September 11 attacks. Saif al Adel, an Egyptian, was tasked with leading al Qaeda until a new full-time emir could take over. Even after Ayman al Zawahiri was named bin Laden's full-time replacement, al Adel will undoubtedly remain in a top position. Al Adel has long been wanted by American officials for his role in the August 1998 embassy bombings in Kenya and Tanzania. After 9/11, he slipped across the border from Afghanistan to Iran. Instead of torturing and killing al Adel, as the Iranian regime does with much of its opposition, al Adel was placed in a loose form of house arrest that really amounted to safe haven. In other words, the Iranians kept al Adel alive, ensuring that he could return to al Qaeda at some point in the future.

Prior to bin Laden's demise, al Qaeda's CEO was working with another high-level terrorist named Atiyah Abd al Rahman to orchestrate a terrorist attack against the U.S. that would have potentially coincided with the tenth anniversary of the 9/11 attacks. Rahman has also reportedly succumbed to a U.S. drone strike in northern Pakistan—where Pakistan's military refuses to take on al Qaeda's strongholds deep inside territory controlled by the Haqqani Network. The Haqqanis themselves are long-time proxies of the Pakistani state, as well as staunch allies of al Qaeda.

Prior to relocating to northern Pakistan where he was killed, Rahman, like Saif al Adel, spent years living in Iran. In July 2011, the Obama Administration's Treasury Department designated six members of an al Qaeda network based in Iran. One of those six al Qaeda members was Rahman. The Obama Administration noted that the al Qaeda network operated as part of "an agreement between al Qaeda and the Iranian government." Moreover, "Rahman was previously appointed by Osama bin Laden to serve as al Qaeda's emissary in Iran, a position which allowed him to travel in and out of Iran with the permission of Iranian officials."[22] Thus, at a minimum, Iran allowed Atiyah and his fellow al Qaeda operatives the room to operate.

Even though the "stateless" paradigm is transparently wrong, it remains the dominant construct used by the U.S. government. A prime example of this paradigm's incoherence can be found in the 9/11 Commission report. In putting forth a "global strategy" for confronting terrorism, the Commission describes al Qaeda as the "stateless network of terrorists that struck us on 9/11."[23] Yet, the Commission's own findings are not consistent with the "stateless" paradigm. On the very same page that the 9/11 Commission labels al Qaeda "stateless," for example, we read: "The first phase of our post-9/11 efforts rightly included military action to topple the Taliban and pursue al Qaeda."[24] A few pages later we learn that the Commission had illustrated "the direct and indirect value of the Afghan sanctuary to al Qaeda in preparing the 9/11 attack and other operations."[25] In particular, Afghanistan gave al Qaeda "the operational space to gather and sift recruits, indoctrinating them in isolated, desert camps."[26] (The relationship between the Taliban and al Qaeda was so tight, in fact, that pre-9/11 Afghanistan has been called a "terrorist-sponsored state."[27])

Before relocating to Afghanistan in the mid-1990s, Osama bin Laden and al Qaeda received refuge in another nation: Sudan. At the time, Sudan was ruled by a prominent member of the international Muslim Brotherhood named Hassan al Turabi. Like bin Laden, Turabi thought the world was embroiled in a clash of civilizations, with his version of Islam on one side and basically everyone else, especially America, on the other.

Under Turabi's watchful eye, bin Laden's al Qaeda began to forge lasting relationships with a variety of state and non-state actors. In particular, bin Laden sought and received Iran's help. For Turabi, the differences between Sunnis and Shiites were inconsequential compared to the Muslim world's differences with the West. Bin Laden adopted this view, too, and was willing to work with Shiites if it improved al Qaeda's prospects for dealing a blow to America. The 9/11 Commission found that bin Laden "showed particular interest in learning how to use truck bombs such as the one that had killed 241 U.S. Marines in Lebanon in 1983."[28] That attack was carried out by Hezbollah, Iran's chief terrorist proxy in Lebanon, and coincided with a simultaneous attack on the headquarters for French paratroopers. The twin suicide bombings, conducted simultaneously, left an indelible impression on jihadists because the attacks were the beginning of a sustained terrorist campaign that drove America out of Lebanon without retaliation. Indeed, the U.S. never developed a deterrence strategy for this terrorist onslaught, which was clearly carried out by Iran and Syria.

Iran and Hezbollah agreed to help bin Laden in his quest to replicate the 1983 bombings. "In late 1991 or 1992," the 9/11 Commission explained, "discussions in Sudan between al Qaeda and Iranian operatives led to an informal agreement to cooperate in providing support—even if only training—for actions carried out primarily against Israel and the United States."[29] The 9/11 Commission continued:

> Not long afterward, senior al Qaeda operatives and trainers traveled to Iran to receive training in explosives. In the fall of 1993, another such delegation went to the Bekaa Valley in Lebanon for further training in explosives as well as in intelligence and security... The relationship between al Qaeda and Iran demonstrated that Sunni-Shia divisions did not necessarily pose an insurmountable barrier to cooperation in terrorist operations.[30]

Iran's and Hezbollah's training was instrumental in al Qaeda's evolution. On August 7, 1998, al Qaeda simultaneously struck the American embassies in Kenya and Tanzania using truck bombs driven by suicide terrorists. The attacks were directly modeled after Hezbollah's 1983 bombings. The 9/11 Commission found that al Qaeda "had begun developing the tactical expertise" for the 1998 embassy bombings when "top military committee members" and "several operatives who were involved with the Kenya cell ... were sent to Hezbollah training camps in Lebanon."[31] Among the al Qaeda operatives who received the training was Saif al Adel, the terrorist who served as interim emir of al Qaeda after bin Laden was killed.[32] That is, bin Laden's interest in the Iranian-backed Hezbollah operations had deadly consequences. With Iran's and Hezbollah's help, more than 200 people were killed in what was al Qaeda's deadliest attack prior to September 11, 2001.

The relationship between al Qaeda and Iran/Hezbollah did not end with the training of some of the 1998 embassy bombers. In a section of its final report entitled, "Assistance from Hezbollah and Iran to al Qaeda," the 9/11 Commission detailed numerous ties between the 9/11 hijackers and Hezbollah officials.[33] The Commission also found that perhaps a majority of the 9/11 hijackers transited Iranian soil en route to their day of terror. The Commission concluded: "We believe this topic requires further investigation by the U.S. government."[34]

Bin Laden and al Qaeda ultimately had to leave Sudan, as international pressure made his hosts uncomfortable. During his African sojourn, however, bin Laden successfully refashioned a network of so-called Arab Afghans who had fought against the Soviets during the 1980s into an international terrorist organization—albeit a fledgling one. After the Sudanese government expelled the terror master, al Qaeda relocated to Afghanistan, almost certainly with the help of Pakistan's Inter-Services Intelligence—the ISI.

Again turning to the 9/11 Commission's final report we learn: "It is unlikely that bin Laden could have returned to Afghanistan had Pakistan disapproved. The Pakistani military intelligence service probably had advance knowledge of his coming, and its officers may have facilitated his travel."[35] During his time away from South Asia, bin Laden had "maintained guest-houses and training camps in Pakistan and Afghanistan."[36] But he needed to broker a deal with the new power inside Afghanistan, Mullah Omar, in order to resettle there.

The ISI made that happen. The 9/11 Commission explains: "Pakistani intelligence officers reportedly introduced bin Laden to Taliban leaders in Kandahar, their main base of power, to aid his reassertion of control over camps near Khowst, out of an apparent hope that he would now expand the camps and make them available for training [Pakistan-backed] Kashmiri militants."[37] The value of Pakistan's assistance to bin Laden at this time cannot be overestimated. After being expelled from Sudan, the 9/11 Commission found, bin Laden "was in his weakest position since his early days in the war against the Soviet Union."[38] He was desperate for a new ally who would host his network and allow him to rebuild. Mullah Omar's Taliban, an ISI proxy, gave him just that. Newly ensconced in Afghanistan, bin Laden rebuilt al Qaeda quickly and within just a few years showed off his group's deadly capabilities. It was from Afghanistan that bin Laden watched the aftermath of the August 7, 1998, embassy bombings and scoffed at the American response. President Clinton authorized missile strikes against a suspicious factory in Sudan and bin Laden's training camps in Afghanistan.

From a tactical perspective, the strikes mostly failed. A few dozen al Qaeda trainees and operatives were killed, but bin Laden escaped. Several Clinton Administration officials and intelligence officers thought they knew why. "Officials in Washington speculated that one or another Pakistani official might have sent a warning to the Taliban or bin Laden," the 9/11 Commission found.[39] Adding to their suspicions was the fact that several

Pakistani military intelligence officials were among the dead at one of bin Laden's camps.

In early 1999, Clinton officials were still exploring ways to get bin Laden. The main obstacle, they feared, was Pakistan. National Security Adviser Sandy Berger "suggested sending one U-2 flight" over Afghanistan in an effort to locate bin Laden.[40] The spy plane would have to fly over Pakistani airspace; Clinton's chief counterterrorism adviser, Richard Clarke, objected on the grounds that Pakistani intelligence "is in bed with" bin Laden and would warn him. "Armed with that knowledge, old wily Usama will likely boogie to Baghdad," Clarke warned.[41] (Clinton Administration officials had received multiple intelligence reports saying that Saddam Hussein wanted bin Laden in Baghdad at the time.)

Ultimately, neither the Clinton nor the Bush Administrations would get bin Laden. He was killed after President Obama authorized a raid on bin Laden's safe haven in Abbottabad, Pakistan—near a Pakistani military cantonment. Given that American officials had worried about the Pakistani military-intelligence establishment being "in bed with" bin Laden more than a decade before, bin Laden's presence in Abbottabad should have come as no surprise. It is also not surprising to learn that the Obama Administration did not trust senior Pakistani military and intelligence officials with the details of the raid beforehand.

The 9/11 Commission's report was completed seven years ago. The "stateless" paradigm it endorsed lives on despite overwhelming evidence that it is logically incoherent. The Commission found that al Qaeda's safe havens in Sudan and Afghanistan were crucial for the organization's development. The assistance Iran and Hezbollah (a state-backed terrorist group) agreed to provide bin Laden directly led to al Qaeda's most successful attack prior to September 11, 2001. And when Osama bin Laden relocated from Sudan to Afghanistan, he almost certainly received assistance from the Pakistani ISI. American officials worried for years about the relationship between the ISI and bin Laden. All of this was cited by the 9/11 Commission. None of it is consistent with the "stateless" paradigm used by American authorities to understand al Qaeda.

A BETTER PARADIGM: THE JIHADIST STATES

During the Cold War, the U.S. government was reluctant to accept the Soviet bloc's sponsorship of terrorism against the West and Israel. Only after the Soviet Union fell and its massive archives were opened to researchers did the full scope of what the U.S. intelligence community missed become obvious. Today, many in the U.S. intelligence community similarly miss the role that jihadist states play in sponsoring terrorist groups, including al Qaeda. Unlike the Communist bloc, the jihadist states do not answer to any one centralized authority. In some cases, they are even rivals for power who sponsor jihadists against one another. Moreover, al Qaeda never answered to any one of these states, even while it sought and received assistance from several of them.

When we speak of jihadist nation-states, it does not mean that the entire government of that nation sponsors terrorism. Typically, it is the military and intelligence establishment of the jihadist states that sponsor terrorists both as a means for extending its power (both internally and externally), and for ideological reasons.

The previous section outlined the roles played by several jihadist states in sponsoring al Qaeda, as detailed by the 9/11 Commission. This list is not exhaustive. To it we should add Syria (which funneled jihadists into Iraq to fight Americans), Saudi Arabia, and Yemen, among others. Not all of these states are equal partners in sponsoring al Qaeda, and sometimes they can even cross swords with bin Laden's creation. For instance, the Saudi Kingdom is clearly in the cross-hairs of al Qaeda in the Arabian Peninsula (AQAP). AQAP seeks to kill Saudi royals and disrupt the Saudi government. And before AQAP took the lead against the Saudis, other branches of al Qaeda orchestrated terrorist attacks inside the Kingdom, too. Indeed, the May 2003 Riyadh bombings demonstrated the degree to which Osama bin Laden had turned against his former ally.

However, even as al Qaeda has targeted the Saudis, we should be mindful of the fact that this is "blowback" in the truest sense of the term.[42] For decades, the Saudi Kingdom was the financial engine of global jihad and remains so, in many ways, to this day. Al Qaeda itself grew out of Saudi and Pakistani cooperation against the Soviets.[43] These two allies of the U.S., which provided the venture with cash and weapons, threw their support behind the most radical groups opposing the Soviets. After the Soviets left Afghanistan, the Pakistanis, with cash from the Saudis, created the Taliban— which, in time, became al Qaeda's most important ally. Everywhere the Saudis have funded mosques and spread Wahhabism, the Saudi state's jihadist religion, extremism and terrorism have followed. Al Qaeda has benefitted from this largesse despite its animosity for the Saudi royals, and some prominent Saudis reportedly continue to fund al Qaeda.

Yemen is the ancestral homeland of Osama bin Laden and, like Saudi Arabia, has been a vital recruiting ground for al Qaeda. AQAP's rise there is no accident. But as Yemen teeters on the brink of complete collapse, the role of Yemen's military in sponsoring jihadism, and specifically al Qaeda, has been widely unappreciated. The second most powerful man in Yemen under President Saleh's regime, General Ali Muhsin al Ahmar, was in fact a long-time sponsor of Osama bin Laden. Al Ahmar, according to a leaked State Department cable, also helped establish the Islamic Army of Aden—which is both affiliated with al Qaeda and a precursor to AQAP. Al Ahmar and the Yemeni military have also long used jihadists as a weapon against their internal opposition, including Houthi rebels.

None of the descriptions provided above is intended to be exhaustive. Each of these states has compiled an extensive history of jihadist sponsorship that would take hundreds of pages fully to recount. Below, some of this evidence is summarized using a unique source: leaked Joint Task Force Guantanamo (JTF-Guantanamo) documents. Particular attention is given to one of the foremost jihadist-sponsoring states on the planet and longtime home to Osama bin Laden before his demise: Pakistan.

LEAKED JOINT TASK FORCE GUANTANAMO (JTF-GTMO) THREAT ASSESSMENTS

Although much of the U.S. government pretends that al Qaeda lacks any state sponsors, it regularly comes across evidence of such sponsorship. In the war against al Qaeda and its affiliates, the best sources are human—men who can tell U.S. officials what the clandestine terror network is doing behind closed doors. The detention facility at Guantanamo Bay, Cuba has housed hundreds of such men since early 2002. Joint Task Force Guantanamo (JTF-GTMO) was set up to interrogate the jihadists detained there and collect intelligence on them from all available sources. The sensitivity of this mission meant that in the years following the September 11 attacks, JTF-GTMO was on the frontlines in the effort to collect intelligence on al Qaeda and its allies. It also meant that JTF-GTMO had to perform its work largely in secret.

Over time, however, the secrecy surrounding JTF-GTMO has succumbed to Freedom of Information Act (FOIA) requests, which were the subject of litigation, as well as leaks. In April 2011, the controversial anti-secrecy organization Wikileaks released formerly secret JTF-GTMO threat assessments for 765 of the 779 detainees held in Cuba. The documents offer key insights into how al Qaeda and associated groups operate.

One particularly interesting document is entitled, "JTF-GTMO Matrix of Threat Indicators for Enemy Combatants."[44] The document lists "indicators used in JTF-GTMO detainee assessments to determine a detainee's capabilities and intentions to pose a terrorist threat if the detainee were given the opportunity." On page 15 of this threat matrix, JTF-GTMO lists "terrorist and terrorist support entities identified as associate forces." The authors of the document explain, "Through associations with these groups and organizations, a detainee may have provided support to al-Qaida or the Taliban, or engaged in hostilities against US or Coalition forces." Three jihadist states, or parts thereof, are listed as associated forces: Iranian intelligence (and Iran's chief terrorist proxy, Hezbollah), the Pakistani Inter-Service Intelligence Directorate (ISID), and Yemeni Intelligence (the Political Security Organization).[45] In other words, the detainees held at Guantanamo were not, in many cases, "stateless" actors.

Leaked JTF-GTMO threat assessments contain numerous examples of how each of these three states sponsors al Qaeda and allied organizations. For instance, one current Guantanamo detainee, an Afghan named Haji Hamidullah, was identified as an "agent of the Iranian Savama (Ministry of Intelligence and Security)" and was "closely associated" with the Taliban, Hezb-e-Islami Gulbuddin (HIG), and al Qaeda.[46] The Iranians allegedly dispatched Hamidullah and his father to Afghanistan to execute a string of terrorist attacks against Western targets. Afghanistan's National Directorate of Security (NDS) reported to American officials that Hamidullah "was responsible for explosions" and "murdered 71 people."

Many of the Guantanamo detainees have connections to Iran, which al Qaeda operatives continue to use for safe transit to Afghanistan. Dozens of Guantanamo detainees used Iranian ratlines on their way to jihad. One ex-Guantanamo detainee, Said al Shihri, was formerly an al Qaeda travel facilitator in Mashhad, Iran.[47] After being released from Guantanamo, al Shihri was enrolled in Saudi Arabia's jihadist rehabilitation program. The rehab did not take, however, and today al Shihri is the number-two leader of AQAP in Yemen.

The leaked JTF-GTMO threat assessments reveal that jihadist states such as Iran are willing to make strange bedfellows with other jihadists when the goal is targeting America. The Taliban and Iran, for example, were long rivals, even enemies. In the late 1990s they nearly went to war with each other after the Taliban executed Shiite diplomats in Mazar-e-Sharif. However, the relationship changed drastically after the September 11, 2001, terrorist attacks.

A Guantanamo detainee named Khairullah Said Wali Khairkhwa was the governor of Herat province in Afghanistan at the time. Khairkhwa, who reportedly had "close ties" to Osama bin Laden, was tasked with mending the Taliban's relationship with Iran. JTF-GTMO's threat assessment for Khairkhwa notes that he attended a "meeting initiated by Iran, possibly Iran's Islamic Revolutionary Guard Corps (IRGC)" on October 3, 2001. The JTF-GTMO file reads: "Iranian officials offered to broker a coalition between the Northern Alliance and the Taliban to unite in their fight against US intervention. The Iranian delegation offered to open the borders to Arabs who wanted to cross into Afghanistan to fight against US and Coalition forces."[48] The Iranian-sponsored coalition of Northern Alliance and Taliban forces did not come to fruition. But Iran did allow Arab jihadists into Afghanistan to fight. And the newly formed relationship with the Taliban would be a lasting one. Iran continues to provide the Taliban with weapons and safe haven to this day. Senior al Qaeda leaders such as Saif al Adel, who was trained by Iran and Hezbollah in the early 1990s, were also sheltered in Iran under a loose form of house arrest for years after the 9/11 attacks.

Leaked JTF-GTMO threat assessments provide stunning new details about Yemen's Political Security Organization (PSO). A current Guantanamo detainee named Abd al Salam al Hilal worked for the PSO, which reported to Yemeni President Ali Abdullah Saleh. While working for the Yemeni government, however, Abd al Salam also served al Qaeda. Abd al Salam allegedly used his position to secure safe transit for al Qaeda operatives traveling to and from Yemen. Some of these terrorists, according to the JTF-GTMO file, likely included the USS *Cole* bombers.[49]

Abd al Salam came under suspicion well before the 9/11 attacks when Italian authorities were monitoring a radical mosque in Milan. In a wire-tapped conversation, Abd al Salam was heard telling another al Qaeda operative:

Well, I am studying airplanes! If it is God's will, I hope to bring you a window or a piece of a plane next time I see you... We are focusing on the air alone... It is something terrifying, something that moves from south to north and from east to west: the man who devised the program is a lunatic, but he is a genius. It will leave them stunned...

We can fight any force using candles and planes. They will not be able to halt us, not even with their heaviest weapons. We just have to strike at them, and hold our heads high. Remember, the danger at the airports. If it comes off, it will be reported in all the world's papers. The Americans have come into Europe to weaken us, but our target is now the sky.[50]

It is easy to see why Italian and American authorities concluded that Abd al Salam probably had foreknowledge of the impending September 11 attacks. But Abd al Salam was not the only member of the PSO who assisted al Qaeda. Abd al Salam also fingered the deputy chief of the PSO, the director of the PSO, the commander of the PSO's deportation department, and another PSO officer as all aiding al Qaeda. Abd al Salam also told authorities that Ali Muhsin, the powerful Yemeni general who helped install President Saleh in office and who was the number two man in Saleh's regime, "was aware" of "these activities."[51]

While Iran and Yemen are mentioned repeatedly in the leaked JTF-GTMO documents, no jihadist state is featured more prominently than Pakistan. Since General Zia ul Haq's reign in the 1970s and 1980s, sponsoring jihadists in Afghanistan, Kashmir, and India has been the official policy of Pakistan's military and intelligence establishment. That policy continued in the 1990s, with the creation of the Taliban, an ISI proxy. And it continued after the September 11 attacks, even as Pakistan reentered an uneasy alliance with the U.S.

Duplicity defines Pakistan's behavior. Pakistan clearly helped America track down numerous al Qaeda operatives, beginning in late 2001. At the same time, however, Pakistan's military continued to sponsor the West's main foes in Afghanistan. Even while providing crucial assistance in the fight against al Qaeda, Pakistan kept the Taliban alive. Mullah Omar relocated to Quetta, and his Pakistani protection became so obvious that his new leadership council came to be called the Quetta Shura Taliban (QST). Gulbuddin Hekmatyar, an old ISI client from the days of jihad against the Soviets, reestablished his base of operations in northern Pakistan. The same is true for the father and son team of Jalaluddin and Siraj Haqqani, who are also longtime clients of the ISI.

These three organizations—the QST, Gulbuddin's Hezb-i-Islami, and the Haqqani network—are the principal insurgency groups in Afghanistan today. The Pakistani military-intelligence establishment has actively aided and abetted them. These three groups have something else in common: they are closely allied with Osama bin Laden's al Qaeda. Siraj Haqqani, who now leads his father's network, sits on al Qaeda's elite Shura council and may have a say in who replaces bin Laden as al Qaeda's top man. Hekmatyar was one of bin Laden's friends from the 1980s. To this day, al Qaeda fights alongside these ISI-backed organizations against the United States and its allies in Afghanistan.

Leaked JTF-GTMO threat assessments provide many new details about the Pakistani military's duplicitous behavior, including its sponsorship not only of al Qaeda's allies, but also of al Qaeda itself. In the leaked file for the aforementioned Haji Hamidullah, we learn:

> December 2002 reporting linked [Hamidullah] to a Pakistani Inter-Services Intelligence Directorate (ISID) initiative to create an office in Peshawar combining elements of the Taliban, HIG, and al Qaeda. The goal of the initiative was to plan and execute various terrorist attacks in Afghanistan.[52]

Another JTF-GTMO file contains an intelligence report saying that "representatives from the Pakistani government and the Inter-Services Intelligence Directorate (ISID)" attended a meeting with Mullah Omar and other top Taliban commanders in February 2005.[53] At the meeting, "Mullah Omar told the attendees that they should not cooperate with the new infidel government (in Afghanistan) and should keep attacking coalition forces."[54]

One JTF-GTMO file contains intelligence reports indicating that the ISID provided training for al Qaeda's allies in Afghanistan, including on remote-controlled Improvised Explosive Devices (RCIEDs).[55] Still another says that, in January 2003, "[t]hree Pakistani military officers provided one month of training" for a group of Taliban commanders "in explosives, bomb-making, and assassination techniques." The Pakistani military training "was conducted in preparation for a planned spring campaign to assassinate Westerners."[56] This same Taliban group went on to kill a Red Cross worker in Afghanistan just a few months later.

Most analysts would probably concede that Pakistan directly sponsors the West's jihadist enemies in Pakistan. However, the deeper lesson still has not been learned. This sponsorship extends, in various ways, to al Qaeda itself. The leaked JTF-GTMO files for two Guantanamo detainees, in particular, illustrate this point clearly. Before his capture in 2007, Harun al Afghani had built a lengthy dossier of terrorist and insurgent activities. According to a leaked JTF-GTMO threat assessment dated August 2, 2007, Afghani worked for both HIG and al Qaeda as an explosives maker and courier.[57] Afghani's extremist career began at a school for refugees and orphans run by September 11 mastermind Khalid Sheikh Mohammed (KSM) and KSM's brother. Afghani spent years with the HIG, and after 9/11 he became part of a special commando unit assembled to help Osama bin Laden escape coalition forces in late 2001. The unit failed to help bin Laden, but Afghani's ties to al Qaeda had just begun.

Afghani worked as a courier for a high-level al Qaeda operative named Abdel Hadi al Iraqi. Al Iraqi, who is also held at Guantanamo, was one of Osama bin Laden's most trusted lieutenants and led the 55th Arab Brigade, a group of al Qaeda fighters who fought alongside the Taliban in pre-9/11 Afghanistan. Afghani's close relationship with al Iraqi demonstrates just how trustworthy al Qaeda found Afghani to be.

The leaked file on Afghani is littered with references to his connections to various terrorists and insurgents working for multiple extremist organizations in Afghanistan and Pakistan. The file also contains some disturbing details about the ISI's support for these organizations. Afghani "is aware of al Qaeda's receipt of advanced information on Pakistani military operations, and al Qaeda's cooperation with other extremist groups," the JTF-GTMO team found. In particular, Afghani allegedly told U.S. authorities that he "spent the night with a large group that left" a training center in Pakistan after they learned "the Pakistani military was about to conduct operations in the area." JTF-GTMO's analysts surmised that Afghani "may have more specific information on the individuals who provided this warning and their level of access to Pakistani [military] planning." Moreover, the file reads, Afghani "has provided information on ISID assistance to extremist groups operating in Pakistan and Afghanistan, and may have additional information on their associations and activities."

Indeed, the JTF-GTMO file on Afghani does contain additional details concerning the ISI's "associations and activities." In October 2006, Afghani "was reported to have returned from Pakistan with 60 rockets, which he intended to use in attacks on the Bagram Airport." Afghani told authorities that "the HIG, Taliban, and al Qaeda had established a weapons depot in eastern Afghanistan, which was managed by" one of his associates. Afghani explained further that "an unidentified Pakistani Inter-Services Intelligence Directorate (ISID) officer paid 1 million (PKR) to one of the operatives involved in transporting ammunition to the depot ... which contained about

800 rockets, AK-47 and machine gun ammunition, mortars, RPGs, and mines ... established in preparation for a spring 2007 offensive."

Pakistan's support for the jihadist insurgents in Afghanistan is not limited to arming and training them. Pakistan has also played a key role in coordinating these groups' assault on Afghan and Western forces. The leaked file for al Afghani, for example, contains this paragraph (emphasis added):

[Afghani] is assessed to have attended a joint operations meeting among extremist elements in mid-2006. A letter describing an 11 August 2006 meeting between commanders of the Taliban, al Qaeda, [Lashkar e Taiba], *Pakistani military and intelligence officials*, and the Islamic Party (probably a reference to the HIG), disclosed that the groups decided to increase terrorist operations in the Kapisa, Kunar, Laghman, and Nangarhar provinces, including suicide bombings, mines, and assassinations.[58]

The JTF-GTMO threat assessment for another detainee, an Afghan named Haji Wali Mohammed, contains even more examples of the Pakistani ISI's sponsorship of al Qaeda. American officials, drawing on intelligence from the Jordanians, identified Mohammed as a "primary" al Qaeda financier who helped fund both the 1998 embassy bombings and al Qaeda's foiled millennium plot in Jordan. The file says that in March 2000, "at the direction of [Osama bin Laden] and with ISID's assistance," Mohammed "facilitated the financing for the purchase of shoulder-fired surface-to-air missiles (SAMs)" that al Qaeda was to deliver to jihadists in Chechnya. Two ISID officers directly "supported" this effort. The JTF-GTMO file reads: "The ISID support included providing a subsidy of $4,000 US for each SAM purchased from suppliers in Afghanistan and Pakistan."[59]

CONCLUSION: A "NEW DETERRENCE"

The intelligence reports cited in leaked JTF-GTMO files show that jihadist states arm, train, fund, and give safe haven to al Qaeda and its allies. Evidence cited in the 9/11 Commission's final report, which insisted that al Qaeda is "stateless," shows the same. Yet, the idea that al Qaeda has existed without help from states has persisted. The purpose of this paper was to highlight just some of the evidence that shows the "stateless" paradigm is both logically incoherent and does not adequately reflect a much more complicated reality. Several jihadist states, or elements therein, have sponsored al

Qaeda and its allies in various ways. They will, in all likelihood, continue to do so even now that Osama bin Laden is dead.

In the decade since the 9/11 attacks, American defense officials began to develop a "new deterrence" strategy for combating the al Qaeda-led terror network. The story of how this new strategy came about is told in great detail by two *New York Times* reporters, Eric Schmitt and Thom Shanker, in their book, *Counterstrike: The Untold Story of America's Secret Campaign Against Al Qaeda*. As Schmitt and Shanker explain, the U.S. government initially concluded that the Islamist terrorist network could not be deterred from striking America. Therefore, it was believed that the deterrence strategies of the past could not be used to defeat this new foe. Over time, however, the U.S. government's thinking evolved and deterrence was seen as a viable strategy.

A close reading of *Counterstrike* reveals that this "new deterrence," which is poorly defined, is not really aimed at al Qaeda's senior leadership, however. Ayman al Zawahiri and his ilk cannot be deterred from striking the U.S. or launching terrorist attacks elsewhere. There are others who can be potentially deterred, however, including arms dealers, financiers and middlemen who are not ideologically committed to al Qaeda's terrorism and yet support it. But these actors, while important, are secondary to the Islamist terror network's most important benefactors: the jihadist states.

The jihadist states should, therefore, be the first priority in a "new deterrence" strategy. A clear message of deterrence should be developed by the U.S. government, making the consequences of terror sponsorship clear. The content of such a message can be debated, but the U.S. cannot afford to ignore the obvious: al Qaeda and like-minded terrorist groups receive substantial support from the jihadist states.

THE ENEMY THREAT DOCTRINE OF AL QAEDA: TAKING THE WAR TO THE HEART OF OUR FOE

Sebastian L. v. Gorka*

As we enter the second decade of the war against al Qaeda and Associated Movements (AQAM), America still does not fully understand the nature of the enemy that most threatens its citizens.

Paradoxically, while the U.S. has in the last 10 years been very successful in militarily degrading the operational capacity of al Qaeda directly to do harm, al Qaeda has become even more powerful in the domain of ideological warfare and other indirect forms of attack. Bin Laden may be dead, but the narrative of religiously motivated global revolution that he embodied is very much alive and growing in popularity. While the U.S. has crippled al Qaeda's capacity to execute mass-casualty attacks with its own assets on U.S. territory, its message has and holds traction with individuals prepared to take the fight to Americans, be it Major Nidal Hasan, Faisal Shahzad, the Times Square attacker, or Umar Farouk Abdulmutallab, the Christmas Day bomber.

Although we have proven our capacity in the last 10 years kinetically to engage our enemy at the operational and tactical level with unsurpassed effectiveness, we have not even begun to take the war to al Qaeda at the

---

* The views expressed in this chapter are solely the author's and do not represent US government policy.

185

strategic level of counter-ideology, to attack it at its heart—the ideology of global jihad. To paraphrase Dr. James Kiras of the Air University, we have denied al Qaeda the capability to conduct complex attacks on the scale of 9/11, but we now need to transition away from concentrating on dismantling and disrupting al Qaeda's network and focus on undermining its core strategy of ideological attack. We need to employ the indirect approach well utilized by our community of Special Forces operators of working "by, with and through" local allies, and move beyond attacking the enemy directly at the operational and tactical level to attacking it indirectly at the strategic level.

There are several reasons for the paucity of our strategic approach to AQAM, many having to do with so-called political correctness. Nevertheless, the fact is, we have forgotten most of the lessons of the last ideological war we fought—the Cold War—including some of the cardinal rules of effective information and psychological operations. We need to remind ourselves how we defeated the last ideological foe we faced, the USSR. In a fashion similar to how America delegitimized the Soviet Union ideologically, we need to bankrupt transnational jihadist terrorism at its most powerful point: its narrative of global religious war. For the sad truth is that for the majority of the last ten years the narrative of the conflict has been controlled by our enemy.[1] Just as in the Cold War, the United States must take active measures to arrive at a position where it shapes the agenda and the story of the conflict, where we force our enemy onto the back foot to such an extent that jihadism eventually loses all credibility and implodes as an ideology. For this to happen we must re-think from the ground up the way in which strategic communications and information operations are run.

Our ability to fight al Qaeda and similar transnational terrorist actors will depend in the first place upon our capacity to communicate to our own citizens and to the world what it is we are fighting for and what the ideology of jihad threatens in terms of the universal values we hold so dear. To quote Sun Tsu, in war it is not enough to know the enemy in order to win. One must first know oneself and why one fights. During the Cold War this happened naturally. Given the nature of the Soviet Union and the nuclear threat it clearly posed to the West, from the first successful Soviet atom-bomb test to the collapse of the USSR in 1991, every day for four decades Americans knew what was at stake and why Communism could not be allowed to spread its totalitarian grip beyond the Iron Curtain. Yet since 9/11 we have institutionally failed to meet our duty to become well informed on the threat doctrine of our enemy. And without a clear understanding of the enemy threat doctrine, victory is likely impossible.

The reasons for our confusion in this area are many but they stem from two serious and connected obstacles. The first is a misguided belief that the religious character of the enemy's ideology should not be discussed, and that we need not address it, but should instead use the phrase "Violent Extremism" to describe our foe and thus avoid any unnecessary unpleasantness. The second is that even if we could demonstrate clear-headedness on the issue and recognize the religious ideology of al Qaeda and its associated movements for what it is, a form of hybrid totalitarianism, we still drastically lack the institutional ability to analyze and comprehend the worldview of this enemy and therefore its strategic mindset and ultimate objectives.

Here it is enlightening to look to the past to understand just how great a challenge is posed by the need for our national security establishment to understand its new enemy. It was only in 1946, with George Kennan's classified "Long Telegram" (later republished pseudonymously as *The Sources of Soviet Conduct*) that America began to understand the nature of the Soviet Union, why it acted the way it did, how the Kremlin thought, and why the USSR was an existential threat to America.[2] Consider now the fact that this document was written three decades after the Russian Revolution, and that despite all the scholarship and analysis available in the United States, it took more than a generation to penetrate the mind of the enemy and come to a point where a counter-strategy could be formulated. Now add to this the fact that today our enemy is not a European secular nation-state, as was the USSR, but a non-European, religiously-informed non-state terrorist group, and we see the magnitude of the challenge.

While initiatives such as Fort Leavenworth's Human Terrain System (HTS) and the teams they provide to theater commanders are well-meant efforts in the right direction of trying to understand the context of the enemy, they still miss the mark on more than one level. To begin with, it is very difficult, if not impossible, to provide the contextual knowledge needed to understand and defeat the enemy if we rely solely upon anthropologists and social scientists, as the HTS does. Today our multi-disciplinary analysis of the enemy and his doctrine just as much requires—if not more so—the expertise of the regional historian and the theologian, the specialist who knows when and how Sunni Islam split from Shia Islam and what the difference is between the Meccan and Medinan verses of the Qur'an. We should ask ourselves, honestly, how many national security practitioners know the answers to these questions, or at least have somewhere to turn to within government to provide such essential expertise.

UNDERSTANDING THE IDEOLOGY OF GLOBAL JIHAD

One of the greatest—self-induced—obstacles we have to understanding our enemy is mirror imaging, seeing Islam as just one more religion like the religions we are most familiar with—Christianity and Judaism. However, if one understands that Islam, not just in its extreme forms, but in its mainstream version, sees politics, economics, law and faith as integral to each other and as part of "shari'a"—the way of life, then one understands that even the phrase "political Islam" is a case of the West using its terminology for something that does not reflect Western concepts and categories. It is therefore pointless to use the phrase "political Islam"; Islam *is* political. The idea that now prevails at the very highest policy levels in the United States government that there are "good Islamists" and "bad Islamists" is patently fallacious if one is familiar with the foundational history of this religion.[3] In fact, you cannot separate politically motivated Islam from jihadi ideology. They feed upon each other and are based upon each other. They cannot be separated in their genetic code from the ideology that informed and shaped the founding of Islam. Muhammad did not simply call himself a prophet, but was at one and the same time a head of state and a successful military commander, not a man of peace, but a battlefield commander.

We must also understand the broader context that brought us al Qaeda and its Associated Movements and see that they are the product of decades, if not centuries, of ideological evolution. AQAM cannot be solely understood as something that had to do with the Afghan War of the 1980s and then the World Trade Center. AQAM must be placed in the broader context of ideological evolution, a context shaped by seminal geopolitical events of the 20th century. Additionally, if we are fully to understand the current threat environment, we need to realize that there are in fact two jihadi camps. There is the kinetic or violent jihadi camp, exemplified by al Qaeda, and there is the non-kinetic jihadi camp, exemplified and led by the Muslim Brotherhood, which, as the results of the so-called Arab Spring have demonstrated, does not need to use violence to achieve its goals. The essential point here is that these two types of actor have the same strategic intent. These are not competitors or enemies. They will have disagreements among themselves, but the nature of these disagreements is almost exclusively tactical, or has to do with matters of timing, but at their core these groups are in the same camp and are united by their ultimate, shari'a-driven goals.

Despite this being the eleventh year of the war, now the longest war the U.S. has engaged in since 1776, we are still not allowed to analyze objectively the enemy threat doctrine of al Qaeda. This phrase, "enemy threat doctrine," simply means studying what the enemy wishes to achieve and how they wish to achieve it. At the beginning of the Cold War, Kennan's 5,000-word analysis of the Soviet Union and why it behaved the way it did explained that the enemy mindset was a product of centuries of imperial attitudes and expansionism, that Josef Stalin was a new embodiment of Peter the Great. His objective explanation eventually helped Paul Nitze write NSC-68, in 1950, which told us that the enemy has an ideology—Communism—and that it must be contained.[4] Without that document, without Kennan explaining the nature of the enemy, without Nitze writing NSC-68, which explained how operationally to contain communism, America probably would not have won in 1991.

To defeat an enemy it is critical to understand his threat doctrine, why he behaves the way he does, the historic, cultural and conceptual explanations for his behavior. But we as national security practitioners are not allowed to do so. Why? In the beginning, we did not have the capacity to understand the threat. On September 11th, 2001, the CIA had merely a handful of people who spoke Pashtun. We knew bin Laden was in Afghanistan, we knew the majority language was Pashtun. We could intercept every single email and satellite phone conversation in Afghanistan. But if those messages and conversations cannot be translated, they are just so much wastepaper. Therefore, having concentrated almost all our efforts since 1946 on trying to understand the USSR and her allies, we did not have the skills to deal with a new enemy. More problematically, it is now not politically correct to discuss this new enemy's threat doctrine since religion is a taboo subject within U.S. government and especially within the national security apparatus of the United States. So much so that the official description for the enemy we face today is the nebulous "violent extremism." This is despite the fact that from Osama bin Laden to Major Nidal Hasan our enemies see themselves as holy warriors, recruiting their followers in mosques and quoting the Qur'an to justify their murderous acts, despite the fact that as Major Hasan opened fire on his fellow officers and their families in Fort Hood, with survivors recounting that he cried "Allah hu Akbar!" or "Allah is Great."

BEGINNING TO UNDERSTAND THE ENEMY: WHAT IS AQAM?

So how do we begin to understand the enemy? I propose three ways to understand AQAM and to understand the nature of al Qaeda's ideology. The first is the most obvious: look at the organizational dynamic, how al Qaeda has evolved over time. The first point to note is that al Qaeda did not spring out of nowhere in 1993. The organization had a "pre-al Qaeda," or zero-phase that was the Arab Services Bureau, also known as the MAK in Arabic. The MAK was created by bin Laden's former mentor and boss, the Palestinian theologian Abdullah 'Azzām. 'Azzām decided that when the Soviets invaded Afghanistan it was a classic case of a foreign invasion of Muslim lands, and defensive jihad was therefore the necessary and legitimate response. 'Azzām realized that the Afghans by themselves could not defeat the Soviet Red Army, and fellow Muslims were therefore called in to assist.

Throughout the 1980s 'Azzām made it his holy mission to recruit other Muslims from around the world to assist their coreligionists in Afghanistan. This is what the MAK was, an organization brought together to recruit, train, and deploy Arab *mujāhidīn*—Jordanians, Yemenis, Saudis—like bin Laden, Egyptians—like Ayman al-Zawahiri, the current head of al Qaeda, to train them in Pakistan and to filter them into Soviet-occupied Afghanistan. This was the beginning of al Qaeda. Then after the Soviets withdrew from Afghanistan in 1988, 'Azzām was assassinated in Pakistan and the whole organization, 50,000 strong, was taken over by bin Laden. Al Qaeda was therefore created out of this Afghanistan guerilla warfare organization.

Looking more closely at the biographies of key al Qaeda players we can identify an interesting dynamic that describes a generational evolution of the new organization now headed by bin Laden. Generation One of al Qaeda, which includes the founding members of the organization, is linked by two factors, age cohort and theater of operations. Generation One includes people who would be in their fifties today, like al-Zawahiri and bin Laden, who fought together against the Soviets in Afghanistan in the 1980s. Generation Two follows from that founding cadre and is made up of the 40-somethings: After bin Laden took control of the organization, looking for a new cause, he asserted that Muslims were suffering in the Balkans. Generation Two is made up of those who were deployed to fight for the Muslims in Bosnia. Generation Three is also linked by age and theater of operation. This generation is made up of the 30-somethings who at the end of the 1990s were sent to Chechnya or other former USSR territories to fight as *mujāhidīn* once again against the Russians. At the same time, the 1990s saw AQAM begin to target not only military occupational forces, but also the "Far Enemy" heartland and its non-military targets as well, be it the first WTC attack in 1993 or the East Africa embassy bombings.

Then after 9/11 a new dynamic developed. As soon as America deployed special forces units and CIA paramilitaries into Afghanistan, the pressure upon 'al Qaeda Central'—the headquarters element of the organization—increased to such an extent that it shifted its operations to the Federally Administered Tribal Areas (FATA) along the border with Pakistan, and then Pakistan proper, where bin Laden would finally be located and killed. And despite the successes of the preliminary phase of the Global War on Terror, al Qaeda was still able from its new locations to inspire further attacks, and in several cases to engage operationally in specific terrorist attacks. Looking at this progression we can understand that al Qaeda is an adaptive threat group which has transformed over time from being a guerilla force fighting military targets in Muslim lands, to being both ideologically and operationally involved with the targeting of civilians outside of any war zone. The history of al Qaeda is thus a story of adaptability and flexibility coupled with a rigid adherence to a religious ideology. For wherever the organization had its base, against whomever it was using violence, it always did so in the name of Allah. Al Qaeda, the enemy threat group, thus has a paradoxical duality: unwavering commitment to its ultimate transcendental cause but a hyperflexible capacity to adjust to a given environment, new theaters of operation, and new targets. It is critical to understand this in order to craft a strategic response.

Looking at the trajectory of U.S. responses to al Qaeda shows how profoundly our interpretation of it—or our misinterpretation—shapes that response. One could start with Charles Krauthammer, who wrote an influential opinion piece on the day after 9/11.[5] In that article Krauthammer said that we now understand the world. The new world order is shaped by the fact that we have an existential threat, and that threat is an organization, not a state. The Soviet Union had been an existential threat from 1948 onwards with its 25,000 nuclear warheads, but now the Soviet Union was gone, replaced by a new threat to our existence in the form of al Qaeda.

This influential article had a clear impact on the Bush Administration following the events of 9/11. However, there were members of the cabinet who disagreed with Krauthammer. Colin Powell, the former Chairman of the Joint Chiefs of Staff, went on record repeatedly stating that al Qaeda was not the enemy; terrorism was the enemy. This is interesting because what is terrorism if not a mode of irregular warfare? Declaring war on a mode of warfare would be akin to saying America is declaring war on air defense or main battle tanks. In the history of warfare we are usually more specific about the nature of the enemy we are facing. Powell's commander, the President, then went on record and said something very different. President Bush said the enemy was not al Qaeda or a form of warfare. In a 2005 speech that would become infamous, the President stated that the enemy is *Islamofascism*.[6] This phrase is very interesting because it includes the term "Fascism," which everyone in America automatically reacts to as being "bad" or "evil," yet also communicates the fact that its followers are exploiting religion. This is a very compact concept; we have a totalitarian ideology that is exclusivist, absolutist, global in its ambitions, but is using the veneer of Islam. After a bad reaction to this phrase, despite the President's repeated assertions that the U.S. is not at war with Islam, the moniker was jettisoned. While one potentially powerful concept was done away with, other descriptions for the enemy abounded. After the invasion of Iraq, the enemy threat group was defined not simply as al Qaeda, but any regime inimical to Washington that may provide weapons of mass destruction to al Qaeda. As al Qaeda moved, under military pressure, from Afghanistan into the FATA region and Pakistan, and later Yemen, statements were made to the effect that "ungoverned spaces" were the enemy. Last but not least, in the last four years another definition of the enemy has evolved.

This very influential concept is associated with General Petraeus and David Kilcullen, his former advisor, and the RAND Corporation, which is the federally funded research facility closest to the Department of Defense. This definition of the enemy sees it as world's first Global Insurgency. Proponents of the view look at al Qaeda and see something unusual about it. In the 20th century the West faced numerous insurgencies; the Viet Cong in Vietnam, the communists in Malaya, the insurgents in Algeria, the Maoists in China, so on. The observation is made that the history of insurgencies describes a pattern. Insurgents focus on the prize of capturing their one particular country: the Vietnamese wanted to become one communist country in Vietnam; the Algerians wanted to capture Northern Algeria from the French; the Malayans wanted to become the government of that nation; and the ultimate insurgent, Mao, wanted to become the Premier of China. Petraeus, Kilcullen and others see al Qaeda as completely different because it is not targeting one country. Al Qaeda is not just about recapturing Afghanistan or Iraq. Al Qaeda wants Jordan, Yemen, Belgium, Spain, the

U.S. It wants everything to be subsumed by the Global Caliphate. The conclusion they thus draw is that al Qaeda is the world's first *global insurgency*, and because of the success of the 'Petraeus Manual,' FM-3-24 on Counterinsurgency, all we need to do is apply our doctrine of counterinsurgency globally. So GWOT, the *Global War on Terror*, should be replaced with GCOIN, *Global Counterinsurgency*. This is not official but it remains a very influential concept. I have written at length on why this is a very problematic idea.[7] The key point about this second lens to our understanding of the enemy, the way we talk about and represent it, is the utter confusion we have demonstrated as a nation in the last ten years. The fact that we can be facing a group that has successfully executed the deadliest terrorist attack in modern history and have completely different descriptions of the threat coming from the highest level of government—from terrorism itself as the foe to a global insurgency—beggars belief. It seems that as the years progress we become more confused and less able accurately to define the threat. This should make us all the more committed to redoubling our attempts at clarity and unity of analysis of the threat. This leads us the third optic for understanding al Qaeda.

The last way we can look at the enemy, which is rarely talked about, and is in fact the most profitable, is al Qaeda in the historic context of Islamic and Arab history. We can go back centuries and centuries, but the most important thing is to place al Qaeda in the last 100 years of Arab and Islamic history, to look at the evolution of the ideology that Patrick Sookhdeo, founder of the Westminster Institute, has accurately called *Global Jihad*.[8] This truly is a global jihad, not a global insurgency, because the individuals involved are not primarily politically motivated; they are primarily religiously motivated, with political goals as important, but secondary.

Five stepping stones in the last 100 years are of core significance to understanding the threat doctrine—the ideology of Global Jihad. The first one is linked to the consequences of World War I. Many commentators have ridiculed bin Laden, Zawahiri and Anwar al-Awlaki for talking about creating a global Caliphate. Commentators have laughed at this concept and pointed to how absurd it would be to create a global religious empire based on the fundamentals of Islam. Those individuals should open a history book, because the Caliphate is not some strange idea cooked up by violent Arabs in a cave in the FATA region of Pakistan. The theocratic Islamic empire existed for centuries in different locations throughout the world; in the Arabian Peninsula, in Mesopotamia, or in Anatolia. The last iteration of the Caliphate existed only 100 years ago in the form of the Ottoman Empire. It is this version of the theocratic empire of Islam that gives us the first date linked to the ideology of Global Jihad.

Problems for the Ottomans began at the start of the 20th century, when they made a geopolitical mistake of historic proportions: they backed the losers in World War I. As a result, they were faced with a very grim future in 1918. They saw the Austro-Hungarian Empire cut up into little parcels and gifted away to new nations such as Yugoslavia. They saw the mighty Russian Empire collapsing into civil war and revolution. The question very quickly became how would they survive having been on the wrong side of World War I? A young and very able Turkish officer by the name of Mustafa Kemal had the answer: the Ottomans would "out-West" the West and show them that their nation could be part of the political community of modern nation-states. Ataturk (Father of Turks), as he would later call himself, decided that the Ottoman Empire would dissolve and become the secular Republic of Turkey. How did Ataturk convince the West not to parcel out the former Ottoman Empire? His first measure was making Arab script illegal. This was a huge change for the Islamic population. Secondly, traditional Islamic and Turkish dress was made illegal. Essentially, overnight, if you worked for the Turkish government, you had to dress like a Westerner instead of in your normal traditional attire and you had to use the roman alphabet.

The third and most important act of Ataturk's in turning the Ottoman Empire into the modern Republic of Turkey was to declare the country secular, officially separating religion from politics. This last measure was implemented by Ataturk in a way that represented a seismic psychological shock to the entire Muslim world, not just to Turks. Ataturk formally dissolved the Caliphate in 1924, thus ending the theocratic empire of Islam. The enormity of this step is a very difficult concept for non-Muslims to comprehend.

The second milestone or psychological shock to Islam, which would later help engender an ideology of jihad, was the consequence of another global conflict, World War II. Two geopolitical factors ran into each other at the end of the war. We have all seen the black and white newsreels of the GIs liberating the death camps and finding piles of bones, shoes, and emaciated bodies. But they also found survivors. Hitler did not kill all the Jews. Therefore in 1945, we had survivors of the Holocaust who had lost their entire families and did not wish to return to their former homes in Germany, Austria or elsewhere in Central or Eastern Europe. This raised this issue of where to send the Jewish survivors of the Holocaust.

At the same time, the British were under attack in Palestine, in the mandate territory that belonged to the Empire. The King David Hotel was bombed and there were calls to free the area from under British control. At this point London decided it had neither the blood nor treasure to maintain Palestine after fighting the Nazis for six years and therefore decided to withdraw. Thus the status of the territory, which had been historically Jewish as well as Arab since antiquity, was indeterminate. The suggestion was made to give the land to the Jews, but, of course, the newly independent Arab nations did not want to lose Palestine to the Jews, since it represented an Islamic "trust", a collective inheritance of the Arabs. Recall that Jerusalem is not important just to Jews and Christians; it is also where Muhammad is supposed to have risen into heaven. In fact, before Muslims prayed toward Mecca they prayed toward Jerusalem. Despite the importance of Palestine to the Arab states and to Islam, the Arabs completely and utterly failed to block the creation of Israel. The Arab leaders therefore lost Palestine, and this was the second monumental shock to the Muslim world of the 20th century. First a Muslim leader had dissolved the religious empire of Islam. Now the Arabs had seen their own leaders lose Palestine to the Jews.

The third milestone is the most important of all and occurs in 1979. One interesting fact about 1979 is that on the lunar calendar that Islam follows this year was actually 1399. There was great expectation associated with the coming of the 15th century and what changes it would bring for Islam. Just as we in the Christian world have had millenarian cults, Islam was pregnant with the idea that something significant was going to happen at the turn of the century. Three very big things did happen. First, we saw the Iranian Revolution, which was seminal in significance for the whole Muslim world despite its being Persian and conducted by Shia. With the deposing of the Shah, Iran sent a message to the West that they fully repudiated the Western model of the nation-state, the separation of church (or mosque) and state, which Khomeini saw as antithetical to Islam. The Revolution would thus see Iran reintegrate faith and politics. This is exactly what you are seeing now in the Arab Spring. From Tunisia to Libya and Egypt we are witness to the reintegration of faith with politics. Iran led the way in 1979 by successfully rejecting what the West sees as one key aspect of modernity. The separation of faith and politics mandated by Ataturk was undone by the events in Tehran and now has become a model for Sunni as well as Shia Muslims.

The second major event of 1979 was the Soviet invasion of Afghanistan. This brought the call to jihad that mobilized people such as Abdullah

'Azzām, bin Laden, and Ayman al-Zawahiri. The last event, which is more important than all of the other events combined, is the siege of Mecca. While the Soviets were becoming embroiled in Afghanistan and the U.S. was trying to rescue its hostages in Tehran, Saudi Arabia witnessed a much more important event. Three hundred jihadists, mostly Saudi but also Yemeni, decided the King of Saudi Arabia was not a true Muslim and that he had betrayed the faith, that Islam was being destroyed from inside by the House of Saud. The jihadists acquired the blessing of several Saudi clerics who agreed with them in saying the King was an apostate and must be removed from power and Islam cleansed. On the very first day of the new century, the jihadists, armed with automatic weapons, captured the Grand Mosque and laid claim to the heart of Islam. For almost two weeks the holiest site in Islam was in the hands of jihadist terrorists.

However, Saudi Arabia in 1979 had no counterterrorism capacity; it had no special forces. Eventually it was the French who would send a group of commandos on a secret mission to assist the King and remove the jihadists (only after they had been formally "converted" to Islam, in order to permit their entry into Mecca).[9] However, in the meantime, the Saudi King found out that the attack mission was sanctioned by Saudi clerics and found out who they were. He then invited them to the Holy Palace and offered them positions as Court Clerics, promising them and their offspring jobs for life if they would guarantee that jihadi ideology would never again threaten the House of Saud or the Saudi regime. Unfortunately for us and for the Muslim world these clerics took the deal offered by the King. More disturbingly, one of the footnotes to that arrangement was that violent jihadi ideology must never again threaten the House of Saud or Saudi Arabia; however its propagation overseas would be not only permissible but also condoned by the House of Saud. How do we know this? One of the most disturbing versions of the Qur'an in English, which has footnotes about Jews and Christians as pigs and donkeys and includes the requirement for good Muslims to acquire weapons of mass destruction to kill the infidel, entitled *The Noble Qur'an*, was until recently the most widely available version of the Qur'an available in federal penitentiaries in the United States.[10] This version of the Qur'an was printed by the government of Saudi Arabia and included the seal of the Grand Mufti of Saudi Arabia. Fortunately six years ago someone in the FBI actually read this version of the Qur'an and it is no longer available in our prisons. However, the important point is that this Qur'an is printed in Saudi Arabia and bears the seal of the Grand Mufti of Saudi Arabia.

The last two connected milestones are the landmark jihadi success stories. 1988 saw the Soviet withdrawal from Afghanistan. If you are bin Laden sitting on a ridgeline watching the Red Army retreat through your binoculars to Uzbekistan who do you think won that war? Of course, he and his 50,000 *mujāhidīn*, not the Afghans. The jihadis believed they had defeated a superpower that three years later would collapse. Thus, not only had the Holy Warriors of Islam militarily defeated a superpower; they had destroyed it, since God was on their side.

The last milestone on the evolution of jihadi ideology was the connected events of 1990 and 1991. This began with Saddam Hussein's invasion of Kuwait, located next to Saudi Arabia. In 1991 bin Laden was still a Saudi national. His father, Mohammed bin Laden, had built the largest contracting company in Saudi Arabia, which had been contracted to repair the Grand Mosque following the 1979 siege. (Most of the highways built in Saudi Arabia from U.S. petrodollars were contracted out to the bin Laden Group and Mohammed bin Laden.) Because of this relationship, Osama bin Laden had very close connections to the House of Saud. He saw his country come under threat from a secular, Arab, Stalinist dictator— Saddam Hussein— whom he would have considered just as much an enemy as the Soviet Union since Hussein was not a "true" Muslim. Osama bin Laden traveled to the royal palace and asked for an audience with the king.[11] Bin Laden said to the king, "My Holy Warriors have just vanquished the Soviet Union. Allow me as a good Saudi national to protect my homeland from the apostate." But in 1990 the Iraqi Army was the largest in the Middle East. It had millions of men in uniform, and the king rejected bin Laden's offer. Bin Laden was further insulted by the king's refusal when the king then asked the U.S. to protect the two holy sites. Remember, if you are bin Laden, it is not America that is coming to help protect his country, it is the "Zionist Crusaders." The Zionist Crusaders, with the blessing of the King of Saudi Arabia, are going to deploy to the holiest country in the Muslim world.

It is clear to me that this is the point when something snapped in bin Laden. He had been the head of a guerilla organization training to fight Russians, Serbs, and Croats who were militarily oppressing Muslims in Central Asia, the Balkans, or the Caucuses. Then something changed. His own king rejected him and relied instead on the Zionist crusaders. This clearly pushed bin Laden to create the al Qaeda as we know it today. The organization went from an international guerilla organization to an international terrorist organization. Within months bin Laden was stripped of his Saudi citizenship for making statements against the king, and within two years, in 1993, the first World Trade Center attack occurred. This is the progression of al Qaeda's ideology of Global Jihad, triggered by key 20th century events. This is how Global Jihad fits into a longer chain of Arab and Muslim events.

Crucial Dates in the Evolution of the Ideology of Global Jihad

1918-1924	End of Caliphate
1945-1948	Creation of Israel
1979	Iranian Revolution, the Siege of Mecca, Soviet Invasion of Afghanistan
1988	Soviet Withdrawal from Afghanistan
1990-1	Fall of USSR and Gulf War I

THE STRATEGIC MINDS BEHIND GLOBAL JIHAD

What is the ideology of al Qaeda and its Associated Movements today? How do we penetrate the mind of the threat group we face across the world and inside our own country? To understand that enemy today, it is important to know at least four key jihadi ideologues. The first individual, Sayyid Qutb, the Egyptian bureaucrat, is the key ideological, doctrinal and strategic master of the Muslim Brotherhood. His book, *Milestones*, is available in any Muslim cultural bookstore in Northern Virginia today. This is the "how to" manual for the Muslim Brotherhood on achieving global victory for Allah. The book is based upon Qutb's two years in America on an exchange program in Colorado, California, and Washington, during which Qutb decided that the United States was a godless, sex-obsessed, materialistic, heretic nation that must be destroyed.

Milestones has a very clear message, one that goes back to the pre-history of Islam. Qutb says the world is again in a state of *jāhiliyya*, mirroring the state of pagan ignorance of Allah that Muhammad found in Mecca when the Koran was revealed to him. Mecca had been a site of pilgrimage for centuries before Muhammad was born, but it was primarily a site of pilgrimage for polytheist pagans to worship their multiple gods. That state of pagan ignorance and worshipping things that are not Allah is called *jāhiliyya*. Qutb reaches back to the 7th century and uses this word and wrenches it into the 1950s and states that we are again in a state of *jāhiliyya* and must cleanse the world of its ignorance of Allah. The only way to do that, according to Qutb, is through jihad, through holy war. In a direct quote, Qutb states, "Islam is not a religion, it is a revolutionary party." It is no accident that this book lifts heavily from Marxist, Leninist and fascist doctrine. Qutb lifts whole concepts, such as the "vanguard" from Lenin and Marx, which will be used by 'Azzām and bin Laden years later. Qutb built a whole new theology of Islamic jihad exploiting Western totalitarian ideologies. Qutb was eventually arrested by Nasser's regime and executed, and he became a martyr to the Muslim Brotherhood cause.

The second individual is Abdullah 'Azzām, who was the creator of the MAK or pre-al Qaeda, and served as bin Laden's former mentor and boss. This man is special in the constellation of jihadi ideologues because he had a PhD in Islamic Jurisprudence from the most important university in Islam, Al Azhar, the university where President Obama gave his infamous Cairo speech in 2009. In Islam, credentialing and reputation are even more important than they are in the West, so the fact that 'Azzām had a PhD in Islamic jurisprudence meant that when he issued a fatwa it was a real fatwa. 'Azzām wrote a book that was a seventy-page fatwa titled *In Defense of Muslim Lands*. In it he argues that because Ataturk dissolved the Caliphate and there is no Caliph who can declare war, jihad is now *fard'ayn*, meaning holy war is now the individual obligation of every good Muslim. This obligation is no longer a collective obligation that would be initiated by the Caliph; instead Muslims must take it upon themselves to self-deploy to defend Muslim lands. 'Azzām went on to say that a Muslim did not need permission from anyone to declare jihad; not parents, wife, or even husband (this last idea being very radical in Arab culture).

The third important ideologue is now the head of al Qaeda since bin Laden's death. His name is Ayman al Zawahiri, an Egyptian from an influential Cairo family. He was not some kind of loser from the fringes of society. One grandfather was the Secretary of the Arab League; the other was the Imam of the Al Azam Mosque. This is a man embedded in the elite of Egyptian society. Zawahiri is a medical doctor who was a member of the Muslim Brotherhood and a founding member of the Islamic Egyptian Jihad or EIJ. He was considered a radical in Egypt, arrested, tortured, and released from prison in 1982. He then went on jihad. He travelled to Pakistan and began to give medical assistance to the jihadis fighting the Soviets, which is where he met bin Laden. This is where we first see the puritanical Wahhabi jihadism of bin Laden meld with this other brand of Egyptian fundamentalism. The melding of these two strains of jihad gives us the al Qaeda we know today.

The last individual is the most important of all but very few people have ever heard of him, even in the American intelligence community. He is Brigadier S. K. Malik. If you read only one person to understand the enemy, read S.K. Malik's book, *The Quranic Concept of Power.* Malik was a General in the Pakistani Army and in 1979 he wrote a book unlike any book in the canon of Western literature. This man is the equivalent of a Thomist theologian combined with von Clausewitz or Jomini. For Malik was a man writing a strategy of war—a theological strategy of war for Islam.

Particularly noteworthy is the identity of those who sanctioned the writing of his book. The foreword was written by the equivalent of our acting Attorney General, who fully endorsed the text. The introduction of the book was written by General Zia ul-Haq, the commander of all Pakistani forces, who, after a coup, became the President of Pakistan. Hence this was not an unrepresentative text by a marginalized author.

The book delivers three messages: First, it repudiates the Clausewitzian concept of war as the continuation of politics by other means (i.e., when other tools such as economics or diplomacy are inadequate to protect the national interest one must use violence or war to achieve those ends). General Malik completely rejects this concept by saying that not only does war have nothing to do with the national interest; in fact it has nothing to do with the nation-state since the nation-state is a heretical Western invention. According to Malik, war only ever has one purpose and that is the realization of Allah's sovereignty on this earth. It does not matter where one is fighting, or when you are fighting, because war can only ever serve the realization of Allah's sovereignty here on earth.

The second message of the book again repudiates Clausewitzian theory and the idea of centers-of-gravity in warfare. In military academies around the world officers are taught to target the enemy's weaknesses and locate so-called centers-of-gravity, to attack those vulnerabilities which, if they are hit hard enough, will cause the enemy to crumble. Malik said that there is no such thing as multiple centers-of-gravity, or even a physical center-of-gravity in war. His book states that there is only one center-of-gravity in warfare, and that is the soul of your enemy, the faith system of the enemy. That is what you must crush if you wish to win in war.

Thirdly, and linked to the latter argument, Malik states that since the soul is the only center-of-gravity that counts, the best weapon in war is terror. A general in the Pakistani Army, endorsed by the President of Pakistan, thus told the world back in 1979 that 9/11 is the kind of attack one should execute if you want to win a war. This is not how the United States or any of her allies understands war. But it is how our enemy does, and so our own understanding must expand to include an enemy who can think this way. Instead, either we have insisted that terrorists are irrational, or we have stripped all religious motivation from them by insisting they are merely violent extremists. If we posit our own motivations for war onto this enemy, we will completely misunderstand him.

AL QAEDA, THE MUSLIM BROTHERHOOD AND THE MODERN WAY OF IRREGULAR WAR

The last topic I wish to discuss revolves around the strategy being used by al Qaeda. Irregular warfare is waged much more often than conventional warfare and this has been the case throughout most of history.[12] Interestingly there are really only two complete theories on how to wage irregular warfare. The first one was developed by Che Guevara. Guevara established what is called the *focoist* concept of insurgencies. To Guevara this meant that one did not have to build a large movement; one just had to lead by example. An insurgent leader only had to go out into the jungle of Latin America and lead by fearless, Marxist example and the people would be in awe of the insurgent, drop their hoes and their pitchforks and join the revolution. Nothing more than personal, catalytic example is required. As history demonstrated, Che Guevara's top-down approach was wrong and that is why he died a young man. The focoist theory does not work.[13]

The other school is the real school of irregular warfare, and that is the *people's war* approach of Mao Zedong. Mao understood how to defeat powerful countries. In fact it is not an overstatement to say that Mao is to irregular warfare what Clausewitz is to conventional inter-state war. Mao wrote that if you wanted to beat a powerful country like the Nationalist Chinese government, the United States or another great nation, you must build your movement from the ground up. You conduct a people's war by going out into the countryside to motivate and recruit the disenfranchised to your cause; you appoint local agitators and you build a "counter-state" or an oppositional shadow government. You must provide services to win over the population, not just apply violence.

Back in 2001, bin Laden was a Guevarist. By hitting the most important economic, military, and political symbols of the United States he expected a groundswell that would motivate the *umma*, the world community of Islam, to rise up in holy war and vanquish the infidel. He did not understand that if you are fighting a very powerful enemy you have to be a Maoist; you must use the indirect approach, as do Hamas and Hezbollah. These organizations understand that you need to win over the population by building health clinics, opening schools, providing welfare aid and building ideologically vetted "cultural centers." These institutions are all parts of the counter-state. What we have seen over the past ten years on the jihadi web blogs is that the enemy is learning and now understands that it is not all about frontal assaults and large-scale symbolic acts of violence, but about building a "mass-base," providing services, establishing no-go areas in the banlieue of Marseille and Paris, providing shari'a-compliant mortgages in Northern Virginia, or Wahhabi-funded "cultural centers" in Minnesota.

STARTING AFRESH: INTELLECTUAL HONESTY AND THE WAR ON AQAM

The official decision in recent years to use the term "violent extremism" to describe the threat is misleading and deleterious to our ability to understand and defeat the enemy we face. America is not at war with all forms of violent extremism. The attacks of September 11th were the work not of a group of terrorists motivated by a generic form of extremism. We are not at war with communists, Fascists, nationalists, or eco-terrorists, but with religiously inspired mass-murderers who consistently cite the Qur'an to justify their actions. Denying this fact simply out of a misguided sensitivity to other Muslims will delay our ability to understand the nature of this conflict and to delegitimize our foe. By analogy, imagine if in the 20th century fight against the Ku Klux Klan federal law enforcement had been forbidden from describing the group they were trying to neutralize as white supremacists or racists, or if during World War II, for political reasons, we forbade our forces from understanding the enemy as a Nazi regime fueled and guided by a fascist ideology of racial hatred, but forced them to call the enemy "violent extremists" instead. We did not do it then and we must not do it now. The safety of America's citizens and our chances of eventual victory depend upon our being able to call the enemy by its proper name: Global Jihadism.[14]

To conclude, the last ten years since September 11th, 2001, can be summarized as a vast collection of tactical and operational successes but a vacuum in terms of strategic understanding and strategic response. To paraphrase a former U.S. Marine who knows the enemy very well and whom I greatly respect, we have failed to understand the enemy at any more than an operational level and have instead, by default, addressed the enemy solely on the operational plane of engagement. Operationally we have become most proficient at responding to the localized threats caused by al Qaeda, but those localized threats are simply tactical manifestations of what is happening at the strategic level and driven by the ideology of Global Jihad. As a result, by not responding to what al Qaeda has become at the strategic level, we continue to attempt to engage it on the wrong battlefield.[15]

The tenth anniversary of the attacks in Washington, in New York, and in Pennsylvania afforded those in the U.S. government who have sworn to uphold and defend the national interests a clear opportunity to recognize what has been accomplished and what needs to be reassessed. We must recommit ourselves to attacking this deadliest of enemies at the level which it deserves to be—and must be—attacked, which is the strategic. Osama bin Laden may be dead, but his ideology of global supremacy through religious war is more vibrant and appealing to audiences around the world than it was on the day before the attacks more than a decade ago. As a result, we must at last remove the often politically constructed obstacles that hinder our capacity to identify the enemy accurately. The executive branch must then produce a comprehensive understanding of the enemy threat doctrine that is Global Jihadism, a document akin to Kennan's foundational analysis that eventually led to the Truman Doctrine and its exquisite operationalization in Paul Nitze's plan for containment, NSC-68.

We must also recognize that this war is potentially more dangerous than even the Cold War. Why did the system of mutually assured destruction (MAD) work during for more than four decades? Because both sides of that conflict enjoyed life too much to press the button. Worldly survival drove not only us, the West, but also our foes, the Soviet Union. But if your enemy is convinced not only that will he go directly to heaven if he dies trying to kill you but that he can also vouch entry into heaven for his best friends and family members, why would he not press that button immediately? Weapons of mass destruction are therefore very attractive to our current enemy, not as bargaining chips, but as keys to paradise.

But instead of going in this direction, acknowledging the ideology that motivates our enemy and using language to reflect that reality, the White House is taking measures to make it even more difficult to discuss the enemy threat doctrine. There are two enemy groups out there that wish us dead or enslaved. The first one, the kinetic terrorists or violent jihadists, is the one

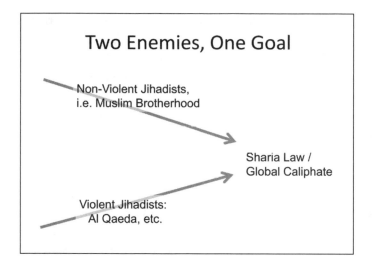

that the media and the U.S. Government obsess over. The second group, which far outweighs the first group in their overall impact and numbers, is the nonviolent jihadists, such as the Muslim Brotherhood. It is vital to understand that these groups are linked. Their strategic end state is exactly the same: a global Caliphate under shari'a law. If we fail to understand this and focus all of our resources on the first group we are going to wake up one morning to realize that we have already lost the war.

Endnotes

Introduction

1. Nashin Arbabzadah, "The 1980s Mujahideen, the Taliban and the Shifting Idea of Jihad," *The Guardian*, April 28, 2011.

2. "The U.S. and the Middle East in a Changing World," speech by Edward P. Djerejian, Assistant Secretary of State for Near Eastern and South Asian Affairs, presented at Meridian House International, June 2, 1992, reprinted in *The DISAM Journal*, Summer 1992, pp. 32-38, http://www.disam.dsca.mil/pubs/Vol%2014_4/ Djerejian.pdf, accessed February 18, 2012.

3. Ibid., p. 45.

4. http://georgewbush-whitehouse.archives.gov/news/releases/2001/09/20010917-11.html, accessed February 29, 2012.

5. *The 9/11 Commission Report: Final Report of the National Commission on Terrorist Attacks Upon the United States*, U.S. Government, p. 51.

6. *National Strategy for Counterterrorism*, The White House, June 2011.

7. Quintan Wiktorowiz, "Anatomy of the Salafi Movement," *Studies in Conflict and Terrorism* 29, 2006, p. 234.

8. *Manhaj* refers to the methodology of implementing the beliefs and laws of Islam. The Salafists espouse a *manhaj* that rejects innovation, reason, and interpretation and aspire instead to a pure adherence to the ways of the Qur'an, the Hadith and the Sunna.

9. Quintan Wiktorowicz, "The New Global Threat: Transnational Salafis and Jihad," *Middle East Policy*, Vol. VIII, No. 4, December 2001, pp. 29-30.

10. Homeland Security Advisory Council, Countering Violent Extremism (CVE) Working Group, Spring 2010, http://www.dhs.gov/xlibrary/assets/hsac_cve_working_group_recommendations.pdf, accessed January 23, 2012.

11. Katharine C. Gorka, "White House Review Threatens Counter-Terrorism Operations," http://www.westminster-institute.org/articles/white-house-review-threatens-counter-terrorism-operations/, accessed February 29, 2012.

12. *Empowering Local Partners to Prevent Violent Extremism in the United States*, The White House, August 2011.

13. "Screening Process for Countering Violent Extremism (CVE) Trainers and Speakers," Joint Staff Action Processing Form, November 10, 2011, Action Number 11-04328. Unclassified.

14. Quintan Wiktorowicz, "The New Global Threat."

Chapter 1

1. Frank Kitson, *Low Intensity Operations: Subversion, Insurgency, and Peacekeeping* (London: Faber and Faber, 1971), p. 78.

2. Stephen P. Lambert, *The Sources of Islamic Revolutionary Conduct* (Washington, DC: Center for Strategic Intelligence Research, Joint Military Intelligence College, 2005), p. 171.

3. Sami Zubaida, "Islam, Religion and Ideology," *openDemocracy*, February 14, 2007.

4. *The 9/11 Commission Report*, http://www.9-11commission.gov/report/911Report.pdf, p. 363, accessed August 12, 2011.

5. "James Glassman on Combating Ideology," *The Washington Note*, July 24, 2008, http://www.thewashingtonnote.com/archives/2008/07/one_of_the_cent/, accessed August 12, 2011.

6. Stephen Ulph, *Towards a Curriculum for the Teaching of Jihadist Ideology, Part II: The Doctrinal Frame* (Washington, DC: Jamestown Foundation, 2010), p. 6.

7. Andrew Gamble, "The Western Ideology," *Government and Opposition*, Vol. 44, No.1, 2009, pp. 1-19.

8. Sarah Johnson, "Is the Deradicalisation of Islamist Extremists Possible in a Secular Society Such as Britain?" *POLIS Journal*, Vol. 2, Winter 2009.

9. Tony Blair, quoted in "Full Text: Blair Speech on Terror," *BBC NEWS*, July 16, 2005.

10. "Tony Blair Denies Military Action Radicalised Muslims," *BBC NEWS*, September 10, 2011.

11. Stephen Ulph, *Towards a Curriculum for the Teaching of Jihadist Ideology, Part I: Introduction—Problems of Perception* (Washington DC: Jamestown Foundation, 2010), p. 2.

12. Mumtaz Ahmad, ed., *State Politics and Islam* (Indianapolis, IN: American Trust Publications, 1986), p. 507.

13. Jacquelyn K. Davis and Charles M. Perry, "Rethinking the War on Terror, Developing a Strategy to Counter Extremist Ideologies: A Workshop Report," March 2007, organized for U.S. Central Command (CENTCOM) with the support of The Defence Threat Reduction Agency (DTRA) under contract IIDTRA1-06-F-0054.

14. Delwar Hussein, "Globalization, God and Galloway: The Islamization of Bangladeshi Communities in London," *Journal of Creative Communications*, Vol. 2, 2007, p. 189.

15. "Islamism," *Almuslih.org*, http://almuslih.org/index.php?option=com_content &view=section&layout=blog&id=13&Itemid=242, accessed September 12, 2011.

16. Ulph, *Towards a Curriculum, Part I*, p. 2.

17. Michael Nazir-Ali, "Behind and Beyond 9/11," *IDEA*, September / October 2011.

18. Lambert, "Sources," pp. 155-157.

19. "Understanding Islamism," International Crisis Group, Middle East/North Africa Report No. 37, March 2, 2005.

20. Ulph, *Towards a Curriculum, Part I*, p. 10.

21. Gabriel Ben-Dor, "The Uniqueness of Islamic Fundamentalism," in Bruce Maddy-Weitzman and Efraim Inbar, eds., *Religious Radicalism in the Greater Middle East* (London: Frank Cass, 1997), p. 241; John L. Esposito, *The Islamic Threat: Myth or Reality?* (New York: Oxford University Press, 1992), pp. 22-23.

22. Bernard Lewis, *The Political Language of Islam* (Chicago: University of Chicago Press, 1991), p. 92.

23. Nasr Hamid Abu Zaid, "Brutality and Civilisation—Violence and Terrorism?" in Jochen Hippler, *War, Repression, Terrorism* (Stuttgart: Institut fur Auslandsbeziehungen, 2006), pp. 301-329.

24. Ulph, *Towards a Curriculum, Part I*, pp. 11-12.

25. Abdel Salam Sidahmed and Anoushirvan Ehteshami, eds., *Islamic Fundamentalism* (Boulder, CO: Westview Press, 1996), p. 1.

26. Laura Guazzone, "Islamism and Islamists in the Contemporary Arab World," in Laura Guazzone, ed., *The Islamist Dilemma: The Political Role of Islamist Movements in the Contemporary Arab World* (Reading: Ithaca Press, 1995), pp. 10-12.

27. Kalim Siddiqui, *Stages of Islamic Revolution* (London: The Open Press, 1996), pp. 30, 74.

28. Ghulam Sarwar, "Challenges Facing Islam and the Muslim Ummah," http://www.defencejournal.com/feb-mar99/challenges-islam.htm, accessed September 1, 2011.

29. Ulph, *Towards a Curriculum, Part I*, pp. 12-13.

30. Ibid.

31. Thomas Hegghammer, "The Ideological Hybridization of Jihadi Groups," in Hillel Fradkin, Husain Haqqani, Eric Brown, and Hassan Mneimneh, eds., *Current Trends in Islamist Ideology*, Vol. 9, Hudson Institute, November 2009.

32. Ayman al-Zawahiri, *Exoneration* (OR *A Treatise Exonerating the Nation of the Pen and the Sword from the Blemish of the Accusation of Weakness and Fatigue*), published in March 2008 on various jihadi websites, http://www.fas.org/irp/dni/osc/exoneration.pdf, accessed April 23, 2010.

33. Ulph, *Towards a Curriculum, Part I*, p. 11.

34. 'Abdullah 'Azzām, *Defence of the Muslim Lands* (Ahle Sunnah Wal Jama'at, nd), pp. 4-6.

35. 'Abdullah 'Azzām, quoted in Raymond Ibrahim, "An Analysis of Al-Qa'ida's Worldview: Reciprocal Treatment or Religious Obligation?" *Middle East Review of International Affairs (MERIA)*, Vol. 12, No. 3, September 2008.

36. Arnaud De Borchgrave, "The Jihad Rages In Cyberspace," UPI, October 24, 2006, http://www.spacewar.com/reports/The_Jihad_Rages_In_Cyberspace_999.html, accessed September 7, 2011.

37. Riaz Hassan, "Globalization's Challenge to Islam," *YaleGlobal*, April 17, 2003, http://yaleglobal.yale.edu/display.article?id=1417, accessed January 21, 2009.

38. Robert A. Saunders, "The Ummah as Nation: A Reappraisal in the Wake of the 'Cartoons Affair'," *Nations and Nationalism*, Vol. 14, No. 2, 2008, pp. 304-305, 310, 312-313, 316.

39. De Borchgrave, "The Jihad Rages."

40. Saunders, "The Ummah as Nation," pp. 304-305, 310, 312-313, 316.

41. Ibid.

42. Ibid., p. 308.

43. *Al-Qaeda's Senior Leadership (AQSL)*, A Jane's Strategic Advisory Services (JSAS) supplement, janes.com/consulting, November 2009.

44. Anwar al Awlaki, "Nidal Hasan Did the Right Thing," *Anwar al Awlaki On-Line*, November 9, 2009, http://www.anwar-alawlaki.com/?p=228target=_blank.

45. Ulph, *Towards a Curriculum, Part I*, p. 11.

46. Olivier Roy, *Globalised Islam: The Search for a New Ummah* (London: Hurst & Co. 2004), p. 284.

47. Sami Zubaida, "Islam, Religion and Ideology," *openDemocracy*, February 14, 2007.

48. Formerly called The Organisation of the Islamic Conference. The OIC has 57 member states and is a major voting bloc in the UN.

49. Abdulaziz Othman Altwaijri, "The Civilizational Role of the Muslim Umma in Tomorrow's World," *Islamic Educational, Scientific and Cultural Organization (ISESCO)*, 2007, http://www.isesco.org.ma/english/publications/Islamtoday/18/P4.php, accessed January 19, 2009. ISESCO is one of the many daughter organizations of the OIC.

50. Saad S. Khan, *Reasserting International Islam: A Focus on the Organization of the Islamic Conference and Other Islamic Institutions* (Oxford: Oxford University Press, 2001), p. 332.

51. Altwaijri, "Civilizational Role."

52. "Canadian PM Criticized by Islamic Group," digital journal, http://digitaljournal.com/article/311505, accessed September 19, 2011.

53. Ulph, *Towards a Curriculum, Part I*, pp. 13-15.

54. *National Security Strategy* (Washington, DC: The White House, May 2010), p. 22, http://www.whitehouse.gov/sites/default/files/rss_viewer/national_security_strategy.pdf.

55. Ewen MacAskill, "CIA Chief Claims al-Qaida Essentially Defeated in Iraq and Saudi Arabia," *The Guardian*, May 30, 2008, http://www.guardian.co.uk/world/2008/may/30/usa.alqaida.

56. "Osama a Casualty of the Arab revolt," *Asia Times Online*, May 3, 2011.

57. Mai Yamani, "Bin Laden's Ghost," *Today's Zaman*, May 3, 2011.

58. J. M. Berger, "The Long War's Long Tail," *Foreign Policy* 30, August 2011.

59. For example, Fred Halliday, the noted academic expert on the Middle East, argued that theology was no explanation for Islamism. A wider framework shorn of religious baggage was needed. Neo-colonialism, economic exploitation, underdevelopment and regime corruption offered a better explanation for jihadi use of violence. See Fred Halliday, "Irregular Warfare and the Modern Middle East: From Mirza Kuchik Khan to Osama bin Laden," lecture delivered at the Conference "Rethinking Jihad," Centre for the Advanced Study of the Arab World, Edinburgh University, September 7-9, 2009.

60. Ulph, *Towards a Curriculum, Part I*, p. 16.

61. De Borchgrave, "The Jihad Rages."

62. Remarks by John Brennan, Assistant to the President for Homeland Security and Counterterrorism, White House Briefing, *Lexisnexis*, August 6, 2009, http://www6.lexisnexis.com/publisher/EndUser?Action=UserDisplayFullDocument&orgId=574&topicId=25188&docId=l:1018813300&start=6.

63. National Security Strategy, May 2010, p. 22, http://www.whitehouse.gov/sites/default/files/rss_viewer/national_security_strategy.pdf.

64. Ulph, *Towards a Curriculum, Part I*, p. 13.

65. "There's Willful Blindness, and Then There's Willful Stupidity," *The National Review Online*, February 11, 2011, http://www.nationalreview.com/corner/259500/theres-willful-blindness-and-then-theres-willful-stupidity-andrew-c-mccarthy#, accessed August 24, 2011.

66. David Cameron, Full transcript, Speech on Radicalization and Islamic Extremism, Munich, Germany, February 5, 2011, *New Statesman*, February 5, 2011.

67. Lorenzo Vidino, "The Muslim Brotherhood in the West: Evolution and Western Policies," The International Centre for the Study of Radicalisation and Political Violence (ICSR), February 2011, pp. 36-38.

68. Ibid.

69. Jamie Bartlett, Jonathan Birdwell, and Michael King, *The Edge Of Violence* (London: Demos, 2010), pp. 49-52.

70. Michael Mumisa, "The civil war among Muslims in Britain," *The Independent (blogs Notebook)*, December 1, 2010.

71. Liberation theology is a Christian theological position that emphasizes justice for the poor and release from the captivity of oppressive social and political conditions, based especially on the book of Exodus. See for example, Naim Ateek, *Justice, and Only Justice: A Palestinian Theology of Liberation* (Orbis Books, Maryknoll, NY, 1989).

72. Bartlett et al, *Edge Of Violence*, p. 53.

73. Lorenzo Vidino, "Europe's New Security Dilemma," *The Washington Quarterly*, October 2009.

74. Ibid.

75. Bartlett et al, *Edge Of Violence*, p. 53.

76. "Theresa May: 'We will not make the same mistakes' on terror," Channel 4 News, June 7, 2011, http://www.channel4.com/news/theresa-may-we-will-not-make-the-same-mistakes-on-terror , accessed March 5, 2012; "Islamist Hatemongers Funded by the Taxpayer with Money Earmarked for Schools," *Daily Mail*, June 8, 2011.

77. *Prevent Strategy*, Presented to Parliament by the Secretary of State for the Home Department by Command of her Majesty, June 2011, p. 8, http://www.homeoffice.gov.uk/publications/counter-terrorism/prevent/prevent-strategy/prevent-strategy-review?view=Binary.

78. Katharine C. Gorka, "White House Review Threatens Counter-Terrorism Operations," http://www.westminster-institute.org/articles/white-house-review-threatens-counter-terrorism-operations/#more-959; Clifford D. May, "What's Islam Got to Do with It?" *National Review Online*, December 15, 2011, http://www.nationalreview.com/articles/285815/what-s-islam-got-do-it-clifford-d-may.

79. *Strategic Implementation Plan for Empowering Local Partners to prevent Violent Extremism in the United States*, Executive Office of the President of the United States, December 2011, p. 1.

80. Lambert, pp. 155-157.

81. Davis and Perry, "Rethinking the War on Terror."

82. "Pulling Together to Defeat Terror," Quilliam Foundation, April 2008, http://www.quilliamfoundation.org/images/stories/pdfs/pulling-together-to-defeat-terror.pdf, accessed November 10, 2008.

83. M. Zuhdi Jasser, "Islamism, not Islam is the Problem," *The Family Security Foundation, Inc.*, May 8, 2007.

84. Peter Riddell, "Sorry, But the Qur'an Does Contain Support for Terror," *Church Times*, September 2, 2005.

85. "What is Progressive Islam?" *ISIM Newsletter*, No. 13, December 2003; Radwan A. Masmoudi, "The Silenced Majority," *Islam 21*, Issue No. 34, May 2003, http://islam21.net/quarterly/Islam21-May03.pdf, accessed August 11, 2005.

86. http://almuslih.com/. See also Robert R. Reilly, "Will the Arab Spring turn into winter?" *Mercatornet*, September 12, 2011, http://www.mercatornet.com/articles/view/will_the_arab_spring_turn_into_winter, accessed September 14, 2011.

87. Jamie Glazov, "Symposium: The Islamic Reformation?" *FrontPageMagazine*, August 13, 2004.

88. "Statement issued by the International Islamic Conference," *The Official Website of The Amman Message*, http://ammanmessage.com/index.php?option=com_content&task=view&id=20&Itemid=34, accessed September 14, 2011.

89. His Majesty King Abdullah II, Speech from the Throne at the opening of the First Ordinary Session of the Fifteenth Parliament, December 2, 2007, http://www.jordanembassyus.org/new/jib/speeches/hmka/hmka12022007.htm, accessed September 14, 2011.

90. Riddell, "Sorry."

91. *AQSL*.

92. Al-Zawahiri, *Exoneration*.

93. Julian Lewis, "Double-I, Double-N: A Framework for Counter-Insurgency," *RUSI Journal*, February 2008.

94. Ibid.

95. Ibid.

96. Ibid.

97. Stephen Ulph, "Vulnerabilities in the Ideology of Jihad," transcript of a lecture at the Westminster Institute, December 10, 2009; and "Memorandum on Developing a Counter Strategy Against the Ideology of the Jihad," Jamestown Foundation, June 2006.

Chapter 2

1. Bertrand Russell, *The Practice and Theory of Bolshevism* (London: George Allen and Unwin, 1920), pp. 5, 29, 114.

2. Carl Jung, *The Symbolic Life*, The Collected Works, Volume 18 (Princeton: Princeton University Press 1939), p. 281.

3. Karl Barth, *The church and the political problem of our day* (New York: Scribner, 1939).

4. Jules Monnerot, *Sociology and Psychology of Communism* (*Sociologie du communisme*), trans. Jane Degras and Richard Rees (London: Allen & Unwin, 1953).

5. Manfred Halpern, *The Politics of Social Change in the Middle East and North Africa*, USAF Project RAND, September 1963, p. 136.

6. Walter Laqueur, *The Origins of Fascism: Islamic Fascism, Islamophobia, Antisemitism* (New York: Oxford University Press, 2006).

7. While fascist systems are consistently chauvinistic, not all resemble the German National Socialists' focus on a purity of lineage. Fascism is better understood in this feature as a form of cultural and spiritual tribalism. Islamism can be considered to share this form of tribalism provided this is understood in the sense of its "exclusive universalism," as if Islam and its values (which admit of no external influence or competition) constituted an overarching super-tribe. Such a conception resolves the conundrum of Islamism as a call to freedom for all mankind (as opposed to the exclusiveness of Nazi Fascism, or the call to domination), but a freedom which is not based on psychological, individualised freedom, but rather on a gradated freedom, with Muslims at the top. The primacy is cultural, and is open to all to accede to. But it is no less exclusivist in the sense that it tolerates no free market-place of ideas, and prescribes severe sanctions against those who attempt to take the openness of access in the opposite direction.

8. Due to Islamic historical and legal tradition, the cultural totalitarianism (as opposed to hegemony) of the "ruling class" of Muslims in this layered society-to-be applies to everything outside this *dhimma*. The totalitarian control is over the external fabric of the shari'a-ruled state, but the exclusivity operates by exclusion, disadvantage and disenfranchisement. The issue is whether one can conceive of an enforced category of inferiority, such as that which the *dhimma* represents, as constituting a negation of totalitarianism, or merely another one of its permutations.

9. While statistically less significant, there is evidence of self-sacrificial acts perpetrated in the cause of political totalitarianisms. For instance, under communism the self-image of the protagonists was that they were fighting for what they conceived was a cosmic good. David Satter notes that "During the Second World War, this attitude was regularly manifested as Soviet soldiers volunteered for suicide missions and threw themselves under tanks, shouting 'For Stalin!'" (David Satter, "The Key to Defeating Radical Islam," in *FrontPage Magazine*, October 20, 2009). Whereas in jihadism dying for the cause is based primarily on the deferred reward, nevertheless, the cause of the martyr is equally invested in the prospect of an Islamic nation on earth.

10. Originally a term referring to the era of pre-Islamic paganism, but used by contemporary Islamists to constitute no longer a historical but a *qualitative* definition of Disbelief, a state of "ignorant depravity".

11. ملثم هنإف هعم نكسو كرشملا عماج نم (Sunan Abī Da'ūd: Book 14, Hadith 2781).

12. Where Islamism, among these parallels, demonstrates greater strength is in the common totalitarian preoccupation with authenticity and the appeal made to the restoration of "true, pristine values." As opposed to the weak cultural embedding of Fascism or Marxism-Leninism, the ideology of Islamism can call upon a long doc trinal tradition extending over a millennium from which to extract elements that underpin the movement. This makes for a much stronger case for indoctrination and adds considerably to the ideology's resilience.

13. Emilio Gentile, "Fascism, Totalitarianism and Political Religion: Definitions and Critical Reflections on Criticism of an Interpretation," in Roger Griffin, ed., *Fascism, Totalitarianism and Political Religion* (New York: Routledge, 2005), p. 33.

14. For instance, the Italian historian Renzo De Felice insisted that there was no connection or valid comparisons to be drawn between Italian Fascism and German National Socialism, which he saw as being a completely different political ideology. He also argued that there were two types of Fascism, Fascism as a *movement* and Fascism as a *regime*, arguing that Mussolini's system was an example only of the latter, that is, a superstructure for his dictatorship and personal power.

15. Cf. Giovanni Gentile and Benito Mussolini, "Il fascismo, oltre a essere un sistema di governo, è anche, e prima di tutto, un sistema di pensiero" ("More than a system of government, Fascism is also, and above all, a system of thought"), "La dottrina del fascism," *Enciclopedia Italiana* (1932).

16. Umberto Eco, "Ur-Fascism," *New York Review of Books*, June 22, 1995.

17. Professor Roger Griffin is a British academic political theorist whose major work *The Nature of Fascism* (1991) established the first new theory of generic Fascism for over a decade, a theory that continues to have an influence on the "new consensus" now emerging in fascist studies among political scientists and historians.

18. Roger Griffin, "The palingenetic core of generic fascist ideology," in Alessandro Campi, ed., *Che cos'è il fascismo? Interpretazioni e prospettive di ricerche* (Rome: Ideazione editrice, 2003), pp. 97-122.

19. Ibid.

20. Roger Griffin, *The Nature of Fascism* (New York: St. Martin's Press, 1991), p. xi.

21. Gentile and Mussolini, "Il fascismo è una concezione religiosa, in cui l'uomo è veduto nel suo immanente rapporto con una legge superiore, con una Volontà obiettiva che trascende l'individuo particolare e lo eleva a membro consapevole di una società spiritual," "La dottrina del fascism," *Enciclopedia Italiana* (1932).

22. The phrase "political religion" has not yet become established, and competes with "secular religion," "religious politics" and "civil religion" for the same semantic space. There are also some claims on the field made by terms such as "millenarianism," given its signifier rôle as the belief in a coming major transformation of society. However, though being an eschatological doctrine it generally lacks the ele-

ment of "forcing the pace" of the awaited transformation understood by the theorists of totalitarianism.

23. Professor Gentile is known for his interpretation of fascism as a "political religion" and has written several works on this theme, including *The Sacralization of Politics in Fascist Italy* (Harvard University Press), *The Origins of Fascist Ideology, 1918-1925* (Enigma), and the aforementioned "Fascism, Totalitarianism and Political Religion: Definitions and Critical Reflections on Criticism of an Interpretation."

24. Gentile, "Fascism," p. 35.

25. Ibid.

26. An indication of this emerging convergence is the inauguration in 2005 of a new academic journal, *Totalitarian Movements and Political Religions*, which has established itself "as an important crossover journal for history, the humanities and the social sciences in probing a wide range of topics in revolutionary movements and regimes, and in the analysis of fascism, communism, totalitarianism, political religion, and many other related subjects." (Griffin, Preface to *Fascism, Totalitarianism and Political Religion*).

27. Roger Griffin, *What is Fascism?*, http://encarta.msn.com, 18 April 2002.

28. لقد انتهى دور الرجل الأبيض ... تفقّـ البشرية اليوم على حافة الهاوية,
Sayyid Qutb, معالم في الطريق ("Milestones on the Way"), Minbar al-Tawhīd wal-Jihād, مقدمة , 2.

29. Hasan al-Bannā', *Toward the Light* (1947).

30. It is best illustrated by Sayyid Qutb's call for the fulfilment of "a mission that, whether the distance be near or far, will accede to the leadership of humanity," Sayyid Qutb, *Milestones*, p. 5.

31. Roger Griffin, "The Sacred Synthesis: The Ideological Cohesion of Fascist Cultural Policy," *Modern Italy.* Vol. 3, No. 1, 1998, pp. 5-23.

32. Thus al-Nabahānī: "While we should consider the Muslim countries as one indivisible society and as a target for the *Da'wah*, we must concentrate our scope of work to one province or specific provinces where we undertake to educate people with Islam so that it springs to life within themselves and so that they live by it and for it... As for the duty of the Muslims, they should work towards turning their land where Islam is not implemented, and which is considered as *Dar al-Kufr* into *Dar al-Islam*." Taq al-Dīn al-Nabahānī, *The Islamic State* (Al-Khilafah Publications), p. 238.

33. For an interesting comparison of the issues of empowerment, universalism and culture shared between Bolshevism and Islamism, see the articles by Frederick Kagan, "The New Bolsheviks, Understanding Al Qaeda," *National Security Outlook*, November 2005, and David Satter, "Soviet Threat is One of Ideas More Than Arms," *Wall Street Journal*, May 23, 1983.

34. Gentile, "Fascism," p. 35.

35. Griffin, "The Sacred Synthesis."

36. Gentile and Mussolini, "Riassume tutte le forme della vita morale e intellettuale dell'uomo. Non si può quindi limitare a semplici funzioni di ordine e tutela, come voleva il liberalismo. Non è un semplice meccanismo che limiti la sfera delle presunte libertà individuali. È forma e norma interiore, e disciplina di tutta la persona," "La dottrina del fascismo," *Enciclopedia Italiana* (1932).

37. Sayyid Qutb, *Milestones*, Chapter 10, تغييرات قفزية ("Far-reaching changes"), p. 97.

38. "Now, if these ministers deem by their majority opinion that alcohol should be permitted then this would be accepted as law. In addition if people deem that prostitution, gambling, paedophilia, killing Muslims (as in the wars on Afghanistan, Iraq and the ongoing war on Islam), homosexuality, permissibility of same-sex marriages etc. is beneficial for the people, then through the process of majority voting, these and other motions would be accepted and implemented as law, such that the people will live and judge by them," Abu Osama, *The Plague of the West*, p. 3.

39. Abū Muhammad al-Maqdisī, المقدسي طارق دين, *Minbar al-Tawhīd wal-Jihād al-Tawhīd wal-Jihād*, n.d.

40. Abd al-Hakim Murad has wittily referred to this preoccupation as "*ummatolatry*," see his *Contentions*, VIII, 40, "Ummatolatry: from Islam to Izlam."

41. Gentile, "Fascism," p. 34.

42. Dr. Muhammad Al Alkhuli, *The Need for Islam*, published on *Islamway*, August 21, 2008, and republished at http://www.islamic-life.com/introducing-islam/article-islam-complete-life.

43. Sayyid Qutb, *Social Justice in Islam*, p. 42. Qutb's argument is that the Church gave up the struggle to show society how to incorporate faith into everyday life by turning to monasticism and separating itself from society. For Qutb, the Protestant Reformation represented the final surrender, and the acceptance of the concept that religion could not act as a system of life.

44. Samir Amin, *Political Islam in the Service of Imperialism*, NewAgeIslam.org, August 16, 2009. De Maistre in his *Essai sur le principe générateur des constitutions politiques et des autres institutions humaines* (*Essay on the Generative Principle of Political Constitutions and other Human Institutions*, 1809), argues that constitutions are not artificial products but come from God. For Isaiah Berlin (*Freedom and Its Betrayal*) his writings are "the last despairing effort of feudalism … to resist the march of progress," and in his essay, "Joseph de Maistre and the Origins of Fascism," Berlin accounts de Maistre the earliest precursor of the Fascist vision of the universe. Bonald was a French counter-revolutionary philosopher and politician and one of the leading writers of the theocratic or traditionalist school. His conservative *Theorie du pouvoir politique et religieux* was condemned by the Directory.

45. Sheikh Abul Ala Maududi, "Islamic Law and Constitution," *The Political Theory of Islam*, 9th edition (Lahore, 1986), pp. 146-147. The use of this citation has aroused the ire of Islamist activists and media watchers, who see such internal parallelism of Islamism with totalitarianism as highly compromising. See, for instance, the objections by the Muslim Council of Britain (http://www.mcb.org.uk/media/responsetobbc.pdf) and the "Islamic Human Rights Commission" (http://www.ihrc.org.uk/show.php?id=1497) to a BBC *Panorama* documentary aired in August 2005.

46. Monnerot, *Sociology and Psychology of Communism*.

47. "Sie bekämpft den jüdisch-materialistischen Geist in und außer uns und ist überzeugt, daß eine dauernde Genesung unseres Volkes nur erfolgen kann von innen heraus auf der Grundlage: Gemeinnutz vor Eigennutz," 25-Punkte-Programm der NSDAP, Munich, February 24, 1920.

48. Sayyid Qutb, *Milestones*, Section III, "The Characteristics of the Islamic Society."

49. Abd al-Qadim Zallum: الديمقراطية نظام كفر يحرم أخذها وأ تطبيقها وأ الدعوة اليها! (*Democracy is a Kufr System, which it is Forbidden to Adopt, Apply or Promote*), p. 22 (Hizb al-Tahrir Publications, 1990).

50. "That the Jama'at's and Lenin's ideas about the "organizational weapon" were similar confirms that the relation of ideology to social action in Maududi's works closely followed the Leninist example," Sayyed Vali Reza Nasr, *The Vanguard of the Islamic Revolution* (I.B Tauris, 1994), pp. 13-14.

51. Sayyid Qutb, *Milestones*, مقدمة , p. 5.

52. For more on this see Ulph, *Towards a Curriculum*, Part III, Chapter 4, "The Ideology of Expansion," available online at http://www.jamestown.org/uploads/media/Ulph_Towards_a_Curriculum_Part3.pdf.

53. They derive this principle from the following Hadith: "The people of my generation are the best, then those who follow them, and then those who follow the latter." (Bukhari 3:48:819 and 820 and Muslim 31:6150 and 6151). The entire period assumed by this therefore extends from the revelation of the Prophet Muhammad (c. 610) to about the time of Ahmad ibn Hanbal's death (855), each generation understood as approximating some eighty years.

54. Abu Baseer al-Tartousi, هذه عقيدتنا وهذا الذي نَدعُو وَ إليها (*This is our Creed and this is what we call for*), www.abubaseer.bizland.com, March 10, 2002.

55. Karen Armstrong, *The Battle for God* (New York: Ballantine Books, 2001).

56. Roger Griffin, "Staging the Nation's Rebirth: the Politics and Aesthetics of Performance in the Context of Fascist Studies," Günter Berghaus, ed., *Fascism and Theatre: The Politics and Aesthetics of Performance in the Era of Fascism* (Oxford: Berg, 1994).

57. Umberto Eco, "Fourteen Ways of Looking at a Blackshirt," *New York Review of Books*, June 22, 1995, pp. 12-15. The obscurity of the message is its strength and

accounts for its versatility. "If you browse in the shelves that, in American bookstores, are labeled New Age," argues Eco, "you can find there even Saint Augustine, who, as far as I know, was not a fascist. But combining Saint Augustine and Stonehenge—that is a symptom of Ur-Fascism."

58. Ibn Hanbal, أصول السنة (*The Foundations of the Sunna*), A. Zumarlee, ed. (April 1991), p. 169.

59. Taqī al-Dīn al-Nabahānī, الشخصية الاسلامية, Part One, 6ᵗʰ edn (Beirut: Hizb al-Tahrir Publications, Dar al-Umma, 2003), pp. 273-284. Eng. trans. *The Islamic Personality*, pp. 153-158.

60. Cf. the Islamist thinker Ismail al-Faruqi, for whom one of the essential features of *tawhīd* is that it "provides a unity to nature, person-hood, and truth that subordinates them to God and, in turn, resolves any concern about a conflict between religion and science," and "legitimates the need to rediscover the Islamic dimension of all knowledge through a process of Islamization." See J. Esposito and J. Voll, *Makers of Contemporary Islam* (Oxford, 2001), p. 30.

61. Al-Nabahānī, ibid.

62. Shaykh Samīr al-Mālikī, الدرر على عظم من على الفلاسفة الملاحدة، ابن سينا، الرازي، الفارابي ... وأشياعهم (*A Response to Those Who Extol the Atheist Philosophers, Ibn Sina, al-Razi, al-Farabi and their Followers*) (n.d.), Section "On Learning the Mundane Sciences," p. 17. فألاصل في هيئة الإباحة... أما الظن بأن كل ما والصل إليه الكفار من علوم على علم المسلمين تعمل والبرارعة فيه هدف نظ خاطئ إذ إيطائ على الواجب على الآلخر همه هم القرخرة الدنيا ومتاعها وعلومها.

63. Sheikh Mohammed Shihabuddin Nadvi, *Rise and Fall of Muslims in Science*, http://www.witness-pioneer.org/vil/Books/SN_science/default.htm.

64. العمل على سلامة المنهاج بحيث تصب كل المناهج العلمية في إطار خدمة الإسلام، وبحيث لا يكون الهدف العلمي البحت... بل يربط طبن هذه العلوم بالإسلام ويقنيها مما امم تحفة الشواطئ من فيها (*Gift of the Monotheists on the Most Important Questions concerning the Fundamentals of the Faith*), compiled in Gaza by the "Jurisprudential Committee in the *Jamā'at al-Tawhīd wal-Jihād*" (2009), pp. 71-72.

65. V. I. Lenin, "Defeat of One's Own Government in Imperialist War," *Selected Works* (New York: International Publishers), vol. 5, p. 147.

66. While historically there were voices that opposed it as a heterodox concept it became doctrinally indigenised among Sunnis once Ibn Taymiyya treated it as a means to counter heterodoxy. By the 18ᵗʰ and 19ᵗʰ centuries Ibn Taymiyya's approach developed under the influence of Hanbali scholars into a fundamental demonstration of *tawhīd*, and consequently an article of faith. While the textual sources are plentiful, the Islamist ideologues found their argumentation for *al-walā' wal-barā'* mostly on *sūras* 3 (*'Imrān*): 28-29, 118-120, 58 (*Al-Anfāl*): 14-22 and the *Sūrat al-Mumtahana* [Q 60:4]: "Verily, we are free from you and whatever

you worship besides Allah, we have rejected you, and there has started between us and you hostility and hatred for ever, until you believe in Allah alone."

67. Raymond Ibrahim, "Osama bin Laden as Robin Hood?" *American Thinker,* September 11, 2008, http://www.americanthinker.com/2008/09/osama_bin_laden_as_robin_hood.html.

68. Al-Sūrī, *The Global Islamic Resistance Call,* Section 12 حكم السكن في ديار المشركين, p. 1160.

69. Muslim historians record that a total of 600-700 Jews of the Banū Qurayza were ordered killed by the Prophet in the fifth year of the *hijra* after the tribe submitted to the judgment of the convert Sa'd bin Mu'adh, who "adjudged by the command of God" that all the able-bodied male persons belonging to the tribe should be executed.

70. *Our Struggle with the Jews,* 12th edn (Dār al-Shurūq), p. 36.

71. His life has an interesting trajectory in terms of the relationship of faith with totalitarianism. Leers joined the Nazi Party in 1929, for whom he wrote the notorious anti-Semitic tract *Juden Sehen Dich An (Jews are Observing You).* He was one of the most important ideologues of the Third Reich and after 1945 continued to specialize in anti-Semitic propaganda. He became the political adviser to the Egyptian Information Department under Muhammad Naguib, and as head of the "Anti-Zionist Propaganda Service," directed among other things the radio broadcasts for the highly influential *Sawt al-'Arab* ("The Voice of the Arabs") which featured anti-Semitic themes, and he oversaw the Arabic translation of *The Protocols of the Elders of Zion* and of Adolf Hitler's *Mein Kampf.* He converted to Islam in 1957 and changed his name to Omar Amin, in honour of the Caliph 'Umar and the Mufti of Jerusalem Hajj Amin el-Husseini. For a good summary of his life and work, see Antonio Rossiello, *Il professore Johann von Leers 'Omar Amin' ed il suo Gotteskampf,* http://forum.politicainrete.net/etnonazionalismo-voelkisch/18037-il-professore-johann-von-leers-omar-amin-ed-il-suo-gotteskampf.html.

72. "Judentum und Islam als Gegensaetze" ("Judaism and Islam as Opposites"), *Die Judenfrage,* Vol. 6, No. 24 (December 15, 1942), p. 278. The citation is discussed in Jeffrey Herf, *The Jewish Enemy* (Belknap: Harvard University Press, 2006), p. 181.

73. See MEMRI Special Report, "Contemporary Islamist Ideology Authorizing Genocidal Murder," No. 25, January 27, 2004.

74. As an indication of the convergence of totalitarianisms, towards the end of his life George Sorel, who was attracted initially to Marxism, became an admirer of Mussolini. The appreciation was mutual, since Mussolini himself said, "I owe most to Georges Sorel. This master of syndicalism by his rough theories of revolutionary tactics has contributed most to form the discipline, energy and power of the fascist cohorts."

75. Gentile and Mussolini, "Respinge quindi il pacifismo che nasconde una rinuncia alla lotta e una viltà—di fronte al sacrificio. Solo la guerra porta al massimo di tensione tutte le energie umane e imprime un sigillo di nobiltà ai popoli che hanno la virtù di affrontarla. Tutte le altre prove sono dei sostituti, che non pongono mai l'uomo di fronte a se stesso, nell'alternativa della vita e della morte," "La dottrina del fascismo," *Enciclopedia Italiana* (1932).

76. Sayyid Qutb, *In the Shade of the Qur'an*, vol.3, trans. and ed. Adil Salahi and Ashur Shamis (Leicester: The Islamic Foundation, 2001), p. 281.

77. See Sayyid Qutb, *Milestones* (Indianapolis: American Trust Publications, 1990), p. 13.

78. 'Abd Allāh 'Azzām, *Martyrs: The Building Blocks of Nations*, quoted by Myatt, *National-Socialism and Islam*.

79. Umberto Eco, "Ur-Fascism."

80. Abū Muhammad al-Maqdisī, القافلة تسير والكلاب تنبح) (*While the Dogs Are Barking, the Caravan Moves On*), published in *Mu'askar al-Battar* 7, March 2004, pp. 7-8.

81. Interview with Muhammad Salāh for a*l-Hayat* (London), December 10, 2007: والجهاد ماض إلى يوم القيامة، والجهاد ماض ليس محصوراً في تنظيم معين كما نظير هذا، لبه وهو شريعة ماضية إلى آخر الزمان. A typical commentary on a Salafist forum illustrates this permanence: "Jihad will continue until the end of time, whatever period of time a person is in, there will always be Jihad happening. There is actually hidden wisdom behind it, but it might not be apparent to you right now, but the more you learn about Allaah and His existence, the more you will understand why certain things have been prescribed." Posted on November 12, 2009 on the *Islamic Awakening* forum, http://forums.islamicawakening.com/f18/jihad-relevant-for-present-past-30191/.

82. Muhammad Farag, الفريضة الغائبة (the "Missing Obligation," or "Neglected Duty"), written in 1981. The work represents one stage on from Sayyid Qutb in the trajectory towards global jihad under al Qaeda in that, doctrinally, he extends the source material for justification of violence beyond the Qur'an to the Hadith literature. He goes so far as to posit jihad as the "sixth pillar" of Islam, a *fard 'ayn* (compulsory religious duty) that must be satisfied directly and immediately.

83. تحقيق المقاصد العظيمة والجليلة التي خلقوا من اجلها وأن من جلها اجلاها هذان المقصدان: اعبد الله وحده ونصرة دينه بالكناية في أعدائه، فمن اجل ذلك كله يحيي المسلم, Abū Muhammad al-Maqdisī, وقفات مع ثمرات الجهاد ("Reflections on the Fruits of Jihad"), *Minbar al-Tawhīd wal-Jihād*, May 2004, p. 57.

84. Examples are: Saudi columnist Muhammad bin 'Abd Al-Latīf Āl Al-Shaykh: *Al-Jazira* (Saudi Arabia), المقدسي وتبرئته ("Al-Maqdis and his acquittal"), July 10 and لكن هم أوسأ من النازيين لضلال بسبب! ("But they are actually worse than the Nazis and more misguided!"), July 24, 2005, where the columnist proposed that jihadism be classified as Europeans classified fascism, a movement "whose thought,

propaganda and propagation is destructive to international security and peace… The two groups drink from the same source… if the denomination differs, the results are still the same." See also 'Abd al-Rahmān al-Rāshid: نويشاف مه ديكأتلاب ("But they surely are Fascists"), *al-Sharq al-Awsat*, August 13, 2006.

85. This, for instance is the view of prominent ex-Islamists such as Ed Hussein (author of *The Islamist*), Maajid Nawaz and Shiraz Maher, both ex-members of the Hizb al-Tahrir.

Chapter 3

1. David M. Levy and Sandra J. Peart, "Soviet Growth and American Textbooks: An Endogenous Past," *Journal of Economic Behavior and Organization*, Vol. 78, 2011, pp. 110-125.

2. The studies on Soviet statistics and freight transportation were published (Gregory Grossman, *Soviet Statistics of Physical Output of Industrial Commodities: Their Composition and Quality* [Princeton, N.J.: Princeton University Press, 1960]; Ernest Williams, *Freight Transportation in the Soviet Union: A Comparison with the United States*, National Bureau of Economic Research, New York, 1959). The summary volume was never written.

3. G. Warren Nutter, "Some Observations on Soviet Industrial Growth," *American Economic Review*, Vol. 47, No. 2, 1957, pp. 618-630; G. Warren Nutter, "Industrial Growth in the Soviet Union," *American Economic Review*, Vol. 48, No. 2, 1958, pp. 398-411.

4. G. Warren Nutter, *The Growth of Industrial Production in the Soviet Union* (Princeton, N.J.: Princeton University Press, 1962).

5. G. Warren Nutter, *The Extent of Enterprise Monopoly in the United States* (Chicago: University of Chicago Press, 1951).

6. One explanation of the origins of the project is that Arthur Burns, who became Chairman of President Eisenhower's Council of Economic Advisers in 1953, had been taken with the uniformity of estimates made by Soviet specialists of the size and growth rate of the Soviet economy. It is thought that he may have sought an independent study to check on those estimates. The NBER would have been a logical choice for the project because of its reputation for objective work and Burns' own long-time association with the bureau. Some trace the origins further back, to the change from the Truman Administration to the Eisenhower and the associated move of Dean Rusk to the Rockefeller Foundation, which later made two grants to the NBER to support the project. In this version, Burns is not directly involved; the impetus may have come from John Foster Dulles, then Secretary of State, whose brother Allen was Director of the CIA, and who knew Rusk well. Whatever the origins, the project was intended to be done by an economist who was outside the circle of American (and European) Soviet specialists.

7. Peter Wiles, "Sinews of Soviet Strength," *Challenge*, July 1962.

8. Nutter was not proficient in Russian, but he had to develop a basic competence in transliteration. He also had the help of several persons fluent in Russian: Israel Borenstein and Adam Kaufman, who are listed as assistants on the book's title page, as well as Marie-Christine (Colbert) MacAndrew, who is mentioned in the preface. But fluency in Russian was one of the prerequisites for membership in the Soviet specialist club.

9. D.R. Hodgman, "Industrial Growth," Abram Bergson (ed.), *Soviet Economic Growth* (White Plains, N.Y., Row, Peterson, 1953), p. 244.

10. Wiles, "Sinews," p. 253.

11. Nutter, "Industrial Growth in the Soviet Union."

12. N.M. Kaplan and R.H. Moorsteen, "An Index of Soviet Industrial Output," *American Economic Review*, Vol. 40, No. 3, 1960, pp. 295-318.

13. James H. Noren, "Soviet Industry Trends in Output, Inputs, and Productivity," U.S. Congress, Joint Economic Committee, *New Directions in the Soviet Economy*, Part II-A, 1966, pp. 271-326.

14. Daniel P. Moynihan, "The Soviet Economy: Boy, Were We Wrong," *Washington Post*, July 11, 1990.

15. For example, during 1870-1913, the Russian annual growth rate was 5.3% while that of the U.S. was 5.1%; from 1928-1940, Soviet output grew at 8.9% per year, while Depression era American output grew at only 1.8% per year. (Nutter, *Growth of Industrial Production*, p. 229.)

16. Wiles, "Sinews".

17. See Steven Rosefielde, "Tea Leaves, and Productivity: Bergsonian Norms for Gauging the Soviet Future," *Comparative Economic Studies*, Vol. 47, No. 2, 2005, pp. 259-273, for an excellent summary of these points.

18. This was well before the development of electronic computing. Later, as the technological revolution went forward, some pro-planning observers thought that the advent of powerful computers would produce dramatically better results for the central planners. Ironically, the technological revolution did more to advance the demise of the system than to secure it.

19. Central Intelligence Agency, "Soviet Capabilities and Probably Causes of Action Through Mid-1959," National Intelligence Estimate 11-4-54.

20. Rush V. Greenslade, "Industrial Production Statistics in the USSR," Vladimir Treml and John P. Hardt, *Soviet Economic Statistics* (Durham, N.C.: Duke University Press, 1972), pp. 155-194. In a critique of Nutter's work published in the *American Economic Review* in 1959, Greenslade lists himself as an employee of the federal government in Washington, D.C., code for the CIA. Rush V. Greenslade and Phyllis A. Wallace, "Industrial Growth in the Soviet Union: Comment," *American Economic Review*, Vol. 49, No. 4, 1959, pp. 687-695.

21. Bergson's specialty was Soviet GNP estimation, so reports dealing with GNP would fall squarely in his area of expertise.

22. A major survey of measurements of Soviet economic growth published in 1957 made no reference to the NBER study in its text or bibliography. G. Ofer, "Soviet Economic Growth, 1928-1985," *Journal of Economic Literature*, Vol. 25, No. 4, 1987, pp. 1767-1833.

23. Friedrich A. Hayek, "Socialist Calculation I: The Nature and History of the Problem," 1935; republished in Friedrich A. Hayek, *Individualism and Economic Order* (Chicago: Regnery, 1948), pp. 119-147.

24. Nutter, *Growth of Industrial Production*, p. 266.

25. Ibid., p. 267.

26. Steven Rosefielde, *Russia in the 21ˢᵗ Century: The Prodigal Superpower* (New York: Cambridge University Press, 2005).

27. Eugene Zaleski, *Planning for Economic Growth in the Soviet Union, 1918-1932* (Chapel Hill, N.C.: University of North Carolina Press, 1962), pp. 270-288, and Eugene Zaleski, *Stalinist Planning for Economic Growth, 1933-1952* (Chapel Hill, N.C. and London: University of North Carolina Press and Macmillan, 1980), pp. 506 ff, show that the Soviet economy was in fact subject to fluctuations. These fluctuations were caused by the central planning system itself.

28. Wiles, "Sinews," p. 45.

29. Rosefielde, "Tea Leaves," msp. 14.

30. Nutter himself did not witness the collapse, having died in 1979.

31. It is beyond the scope of this paper to examine the huge literature on these transitions. One point is worth emphasizing: the reforms in these countries (and elsewhere) were always strongly conditioned by the informal institutions that had been developed over many years, institutions that reflected their cultural and religious heritages. See Svetozar Pejovich, *Law, Informal Rules and Economic Performance* (Northampton, MA: Edward Elgar, 2008), for development of these points.

32. Of course, many individuals and groups benefit from the partial planning of regulation, taxation, and so forth. Advocacy in that sense has nothing to do with beliefs about planning per se.

Chapter 4

1. This chapter is partially adapted from the author's address at the George Bush School of Government and Public Service, Texas A&M University, January 28, 1999, "Emboldening Domestic Resistance to Communism: Presidential Rhetoric and the War of Information and Ideas Against the Soviet Union." The author would like to thank Amanda Caligiuri, a graduate student at The Institute of World Politics (IWP), and IWP intern Michael Watson, for their invaluable research assistance.

2. See, for example, one of the fashionable books of the day: H. Gordon Skilling and Franklyn Griffiths, eds., *Interest Groups in Soviet Politics* (Princeton, NJ: Princeton University Press, 1971).

3. See Nathan Leites, *The Operational Code of the Politburo* (New York, NY: The RAND Corporation, 1951).

4. Karl Marx, "Theses on Feuerbach," in Robert C. Tucker, ed., *The Marx-Engels Reader* (New York, NY: W.W. Norton & Company, Inc., 1972).

5. See Vladimir Lenin, "The Tasks of the Youth Leagues," Robert C. Tucker, *The Lenin Anthology* (New York: W. W. Norton & Co., 1975) pp. 667ff.

6. Alain Besancon, *The Soviet Syndrome* (New York, NY: Librairie Hachette, 1976).

7. Interview with Leszek Kolakowski, 1988.

8. Alexander Solzhenitsyn, "The Smatterers," Alexander Solzhenitsyn, ed., *From Under the Rubble* (Boston: Little, Brown and Co., 1975), p. 275.

9. See, for example, Stephen Young, "How North Vietnam Won the War," *Wall Street Journal*, August 3, 1995, p. A8.

10. For an examination of how the Soviets analyzed the correlation of forces, see my *Soviet Perceptions of U.S. Foreign Policy* (Ithaca: Cornell University Press, 1982).

11. It should be noted that, by the 1970s, Soviet ideology had been forced by the pressures of political realities within the Soviet empire to recognize that "objective, material factors" were not necessarily decisive in establishing the "basis" of socio-political order. The Kremlin's ideologists had to wrestle with the unforeseen and unwelcome reality of a "subjective factor"—viz., weak ideological commitment on the part of the Czechoslovak Communist Party, which, in the "Prague Spring" of 1968, called for "socialism with a human face," thus implying that Soviet socialism was bereft of such a human face. This reality compelled the CPSU to fight this weakness with a heavy dose of subjectivism: more ideological propaganda, combined with the violence of the Brezhnev Doctrine-inspired invasion. For a brilliant, thorough, and neglected analysis of this situation, see R. Judson Mitchell, *Ideology of Superpower* (Stanford: Hoover Institution Press, 1982).

12. The Islamic concept (developed by Hanafi jurisprudence) divides the world between the "house of war" (*Dar al-Harb*) and the house of Islam (*Dar al-Islam*). The latter concept is sometimes also called the *Dar as-Salaam* (or "house of peace").

13. For the classic analysis of this and other key elements of Soviet strategy, see Robert Strausz-Hupé, William R. Kintner, James E. Dougherty, and Alvin J. Cottrell, *Protracted Conflict: A Challenging Study of Communist Strategy* (New York, NY: Harper & Brothers, 1959). The reader will note the similarity of the Soviet concept of the division of the world and that of Islamic jihadism (the house of war and the house of Islam).

14. There have been numerous Soviet lexicons of political terms as well as Western dictionaries of Soviet semantics. See, for example, Ilya Zemtsov and Gay M. Hammerman, eds., *Lexicon of Soviet Political Terms*, (Fairfax, VA: HERO Books, 1984); Raymond S. Sleeper, ed., *A Lexicon of Marxist-Leninist Semantics*

(Alexandria, VA: Western Goals, 1983); and A. M. Rumyantsev, ed., *A Dictionary of Scientific Communism*, (Moscow: Progress Publishers, 1984).

15. See Juliana Pilon, "The United Nations Library: Putting Soviet Disinformation into Circulation," Heritage Foundation *Backgrounder* 487, February 18, 1986.

16. See, for example, former Soviet KGB chief Yuri Andropov's memorandum to the Politburo reviewing KGB financing and influence over the Black Panther Party in the United States: Vladimir Bukovsky, *Moskiewski Proces* (Warsaw: 1998), p. 37. This book, published as *Judgment in Moscow* in English, is not widely available but has been translated from Russian into French in 1995, German in 1996, and Polish in 1998, the last of which this writer used.

17. See documentary evidence of the use of "liberation theology" as an instrument of subversion in the documents of Grenada's ruling communist party—the New Jewel Movement. Here, the chief of Grenada's secret police recommends inviting Cuban and Sandinista authorities on liberation theology to come to Grenada to undermine the theological integrity of churches on the island. See Keith Roberts, "Analysis of the Church in Grenada," cited in Herbert Romerstein and Michael Ledeen, eds., *The Grenada Documents: An Overview and Selection* (Washington, DC: U.S. Department of State and U.S. Department of Defense, 1984), p. 5-5 (this is a selection of documents from the larger Grenada Archive which resides in the National Archives). See also U.S. Department of State, Soviet Active Measures: The Christian Peace Conference, May 1985, cited in Sven Kraemer, ed., *The Soviet Union Fights the Cold War*, a collection of primary source documents of the Reagan Administration published as a CD-ROM (Washington, DC: American Foreign Policy Council, November 1999); U.S. Department of State, *Soviet Influence Activities: A Report on Active Measures and Propaganda, 1986-87* (Washington, DC: August 1987), p. 7.

18. See, for example, the extraordinary account of Soviet bloc promotion of narcotics in the West in Joseph D. Douglass, Jr., *Red Cocaine: The Drugging of America* (Atlanta, GA: Clarion House, 1990). As this writer can testify from personal experience, no U.S. government agency, when confronted with the powerful defector testimony presented in the Douglass book, was willing to verify it or collect further information on it. Corroborating the material in this book was evidence that emerged from the Italian investigation of the assassination attempt on Pope John Paul II, where the Bulgarian state corporation, Kintex, was found to be involved in this activity; testimony from East German intelligence official, Alexander Schlalck-Golodkowski, on East German involvement (see, for example, Rachel Ehrenfeld, "The Drugs and Terror Connection," The Sagamore Institute, September 1, 2001); and evidence on Nicaraguan Sandinista involvement as well (see https://www. cia.gov/library/reports/general-reports-1/cocaine/contra-story/append.html). The Soviet policy of promoting sexual libertinism proceeded from Bolshevik strategy to use this instrument in the years immediately following

the October Revolution to break down the traditional social structures of society. See Alix Holt, trans. and ed., *Selected Writings of Alexandra Kollontai* (Westport, CT: L. Hill, 1977) and Gregory Carleton, *Sexual Revolution in Bolshevik Russia* (Pittsburgh, PA: University of Pennsylvania Press, 2005).

19. For an account of the communist cultural subversion, see Stephen Koch, *Double Lives: Spies and Writers in the Secret Soviet War of Ideas Against the West* (New York, NY: The Free Press, 1994). For a first-hand defector account of Soviet use of agents of influence, see Stanislav Levchenko, *On the Wrong Side: My Life in the KGB* (Washington, DC: Pergamon-Brassey's International Defense Publishers Inc., 1988).

20. See, for example, Joseph Finder, *Red Carpet* (New York, NY: Holt, Rinehart, and Winston, 1983).

21. For an overall examination of communist subversion, see William Kintner, *The Front is Everywhere* (Norman, OK: University of Oklahoma Press, 1950); and Peter Collier and David Horowitz, *Destructive Generation: Second Thoughts About the '60s* (New York, NY: The Free Press, 1996); and the considerable literature on Soviet front organizations: James L. Tyson, *Target America: The Influence of Communist Propaganda on U.S. Media* (Chicago: Regnery Gateway, 1981); Clive Rose, *The Soviet Propaganda Network: A Directory of Organizations Serving Soviet Foreign Policy* (London: Pinter Publishers Limited, 1988); Maria Leighton, *Soviet Propaganda As a Foreign Policy Tool* (New York, NY: Freedom House, 1981); Federal Bureau of Investigation, Soviet Active Measures in the United States, 1986-1987 (Washington, DC: June 1987); and Juliana Pilon, "At the U.N., Soviet Fronts Pose as Nongovernmental Organizations," Heritage Foundation *Backgrounder* 549 (Washington, DC: December 1, 1986).

22. NSDD-75 "U.S. Relations with the USSR," January 17, 1983, p. 1.

23. Ibid., p. 3.

24. Ibid., p. 4.

25. See Strausz-Hupé et al., *Protracted Conflict*.

26. Speech to the National Association of Evangelicals, Orlando, Florida, March 8, 1983.

27. Memorandum to the President: "The Truth and the Strength of America's Deterrent," January 1983, cited in Richard Reeves, *President Reagan: The Triumph of Imagination* (New York: Simon & Schuster, 2005), pp. 139-140.

28. Ronald Reagan, "Remarks on Signing the Captive Nations Week Proclamation," The White House (Washington, DC: July 19, 1982). Available online: http://www.reagan.utexas.edu/archives/speeches/1982/71982b.htm.

29. Ronald Reagan's Presidential Press Conference, on January 29, 1981 covered in Hedrick Smith, "News Analysis: Reagan Putting his Stamp on U.S. Policies: at Home and Abroad, a Change, of Course," *New York Times*, January 30, 1981. Available online: http://www.nytimes.com/1981/01/30/world/analysis-reagan-put-ting-his-stamp-us-policies-home-abroad-change-course.html.

30. Lenin, "The Tasks of the Youth Leagues."

31. See this author's chapter, "Themes of Soviet Strategic Deception and Disinformation," Brian D. Dailey and Patrick J. Parker, eds., *Soviet Strategic Deception* (Lexington, KY: Hoover Institution Press, 1987), pp. 55-75.

32. One of the contemporaneous examples of this theme was the *Washington Post's* portrayals of former KGB chief and new Communist Party General Secretary and former KGB chief Yuri Andropov as a modern, moderate liberal, "the first intellectual" in the post of General Secretary, who enjoyed modern art, theater, jazz, scotch whisky, and even talking to dissidents. See, for example, Dusko Doder, "Andropov Shows a Talent For Consolidation of Power," *The Washington Post*, November 21, 1982, p. A1, and Dusko Doder, "Andropov Seen Bringing New Decisiveness," *Washington Post*, December 12, 1982, p. A1.

33. U.S. Department of State, "White Paper on Communist Interference in El Salvador" (Washington, DC: February 1981).

34. U.S. Department of Defense, *Soviet Military Power*, 1981, 1983, 1984, 1985, 1986, and 1987 Reports, cited in Kraemer, *The Soviet Union Fights the Cold War*.

35. Ronald Reagan, Address to the Nation on Strategic Arms Reduction and Nuclear Deterrence, The White House (Washington, DC: November 22, 1982).

36. General Advisory Commission on Arms Control and Disarmament, *A Quarter Century of Soviet Compliance Practices under Arms Control Commitments, 1958-1983*, December 1983 (released to Congress in October 1984). Subsequently, the Administration submitted annual reports to Congress on Soviet compliance practices.

37. See Joseph D. Douglass, Jr., *Why the Soviets Violate Arms Control Treaties* (Washington, DC: Pergamon-Brassey's International Defense Publishers Inc., 1988).

38. Although the Carter Administration had issued reports on human rights violations, it diluted the strategic significance of Soviet violations by morally equating with them those of authoritarian regimes that both opposed the USSR and supported the United States. This policy of "moral equivalence" was reversed by the Reagan Administration on the grounds that the number, scope, and systematic character of Soviet violations made those of such authoritarians as the Shah of Iran, who had been targeted by the Carter Administration, pale in comparison. For a critique of the Carter policy see, Jeane Kirkpatrick, "Dictatorships & Double Standards," *Commentary*, November 1979.

39. Ronald Reagan, "Statement on Soviet Human Rights Policies," October 18, 1983. Available online: http://www.reagan.utexas.edu/archives/speeches/1983/101883b.html.

40. These reports by the USIA (formerly called the U.S. International Communication Agency—USICA) were not distributed within the United States, pursuant to the Smith-Mundt Act, and hence are very difficult to find. One source

of some of the most prominent of these reports is Kraemer, *The Soviet Union Fights the Cold War*. Some relevant reports on the CD-ROM include: "Afghanistan: The Struggle to Regain Freedom" (Washington, DC: US Information Agency, 1982); "Afghanistan: The Struggle in its Fifth Year," (Washington, DC: US Information Agency, June 1984); "Poland: A Season of Light and of Darkness" (Washington, DC: US International Communication Agency, 1982); "Cuba's Renewed Support for Violence in Latin America: a Special Report" (Washington, DC: US International Communication Agency, December 1981); and "Cuban Armed Forces and the Soviet Military Presence" (Washington, DC: US International Communication Agency, 1982).

41. See: U.S. Department of State, *Soviet Influence Activities: A Report on Active Measures and Propaganda, 1986-1987* (Washington, DC: October 1987) in Kraemer, *The Soviet Union Fights the Cold War*.

42. Part of the Administration's effort to expose Soviet influence operations was its release of several publications on the apparatus of subversion and political action. These included: U.S. Department of State, *The International Department of the CPSU Central Committee* (see The Federal Bureau of Investigation, *Soviet Active Measures in the United States 1986-1987* [Washington, DC]); U.S. Department of State, *Active Measures: A Report on the Substance and Process of Anti-U.S. Disinformation and Propaganda Campaigns* (Washington, DC: August 1986); U.S Department of State, *Soviet Influence Activities: A Report on Active Measures and Propaganda, 1986-1987*; United State Information Agency, *Soviet Active Measures in the Era of Glasnost*, A Report to Congress by the United States Information Agency, March 1988; U.S. Department of State, *Soviet Active Measures: Forgery, Disinformation, Political Activities* (Washington, DC: October 1981); and the U.S. Department of State's shorter reports on Soviet active measures, some of which came under the title of a Foreign Affairs Note (many of these appear in Kraemer, *The Soviet Union Fights the Cold War*).

43. Aleksandr Solzhenitsyn, *The Mortal Danger* (New York: Harper Torchbooks, 1980), pp. 50-53. (This was first published as "Misconceptions about Russia Are a Threat to America," *Foreign Affairs*, Spring 1980.)

44. Ibid., p. 129. (This quotation appeared also in "The Courage to See," *Foreign Affairs*, Fall 1980.)

45. Interview of President Ronald Reagan by Radio Free Europe/Radio Liberty, Washington, DC. June 14, 1985.

46. See, for example, Richard Cummings, "Special Feature: The 1981 bombing of RFE/RL," Radio Free Europe/Radio Liberty Archive, February 9, 1996. See also "Voices of Hope: the Story of Radio Free Europe and Radio Liberty," Hoover Institution Archival Exhibit, 2010.

47. See Arch Puddington, *Broadcasting Freedom: The Cold War Triumph of Radio Free Europe and Radio Liberty* (Lexington: University Press of Kentucky, 2000). See

also Michael Nelson, *War of the Black Heavens: The Battles of Western Broadcasting in the Cold War* (Syracuse, NY: Syracuse University Press, 1997).

48. Nelson, *War of the Black Heavens.*

49. Lech Walesa, Press Conference at RFE/RL on the Role of the Radios in Poland's Struggle for Freedom (Washington, DC, 1989), as quoted in A. Ross Johnson, "A Brief History of RFE/RL" (Washington, DC: December 2008), http://www.rferl.org/section/history/133.html. From the author's recollection, the quotation recorded in this account is slightly incorrect; hence, the author has added the extra words in brackets.

50. Donnie Radcliffe, "Vaclav Havel, Face to Face with the Voice," *Washington Post*, February 27, 1990.

51. Ronald Reagan, Address to Members of the British Parliament, London, England, June 8, 1982. Available online: http://www.reagan.utexas.edu/archives/speeches/1982/60882a.htm.

52. Source: The National Endowment for Democracy.

53. Peter Schweizer, *Reagan's War* (New York, NY: Doubleday, 2002), pp. 187-188.

54. Ronald Reagan, Speech at Moscow State University, May 31, 1988.

55. Ibid.

56. The Kremlin's fear of the truth was great enough that it went to ridiculous lengths to suppress it—even in the case of this small (3' x 6') billboard. Since it was illegal to tread on lawns in Moscow, the Soviets planted a patch of grass on the broad sidewalk adjacent to the billboard so that passersby had to stand some six feet away from the billboard, thus making it impossible to read the texts displayed there. The USIA retaliated by increasing the print size, albeit at the expense of the volume of text.

57. Ted Vollmer, "Human Rights Measure OKd for County Ballot," *Los Angeles Times*, January 4, 1984, p. C1.

58. NSC-NSDD-32 "U.S. National Security Strategy," May 20, 1982.

59. See the details of this covert program as outlined by eyewitnesses in Peter Schweizer, *Victory: The Reagan Administration's Secret Strategy that hastened the Collapse of the Soviet Union* (New York: Atlantic Monthly Press, 1994). The four parts of the program are cited on p. 75. Details of the media assistance effort are cited on pp. 89-90, 146, 225.

60. Ibid., p. 76.

61. Ibid.

62. Ibid., pp. 70, 75, 86, 88. 89, 123, 160, 164, 165, 227, 228, 257, 258.

63. Ibid., pp. 265, 281.

64. Ibid., pp. 159, 256.

65. This writer personally met one of these Alpinists who shared with me reports of these contacts.

66. Schweizer, *Victory*, pp. 184, 228.

67. Ibid., p. 267.

68. Ibid., p. 156.

69. Ibid., p. 177.

70 Ibid., pp. 175-176

71. Ibid., p. 178.

72. Ibid., p. 208.

73. Ibid., pp. 271-272.

74. Ibid., pp. 273-274.

75. For an expanded analysis of the three internal crises reviewed here, see John Lenczowski, *The Sources of Soviet Perestroika* (Ashland, OH: Ashbrook Center, Ashland University, 1990).

76. See Milovan Djilas, *The New Class: An Analysis of the Communist System* (New York, NY: Praeger, 1957); and Michael Voslensky, *Nomenklatura: The Soviet Ruling Class* (Garden City, NJ: Doubleday & Company, Inc., 1984), for early and late descriptions of the communist privileged elite.

77. This pattern of freeze and thaw is fully explained in Alain Besancon, *The Soviet Syndrome* (New York, NY: Librairie Hachette, 1976).

78. For a systematic analysis of the Soviet cultural offensive, see John Lenczowski, *Soviet Cultural Diplomacy: A Multi-faceted Strategic Instrument of Soviet Power*, 1991, available online: http://www.iwp.edu/doclib/200607710_cultural_diplomacy.pdf.

79. TASS, October 31, 1987, Foreign Broadcast Information Service Daily Report —Soviet Union, November 5, 1987, p. 54. This quotation is cited in John Lenczowski, "Military *Glasnost*' and Strategic Deception," *International Freedom Review*, Vol. 3, Number 2, Winter 1990, p. 6, available online: http://www.iwp.edu/docLib/20110628_MilitaryGlasnost.pdf.

80. Mikhail Gorbachev, Speech on the Anniversary of the October Revolution, November 1987. This is also quoted in Lenczowski, "Military *Glasnost*' and Strategic Deception," p. 6.

81. Properly speaking, *glasnost*' means "publicity" or possibly "giving voice to people under controlled circumstances." Insofar as it has any relation to "openness," it could conceivably be defined as "controlled openness." Suffice it to say that the term has been used misleadingly to describe what Soviet and Tsarist propagandists wished to portray as freedom of speech.

82. See Lenczowski, "Military *Glasnost*' and Soviet Strategic Deception."

83. The Soviets justified the invasion of Baku on the basis of an ostensible need to create civil peace between Azeris and Armenians in Baku. The conflict between the two national groups, however, was deliberately exacerbated by the KGB, which orchestrated a pogrom of Armenians living in that city and gave media platforms (such as prime-time television) to Azeri chauvinist extremists who incited anti-Armenian violence.

Chapter 6

1. See: Robert M. Gates, *From the Shadows: The Ultimate Insider's Story of Five Presidents and How They Won the Cold War* (New York: Simon & Schuster Paperbacks, 1996), pp. 202-206.

2. Ibid., p. 203.

3. Ibid., p. 204.

4. Ibid.

5. Ibid., p. 202.

6. Ibid., p. 204.

7. Ibid.

8. Ibid., p. 205.

9. Ibid.

10. Ibid.

11. Ibid.

12. Ibid.

13. Ibid., p. 206.

14. Ibid.

15. Ibid.

16. Ibid.

17. See Christopher Andrew and Vasili Mitrokhin, *The World Was Going Our Way: The KGB and the Battle for the Third World* (New York: Basic Books), pp. 246-259.

18. Andrew and Mitrokhin, p. 247.

19. Ibid., pp. 246-248.

20. Ibid., pp. 247-248.

21. The biggest exception is Major Nidal Malik Hasan's shooting spree at Fort Hood, Texas, in November 2009. However, it should be noted that Hasan was repeatedly in contact with al Qaeda cleric Anwar al Awlaki in the months leading up to the attack. Awlaki was safely ensconced in his safe haven in Yemen.

22. See: http://www.treasury.gov/press-center/press-releases/Pages/tg1261.aspx.

23. *The 9/11 Commission Report*, 2004, p. 363.

24. Ibid.

25. Ibid., p. 366.

26. Ibid.

27. This phrasing has been used many times. See, for example: http://www. embassyofafghanistan.org/speeches/speech22.html.

28. *The 9/11 Commission Report*, p. 61.

29. Ibid.

30. Ibid.

31. Ibid., p. 68.

32. That Saif al Adel was one of the trainees emerged during the 2001 trial of some of the al Qaeda operatives responsible for the 1998 embassy bombings.

33. *The 9/11 Commission Report*, pp. 240-241.

34. Ibid., p. 241.

35. Ibid., p. 64.

36. Ibid.

37. Ibid.

38. Ibid., p. 65.

39. Ibid., p. 117.

40. Ibid., p. 134.

41. Ibid.

42. I will not deal with the myths about Osama bin Laden, al Qaeda, and the Taliban being creations of, or sponsored by, the CIA here. Suffice it to say, there is no evidence to back up those myths.

43 For an excellent summary of al Qaeda's origins in the war against the Soviets, as well as the roles played by the Saudis and Pakistanis, see Steve Coll, *Ghost Wars: The Secret History of the CIA, Afghanistan, and Bin Laden, from the Soviet Invasion to September 10, 2001* (New York: Penguin Books, 2004).

44. The document is available on the *New York Times'* web site: http://www.nytimes.com/interactive/2011/04/24/world/guantanamo-guide-to-assessing-prisoners.html.

45. It should be noted here that many charities backed by the Saudi royals were also listed as associate forces. These charities include Al Haramayn International Foundation, Benevolence International Foundation, Muslim World League, World Assembly of Muslim Youth, International Islamic Relief Organization, and Saudi High Commission for Relief.

46. Thomas Joscelyn, "The Gitmo Files: An Agent of Iran," *The Long War Journal*, May 18, 2011. Available online: http://www.longwarjournal.org/archives/2011/05/the_gitmo_files_an_i.php#ixzz1PuvmohTL.

47. JTF-GTMO MEMO, "Subject: Recommendation for Continued Detention Under DoD Control (CD) for Guantanamo Detainee, ISN US9SA-000372DP (S)," April 13, 2007.

48. JTF-GTMO MEMO, "Subject: Recommendation for Continued Detention Under DoD Conrol (CD) for Guantanamo Detainee, ISN US9AF-000579DP (S)," March 6, 2008, p. 3.

49. Thomas Joscelyn, "Yemeni government official doubled as al Qaeda operative, leaked assessment shows," *The Long War Journal*, April 26, 2011. Available online: http://www.longwarjournal.org/archives/2011/04/yemeni_government_of.php#ixzz1Pv8la7lp.

50. A partial transcript of the wiretap can be found on the New York Times' web site, in declassified files: http://projects.nytimes.com/guantanamo/detainees/1463-abdul-al-salam-al-hilal.

51. JTF-GTMO MEMO, "Subject: Recommendation for Continued Detention Under DoD Control (CD) for Guantanamo Detainee, ISN US9YM-001463DP (S)," September 24, 2008, p. 9.

52. JTF-GTMO MEMO, "Subject: Recommendation for Continued Detention Under DoD Control (CD) for Guantanamo Detainee, ISN US9AF-001119DP (S)," April 23, 2008, p. 7.

53. JTF-GTMO MEMO, "Subject: Update Recommendation to Transfer to the Control of Another Country for Continued Detention (TCRD) for Guantanamo Detainee, ISN: US9AF-000118DP (S)," June 3, 2005, p. 3.

54. Ibid.

55. JTF-GTMO MEMO, "Subject: Update Recommendation to Retain in DoD Control (CD) for Guantanamo Detainee, ISN US9AF-001037DP (S)," July 1, 2005, p. 4.

56. JTF-GTMO MEMO, "Subject: Recommendation for Continued Detention Under DoD Control (CD) for Guantanamo Detainee, ISN US9AF-001030DP (S)," May 19, 2008, p. 5.

57. JTF-GTMO, "Subject: DAB Assessment of Guantanamo Detainee, ISN US9AF-003148DP (S)" ("JTF-GTMO Memo on Harun al Afghani") August 2, 2007.

58. JTF-GTMO Memo on Harun al Afghani, p. 7.

59. JTF-GTMO MEMO, "Subject: Recommendation for Continued Detention Under DoD Control (CD) for Guantanamo Detainee, ISN US9AF-000560DP (S)," October 23, 2008, p. 6.

Chapter 7

1. For further details on the enemy narrative, our flawed response, and the principles of effective strategic communications, see Sebastian L. v. Gorka and David Kilcullen, "Who's Winning the Battle for Narrative: Al-Qaida versus the United States and its Allies," James J. F. Forest, ed., *Influence Warfare—How Terrorists and Governments Fight to Shape Perceptions in a War of Ideas* (Westport, CT: Praeger Security International, 2009), pp. 229-240.

2. The declassified text of Kennan's original cable can be found at http://www.ntanet.net/KENNAN.html. The pseudonymous article he later wrote for a broader audience in *Foreign Affairs* is at http://www.historyguide.org/europe/kennan.html (both accessed February 15, 2012).

3. The worst example of this unfortunately influential argument can be found in Quintan Wiktorowicz, "The New Global Threat: Transnational Salafis and Jihad," *Middle East Policy*, Vol. VIII, No. 4, December 2001, pp. 29-30. The author is a senior advisor to the administration.

4. The unclassified NSC-68 makes fascinating reading and is available at http://www.airforce-magazine.com/MagazineArchive/Documents/2004/December%202004/1204keeperfull.pdf (accessed February 15, 2012).

5. "To War Not to Court," *The Washington Post*, September 12, 2001, http://www.washingtonpost.com/ac2/wp-dyn?pagename=article&node=digest&contentId=A14320-2001Sep11 (accessed March 14, 2012).

6. The speech was made at the National Endowment for Democracy, October 6, 2005. In it the President said, "Islamic terrorist attacks serve a clear and focused ideology, a set of beliefs and goals that are evil, but not insane. Some call this evil Islamic radicalism; others, militant Jihadism; still others, Islamo-fascism." The full transcript is available at http://www.washingtonpost.com/wp-srv/politics/administration/bushtext_100605.html (accessed March 14, 2012).

7. In short, the belief that you can take FM-3-24 on COIN, which is not a strategic text but rather a doctrinal field manual, and create a strategy is a mistake. Field manuals are "how-to" books, similar to using your car manual to change a tire when you get a flat. FMs do not answer the "why" question and are not written to give a strategic framework and logic of response. For the full details of how problematic a concept Global Counterinsurgency is, see Stephen Sloan and Sebastian L. v. Gorka, "Contextualizing COIN," *Journal of International Security Affairs*, No. 16, Spring 2009, pp. 41–48, available at http://www.securityaffairs.org/issues/2009/16/sloan&gorka.php (accessed March 13, 2012).

8. See Patrick Sookhdeo, *Global Jihad: The Future in the Face of Militant Islam* (McLean, VA: Isaac Publishing, 2007).

9. For the full story see Yaroslav Trofimov, *The Siege of Mecca* (New York, NY: First Anchor Books, 2008).

10. *Interpretation of the Meanings of the Noble Qur'an in the English Language: A Summarized Version of At-Tabari, Al-Qurtubi and Ibn Kathir with comments from Sahih Al-Bukhari*, summarized in One Volume by Dr. Muhammad Taqi-ud-DinAl-Hilali and Dr. Muahhamd Muhsin Khan (Riyadh, Saudi Arabia: Darussalam Publishers and Distributors, 1996).

11. For fuller details see Lawrence Wright, *Looming Tower—Al-Qaeda and the Road to 9/11* (New York, NY: Knopf, 2006).

12. For data on how much more prevalent irregular warfare is than conventional or regular warfare, see Sebastian L. v. Gorka and David Kilcullen, "An Actor-Centric Theory of War," *Joint Forces Quarterly*, No. 60, 1st quarter 2011, available at http://www.ndu.edu/press/lib/images/jfq-60/JFQ60_14-18_Gorka-Kilcullen.pdf (accessed March 12, 2012).

13. For some of the best comparative analysis of irregular warfare, focoist versus Maoist, see the works of Thomas A. Marks, for example the seminal *Maoist People's War in Post-Vietnam Asia* (Bangkok: White Lotus, 2007).

14. For the best work on understanding the enemy we now face see Patrick Sookhdeo's *Global Jihad* and the analytic work of Stephen Ulph, including *Towards a Curriculum for Teaching Jihadist Ideology* (Jamestown Foundation), available at http://www.jamestown.org/single/?no_cache=1&tx_ttnews%5Btt_news%5D=3699 9. For an overview of the key thinkers and strategists of Global Jihadi ideology see Sebastian L. v. Gorka: *Jihadist Ideology: The Core Texts*, lecture to the Westminster Institute, audio and transcript available at http://www.westminster-institute.org/articles/jihadist-ideology-the-core-texts-3/#more-385.

15. COL (ret.) Andrew N. Pratt, Director of the Program for Terrorism and Security Studies, George C. Marshall Center, email communication, June 2011.

ABOUT THE AUTHORS

DR. SEBASTIAN L. V. GORKA

Dr. Sebastian L. v. Gorka is Director of the Homeland Defense Fellowship Program of National Defense University's College of International Security Affairs, and Military Affairs Fellow with the Foundation for Defense of Democracies. An international authority on irregular warfare, terrorism and national security, he also teaches at Georgetown University, the John F. Kennedy Special Warfare Center and School, and the FBI Academy. A graduate of London University and Corvinus University, Budapest, he was Kokkalis Public Policy Fellow at Harvard's Kennedy School of Government. Most recently, Dr. Gorka advised U.S. Special Operations Command and the Pentagon on the new Joint Operating Concept for Irregular Warfare.

THOMAS JOSCELYN

Thomas is a Senior Fellow and Executive Director of the Center for Law and Counterterrorism at the Foundation for Defense of Democracies. Most of Thomas's research and writing has focused on how al Qaeda and its affiliates operate around the world. He is a regular contributor to the *Weekly Standard* and its online publications, the *Daily Standard* and *Worldwide Standard*. He is the Senior Editor of *The Long War Journal*. His work has also been published by *National Review Online*, the *New York Post*, and a variety of other publications. Thomas is the author of *Iran's Proxy War Against America*, which details Iran's decades-long sponsorship of America's terrorist enemies. He makes regular appearances on radio programs around the country and has appeared on MSNBC. Thomas served as the senior terrorism adviser for Mayor Giuliani's 2008 presidential campaign. In 2006 he was named one of the Claremont Institute's Lincoln Fellows. He holds a BA in Economics from the University of Chicago.

Dr. John Lenczowski

John Lenczowski is the founder and president of The Institute of World Politics, an independent graduate school of national security and international affairs in Washington, D.C. From 1981 to 1983 Dr. Lenczowski served in the State Department in the Bureau of European Affairs and as Special Advisor to the Under Secretary for Political Affairs. From 1983 to 1987 he was Director of European and Soviet Affairs at the National Security Council. In that capacity, he served as principal Soviet affairs adviser to President Reagan. He has been associated with several academic and research institutions in the Washington area, including Georgetown University, the University of Maryland, the American Enterprise Institute, the Ethics and Public Policy Center, the Council for Inter-American Security, and the International Freedom Foundation. He has also served on a Congressional staff. He is the author of *Soviet Perceptions of U.S. Foreign Policy* (1982), *The Sources of Soviet Perestroika* (1990), and *Cultural Diplomacy: A Multi-faceted Strategic Asset of Soviet Power* (1991). His most recent publication is the newly released *Full Spectrum Diplomacy and Grand Strategy: Reforming the Structure and Culture of US Foreign Policy*.

Prof. John H. Moore

From 1990 until 1996, Dr. Moore was an administrator and faculty member at George Mason University. He was Director of the University's International Institute from 1990 to 1995. In June 1985, President Reagan appointed Dr. Moore as Deputy Director of the National Science Foundation, a position he held until he joined George Mason University in 1990. He was Associate Director and Senior Fellow of the Hoover Institution at Stanford University before moving to the National Science Foundation. Dr. Moore has also served on the faculties and staffs of the University of

Virginia, the University of Miami and Emory University. Dr. John H. Moore served as the president of Grove City College from 1996 to 2003. Dr. Moore earned an undergraduate degree in chemical engineering and a master's degree in business administration from the University of Michigan. His doctorate in economics was awarded by the University of Virginia in 1966. He has published numerous books and articles on a range of subjects including science policy and the economic systems of Eastern and Central Europe.

ROBERT R. REILLY

Robert Reilly has taught at the National Defense University, and served in the Office of The Secretary of Defense, where he was Senior Advisor for Information Strategy (2002-2006). He participated in Operation Iraqi Freedom in 2003, as Senior Advisor to the Iraqi Ministry of information. Before that, he was director of the Voice of America, where he had worked the prior decade. Mr. Reilly has served in the White House as a Special Assistant to the President (1983-1985), and in the U.S. Information Agency both in D.C. and abroad. In the private sector, he spent more than seven years with the Intercollegiate Studies Institute, as national director and then president. He was on active duty as an armored cavalry officer for two years, and attended Georgetown University and the Claremont Graduate University. He has published widely on foreign policy "war of ideas" issues, and classical music. His latest book is *The Closing of the Muslim Mind: How Intellectual Suicide Created the Modern Islamist Crisis*. He is currently Senior Fellow at the American Foreign Policy council.

DR. PATRICK SOOKHDEO

Patrick Sookhdeo received his PhD from the School of Oriental and African Studies of the University of London, and he is a leading expert on jihadist ideology and radical Islam, advising governments around the globe. He has spoken at many military and security events and is the author of numerous books, including *Global Jihad: The Future in the Face of Militant Islam*, *Understanding Shari'a Finance: The Muslim Challenge to Western Economics*, and *Faith, Power, and Territory: A Handbook of British Islam*. He is currently Visiting Professor at the Defence Academy of the UK, Adjunct Professor at the George C. Marshall European Center for Security Studies, Guest Lecturer at the NATO school, Oberammergau, Germany, and lecturer at ARRC Germany on Islam and Islamic terrorism. He is also involved in pre-deployment training for UK armed forces, and serves as adviser to Permanent Joint Headquarters UK. He has briefed SOCOM and the FBI. He has also served as Cultural Adviser to RC South, Afghanistan (2010), to ISAF, in Kabul, Afghanistan (2007) and to GOC, Basra, Iraq (2007).

STEPHEN ULPH

Stephen Ulph is a Senior Fellow at the Jamestown Foundation, Washington DC, where he specializes in the analysis of jihadist and Islamist ideology and regularly lectures on aspects of Islamist and jihadist ideology impacting on western democracies and the course of the war on terrorism. The core of his research focuses on the doctrinal underpinning, taking as its starting point the Islamists' and jihadists' own points of departure. Mr. Ulph was the founder editor of *Terrorism Focus* and also the founder editor of the journals *Terrorism Security Monitor* and *Islamic Affairs Analyst* for Jane's Information Group. His expertise has informed the U.S. Senate Select Committee on Intelligence, the U.S. National Counter-Terrorism Center, the U.S. State Department, the Office of the Vice-President and other government agencies through numerous briefings. His publications include an analysis on the course of jihadism in Syria for the CTC at the US Military Academy, West Point, an ideological analysis of the "Virtual Border Conflict" (the online arena for Islamist extremism) for *The Borders of Islam*, an academic publication exploring Samuel Huntingdon's thesis, and a 4-part reference work, *Towards a Curriculum for the Teaching of Jihadist Ideology*, available online at the Jamestown Foundation.

About the Westminster Institute

The Mission of The Westminster Institute is to promote individual dignity and freedom for people throughout the world. The Institute fulfills this mission by sponsoring high-quality independent research by scholars and policy analysts, with a particular focus on the threat posed by extremism and radical ideologies. The Westminster Institute is a fully independent, non-profit organization that is funded by contributions from individuals and private foundations. The Institute was created in April 2009 and since that time it has held numerous briefings and events. Recent events include:

- *Understanding Security in Pakistan's Tribal Areas*, with Thomas Wilhelm, Director, the Foreign Military Studies Office

- *Islamism and the Future of the Christians of the Middle East*, with Prof. Habib C. Malik, Lebanese American University

- *How Terrorist Groups End*, with Dr. Christopher C. Harmon, Marine Corps Research Center

- *Lone-Wolf Shooters Motivated by Al Qaedist Ideology*, with Madeleine Gruen, Senior Analyst, NEFA Foundation

- *Khalid Shaikh Mohammed, Mastermind: The Many Faces of the 9/11 Architect*, with author Richard Minter

- *Arab Spring or Christian Winter?* with author Robert R. Reilly

- *Global Jihad: The Threat Doctrine and Strategic Response*, with Dr. Sebastian Gorka, Foundation for Defense of Democracies

- *Combating Terrorist Financing and Illicit Networks*, with Celina Realuyo

- *Lessons from the Battlefield: Counter-Insurgency for Domestic Law Enforcement*, with Lieutenant Michael J. Domnarski and Trooper Michael Cutone, Massachusetts State Police

- *Muslim-Christian Violence in Nigeria*, with The Most Rev. Dr. Ben Kwashi, Archbishop of Jos Province, Nigeria

- *Responding to Islamism: Lessons from Dietrich Bonhoeffer, Karl Barth, and Bishop George Bell*, with Dr. Patrick Sookhdeo, Barnabas Fund

- *The Rise of Political Islam and the Ideology of Jihad*, with Dr. Sebastian Gorka, Foundation for Defense of Democracies

- *Intelligence and Counter-Intelligence Challenges of Militant Islam*, with Dr. John J. Dziak, Dziak Group Inc. Intelligence Consulting

To receive notification of upcoming events and/or publications, please sign up for the Westminster Institute mailing list, at www.westminster-institute.org. You can also follow us on Facebook.